The Vision
of a Contemporary University

The Vision
of a Contemporary University

A CASE STUDY OF EXPANSION AND DEVELOPMENT
IN AMERICAN HIGHER EDUCATION, 1950–1975

Russell M. Cooper
and
Margaret B. Fisher

A University of South Florida Book

University Presses of Florida
Tampa

University Presses of Florida is the central agency for scholarly publishing of the State of Florida's university system. Its offices are located
at 15 NW 15th Street, Gainesville, FL 32603. Works published by
University Presses of Florida are evaluated and selected for publica-
tion by a faculty editorial committee of any one of Florida's nine
public universities: Florida A&M University (Tallahassee), Florida
Atlantic University (Boca Raton), Florida International University
(Miami), Florida State University (Tallahassee), University of Central
Florida (Orlando), University of Florida (Gainesville), University of
North Florida (Jacksonville), University of South Florida (Tampa),
University of West Florida (Pensacola).

Library of Congress Cataloging in Publication Data
Main entry under title:

Cooper, Russell Morgan, 1907–1975
  The vision of a contemporary university.

  "A University of South Florida book."
  Includes index.
  1. Florida. University of South Florida, Tampa—
History. I. Fisher, Margaret Barrow, 1918–   joint author. II. Title.
LD1799.8.F6C66   378.759'65   80–29022
ISBN 0–8130–0702–X

Printed in U.S.A.

Dedication

The people of Florida had a vision of a university system serving the whole state. The people of the Tampa Bay area had a vision of a new university that would realize values in lifelong learning for themselves and their children. Together they worked to bring the University of South Florida to life.

To these people, who strengthen the community of scholars from generation to generation, we dedicate this book.

Contents

Foreword

In 1974, M. Cecil Mackey, then President of the University of South Florida, asked Dr. Russell M. Cooper, Dean of the College of Liberal Arts from 1959 to 1971, to write a history of the University of South Florida. The purpose was to be twofold: to record the birth and growth of the University while many of its founders were still available to contribute to the writing and to celebrate the University's twentieth anniversary in 1976. Dr. Cooper accepted that responsibility, but, unfortunately, the goal was not achieved in time for that celebration. Russell Cooper died unexpectedly in 1975, after completing six chapters of the intended twelve.

Colleagues read Cooper's unfinished manuscript and agreed that it was a document worthy to be continued. But at that time no suitable arrangement could be made for the completion of the book. Interest further waned when President Mackey left the institution in August 1976 to assume the presidency of Texas Technological University.

William Reece Smith, Jr., was Interim President of the University of South Florida from September 1, 1976, through September 21, 1977. It was during his term of office that Dr. Margaret Fisher, an early and influential staff member of the University of South Florida and recently retired from the University, was commissioned to complete the manuscript. Dr. John Lott Brown, who became President of the University of South Florida in October 1977, encouraged the project, and arrangements were made for the work's publication by University Presses of Florida.

After a long gestation, President Mackey's idea and Dean Cooper's manuscript have finally become a book, approximately five years after its intended completion but in time for the University of South

Florida's Silver Anniversary. Fittingly, it was published during the same academic year (1980–81) that another tribute was made to the book's original author: the Arts and Letters building was named after Russell M. Cooper.

Although much has happened in the life of the University of South Florida since 1976, Margaret Fisher and I decided that the original date for closure (1975/76) was still the appropriate one because it followed Russell Cooper's design and intent.

I want to thank the charter faculty members and others who painstakingly read the typed manuscript of this book for accuracy of facts and interpretations. Their assistance has helped to make this book, as one such reader has stated, "a rare combination of history and philosophy."

William H. Scheuerle

Preface

On September 26, 1960, the University of South Florida was born. After four years of planning, building, and recruiting, its doors opened to the first 1,997 students.

The fourth state university in Florida was something of a pioneer; Murray G. Ross declares in his volume *New Universities in the Modern World,* "As a completely new and separate institution, rather than a branch of one of the existing state universities, the University of South Florida thus became the first new institution of its kind to be conceived, planned, and built in the United States in the twentieth century."

Fifteen years later the youthful institution is coming of age, in some ways surpassing and in others confounding the hope of its founders. It has grown into a complex of ten colleges [1975], three regional centers, over 20,000 students, and a hundred or more buildings valued at around $100 million. As of 1975, graduate programs offer master's degrees in sixty-two fields and a doctorate in seven; medical and nursing colleges also offer graduate and professional degrees.

The progenitors of the University have brought their offspring into a remarkable adolescence through many moments of apprehension and bewilderment. For the University has developed a character rather different from their early dreams—perhaps better, perhaps worse, but certainly different. Were these changes inherent from the beginning? Have they come from new pressures in the constituency, or from the peer pressure of other universities?

This book seeks to assess the forces, both organic and environmental, that have shaped the development of the University and to explore the sources and consequences of decisive actions on plans, policies, and programs. Who made the decisions and why? How have plans and policies worked out in practice?

During the turbulent sixties and early seventies, unrest, violence, and political agitation severely buffeted higher education all across the United States. In the graphic context of a single campus, the meaning and impact of these forces and movements may take on a sharper focus and greater clarity. To some degree every university reflects the experience of the whole system of higher education, and the story of one university going through its formative years in a time of change and growth in society may reflect in various ways the experience of two critical decades of nationwide expansion and development. The University of South Florida is certainly not the nation's best or most important university; but its conception, growth, and development were directly influenced by state and national policy. As a new institution unfettered by tradition, the University may reveal more clearly than older universities the impact of contemporary issues, problems, changes, and opportunities that affected the general system of higher education.

Even though it draws upon historical materials, this book is not merely a chronicle of events. Nor is it a public relations document, for it reports failures as freely as successes. It seeks to interpret the source, meaning, and impact of certain movements of the period 1950–75 in the life of a single university. By examining these developments in some depth, we may hope to understand the modern university better as an institution and to gain insight into the process and progress of American higher education.

The author was Dean of the Liberal Arts College of the University of South Florida from 1959 to 1971 and participated in many of the decisions reported here. While he had an intimate acquaintance with the University's founders and with various factors at work in the course of its development, this very closeness made objectivity difficult. Fortunately much documentation was available in the University Archives and administrative offices, and most of the founders were available to give testimony.

The study could never have been done without the cordial cooperation of administrators, faculty, students, and librarians. The present University administration encouraged the study and scrupulously refrained from any effort to influence its contents. The author, therefore, assumes complete responsibility, with appreciation for the invaluable assistance that came from every quarter.

Russell M. Cooper
Tampa, 1975

☆   ☆   ☆

Dean Cooper completed six chapters covering the Florida Plan for higher education, the creation of the University, and the history of each of its colleges. I have tried to realize the whole work as he envisioned it, setting the experience of one new university in the context of some critical tasks confronting American higher education after World War II.

My own contributions to the work deal with interdisciplinary methods of instruction and governance and with the experience of New Students having no family tradition of higher education. On some of these matters, the University's experience illustrates the findings of a nationwide study of New Students in the 1950s and 1960s, *Beyond the Open Door,* by K. Patricia Cross. Cross found that "equalitarian" principles applied to plans for opening new doors to lifelong learning as a *birthright*, while "beyond the open door," "meritocratic" principles of an *earned right* to education continued to prevail in universities following an "academic lockstep" and screening students up or out in the passage to a degree. Changing the system of higher education, turning away from scalar assumptions and meritocratic practices toward developmental principles of instruction and governance, away from the lockstep toward a "swinging door" for lifelong learning, tell much of the story of higher education in these decades.

The experience of the University of South Florida was equalitarian in one important respect: every member for the past twenty years has had an equal responsibility to contribute in some fashion toward its growth and development. All contributed generously. A study honoring all contributions would have to name thousands and would require a comprehensive institutional history, which this work does not contemplate.

Neither Dean Cooper nor I intended to provide an exhaustive review of the rich literature of the period. We have summed up those works that particularly influenced us, those we shared with colleagues, and those assessing significant trends of the time. I have included some studies published since 1975 that give added insight into certain factors affecting the University.

I found the focus on *process* to characterize most of the significant developments of the period. But any process followed at the University usually had to be reconstructed from personal notes and recollections; existing documents usually reflected the outcome more fully than the process involved. I am grateful to more people than I can name for help in understanding how things were done. My interpretation may differ from that of other participants and does not always follow received tradition. For these differences, and for any errors, I have full responsibility.

I cannot think, however, that Russell Cooper and I have erred in considering the process of teaching and learning to be the vital center of a contemporary university or in viewing American higher education as one of the great life-sustaining systems in our society and in the entire culture of cities. A deeper understanding of the enjoyment of learning as a process that brings people together and sustains their whole life and work may be a valuable outcome of this period of growth and diversification in higher education.

William Scheuerle deserves most of the credit for seeing the project through, and I thank him for his generous advice and assistance. Julia and Lucile Cooper provided heartwarming encouragement and suggestions. I hope they will find this work worthy to stand beside the many contributions that Russell Cooper made to higher education.

Margaret B. Fisher
Tampa, 1980

1
Gestation

Between the Tides

In the nationwide expansion of higher education during the third quarter of the twentieth century, one of the many new colleges and universities established was the University of South Florida. As World War II was ending, leaders in higher education and government began to plan for an oncoming tide of students clamoring for admission to colleges and universities. Actually, two tides were converging on higher education, and either could engulf the entire system. The birth rate had steadily been increasing, and its effect on the colleges would reach its peak by the mid-1960s. How many thousands of new students might enroll and what advanced studies and degrees they might pursue depended also upon rising expectations for higher education, reflected in the steady increase in the proportion of youth aged 17 to 21 who were enrolled in college and the increasing enrollment of adults beyond the customary college age.

In 1947 President Truman received the final report from his Commission on Higher Education, which predicted that enrollments nationwide would swell from 3 million in 1947 to more than 4 million by 1960. A "National Inventory of Talent" conservatively estimated that at least 49 percent of the adult population had reasonable expectations of completing a two-year program of general and vocational education and at least 32 percent had the ability to complete "advanced liberal or specialized professional education." An increase of some 170 percent in graduate enrollment appeared to be necessary in order to provide some 250,000 new college teachers and nearly as many new professionals for other social systems. The commission advised the universities to prepare without delay to meet these needs.

1

The report reinforced the equalitarian thrust toward a "birthright" in educational opportunities: "American colleges and universities . . . must become the means by which every citizen, youth and adult, is enabled and encouraged to carry his education, formal and informal, as far as his native capacities permit." Noting the need for more diversified programs and methods of instruction, it recommended an increase in new types of postsecondary institutions, especially two-year community and junior colleges offering both terminal programs and continuing education for adults. The commission particularly urged all colleges and universities to capitalize more fully on expertise in research by cultivating more systematically the art of teaching.[1]

The projections for expansion and diversification proved to be realistic. In 1951 about 24 percent of the college-age group was enrolled and by 1967 nearly 47 percent.[2] An increasing number and proportion of undergraduates were adults beyond the traditional college age. Clark Kerr declared that "We are witnessing everywhere the demise of two long-held notions, that higher education ought to be restricted to a small elite minority, and that only a small percentage of the country's population is capable of benefiting from some kind of higher education."[3]

These equalitarian trends emerged in a system that operated predominantly on the meritocratic principle of admitting students on the basis of their ranking at high school graduation according to grades and scores on standardized tests. Breaking away from aristocratic and elitist traditions of admission by right of family inheritance or by the grace and favor of a distinguished scholar or wealthy patron, the American educational system had primarily substituted grades for grace and financial aid for favor. Out of this meritocratic principle of an "earned right" in higher education evolved an even stronger equalitarian emphasis on a birthright in lifelong learning for all Americans. Policies and plans developed by the 1947 commission aimed at a rapid expansion of opportunities to match the consequent rise in expectations for higher education.[4]

The Florida Plan

In keeping with well-established constitutional principles, the commission recommended a program that depended on the states for action, according to their primary responsibility for education, with federal assistance for part of the added capital investment. Each state had distinctive needs and opportunities to consider in coping with a growing population and rising expectations.

In Florida, rates of population growth were compounded by increasing in-migration affecting the entire educational system. Since 1900 the state's population has doubled about every 20 years— 2,771,000 in 1950, 4,952,000 in 1960, 6,789,000 in 1970, and nearly 9 million projected for 1980. Florida also confronted the urgent need for racial integration in the public schools, colleges, and universities, along with the need to increase substantially the total number of educational institutions.

In 1954 nine accredited private colleges and universities and three state universities had a combined enrollment of 36,000 and a total capacity of approximately 38,000. The state universities were approaching the limits of land available for expansion and could hardly accommodate enrollment growth of even modest size. Florida had always "exported" a substantial number of college students, but out-of-state institutions, faced with their own expanding populations, could not absorb an increasing number of students from Florida.

The Board of Control, which coordinated planning and policy for the three state universities, initiated a comprehensive planning study in 1954. With approval from the Cabinet–Board of Education (the elected members of Florida's Cabinet play this dual role), the Board of Control appointed a Council for the Study of Higher Education, enlisting five distinguished educators from outside the state: John E. Ivey, chairman; A.J. Brumbaugh, director; Earl J. McGrath, Floyd W. Reeves, and John Dale Russell.

Late in 1956 the council delivered its report, *Higher Education and Florida's Future,* a one-volume summary of recommendations buttressed by several volumes of analytic evidence. This laid the groundwork for planning and action to expand both the university and the community college systems. The evidence demonstrated without question that the state's tasks were even more urgent than had generally been recognized.

For example, enrollment was projected to rise from 36,000 in 1954 to more than 132,000 by 1970.[5] (Actual figures for 1970 exceeded 240,000.) Areas of greatest population growth, remote from the established state universities, had no resources aside from nine private institutions with limited capacity to expand and five two-year junior or community colleges. Accordingly the council focused on demographic factors in a comprehensive plan that would provide access to higher education for all Florida residents. New institutions would be located where students could commute, reducing construction expenses for the state and living expenses for the students. The expanded, urban-centered system would have two distinct institutional networks.

The most extensive network—18 new two-year community colleges plus 5 existing ones—would eventually expand to 28, the last opening in 1973. These community colleges would have 99 percent of the population within commuting distance.

Universities would provide regional access and offer selective admission to the top half of high school graduating classes and to community college graduates with an Associate of Arts degree. The "Brumbaugh Report" proposed three new universities, the first to be established as soon as possible in the Tampa Bay area, another on the lower east coast (Florida Atlantic University at Boca Raton), and a third in the Orlando area (Florida Technological University, later renamed the University of Central Florida). Two more universities on the east coast (the University of North Florida at Jacksonville and Florida International University at Miami) and one to serve the panhandle (the University of West Florida at Pensacola) were added to the plan as population continued to increase.

The council's report combined an equalitarian access model for the open-admission community colleges with the traditional meritocratic ladder in the universities, designed for selective admission on the principle of an "earned right" to enter and progress toward four-year and higher degrees. The Florida Plan capitalized on this combination of principles and integrated the two networks by paralleling A.A. degree programs with general education requirements for B.A. degrees and by designing four of the new universities (at Pensacola, Jacksonville, Miami, and Boca Raton) specifically to serve community college graduates and offer only the last two years of study for the bachelor's degree plus some master's programs.

The council recommended that "addition of graduate instruction should be governed by demand both in the new institutions and on a system-wide basis."[6] The new institutions should offer only the bachelor's degree in liberal and applied arts and sciences, including a few professional fields carefully selected to meet clearly demonstrated demand. Their first objective was to develop fully accredited baccalaureate programs; then the Board of Control might consider plans for studies at the master's level. In general, graduate and professional education should develop primarily around the established programs at the University of Florida and Florida State University.

The council's rather cautious approach to the role and scope of new universities and the extent to which students might proceed beyond the "open door" was consistent with the fairly conservative estimates of the 1947 President's Commission. How many New Students taking these opportunities would prove equal in performance to those selected by traditional standards for admission could not be predicted. In the 1950s national and state plans had to focus primarily on expanding opportunities for undergraduate studies and continuing education. The actual experience of New Students would strongly influence the future development of Florida's universities and community colleges.

"The Brumbaugh Report" was truly prophetic in its vision and comprehensive in scope. Its recommendations accommodated future changes, which could not be predicted in every respect. The council urged the Florida Cabinet and legislature to develop stronger planning capabilities in order to keep pace with general economic growth and development as well as expanding educational systems. The state quickly and effectively carried out the council's plan and timetable for expansion of the university system while enlarging its general resources for planning.

Even before the council produced the final report, the Board of Control took the first steps to establish the new university recommended for the Tampa Bay area. It looked for a site that would be near the center of projected population growth in the designated seven-county service area around Hillsborough and Pinellas counties and would provide ample land for future expansion. Several sites were surveyed in Tampa and St. Petersburg, and the two cities hotly contended for the new institution. In December 1956, the board decided on a 1,694-acre tract northeast of Tampa. Nine or ten miles from the central business district and adjoining a new industrial park, the area would be a major center for commercial and residential development in the decades to come.

On December 18, 1956, the Cabinet–Board of Education formally created the new four-year institution and approved the recommended location. The 1957 legislature appropriated $8,602,000 for construction and $140,000 for salaries and expenses during the two years of planning for classes to open in September 1960.

A Question of Identity

John S. Allen was acting President of the University of Florida when the Board of Control nominated him to be president of the first "expansion" institution. His appointment was approved in July 1957, and he took office August 1. Allen had participated in planning for the new school through the university system's Council of Presidents and Board of Control. He was thoroughly familiar with the plans, policies, site selection, cabinet authorization, and legislative appropriations affecting its role and scope.

A professor of astronomy, Allen left Colgate University to direct the Division of Higher Education of New York State from 1942 to 1948. Then he joined the administration of the University of Florida under President J. Hillis Miller. His experience in administration of public and private universities and a state system of higher education, and his knowledge of the educational problems and political realities of Florida, gave him the resources desired by the Board of Control to bring the new institution into the national mainstream of higher education and into service for the people of Florida.

The new institution had a president and a campus. Now it needed a name that would declare its identity and role. The Board of Control had not yet determined either the shape of the university system or the role of new institutions within it. Nevertheless it had to set the identity of the one in Tampa. Should this new enterprise be a college or a university?

THE CALIFORNIA MODEL

Because California had experienced explosive growth earlier than some other states, many educators and public officials looked to its system as a model for expanding educational opportunities in their own constituencies. Beginning in 1953, California's system of higher education reorganized to form a meritocratic pyramid, with access increasing in selectivity from the open-admission community colleges at the lowest level, to the graduate schools at the apex. The University of California expanded beyond the original campuses at Berkeley, Davis, and Los Angeles. These highly selective universities admitted only the most proficient high school graduates, those considered most likely to progress beyond the bachelor's degree. Their undergraduate and graduate instruction had a strong orientation toward distinction in research.

State colleges with selective admission were responsible for most of the traditional bachelor's degree programs and offered master's studies in some fields of high demand; they served approximately the upper half of high school graduating classes. Community colleges provided open access to a variety of vocational, general, and continuing education programs. The most able and proficient students from state colleges and community colleges could advance to a university and to the highest degrees through successive screenings at each step on the traditional meritocratic ladder.

PYRAMID OR FLAGSHIP?

The Brumbaugh Report made no recommendation for the design of Florida's system, though its authors inclined toward the California model. The Board of Control and Cabinet–Board of Education had gone only so far as to adopt access models similar to California's: open admission to community colleges and selective admission to universities. There had been no decision to adopt a graduated system of any particular kind. Many other educators and state officials, however, strongly advocated adopting California's pyramidal model in its entirety. On this basis, the new institution in Tampa and others like it would be state colleges offering only the baccalaureate degree.

Some advocates proposed that the University of Florida administer FAMU, FSU, and the new universities as its branches under a central administration. But because FSU advanced an equal claim to become the apex of such a pyramid, other proposals suggested two "flagships," one in Gainesville and one in Tallahassee. Florida A&M and the new universities might offer some graduate and professional studies at the master's level by extension from the flagships.

Many state officials were convinced that Florida needed no more than one or two centers for research and graduate and professional education. They feared that further expansion of opportunities would dilute limited financial resources so much that high quality in advanced studies and research could not be sustained anywhere in the university system. Equality of opportunity through the "open door" of community colleges should apply at entry from high school. Past that point, the traditional meritocratic ladder, selecting fewer and fewer students for advanced degrees, was considered essential in order to maintain quality.

Governor LeRoy Collins felt strongly that Florida should concentrate research and graduate study in the leading universities at Tallahassee and Gainesville. The Board of Control recommended the same salary scale for the president of the new university and the presidents of the University of Florida and Florida State University. But Collins persuaded the Cabinet–Board of Education to reduce the presidential salary scale for the new university by $2,500—in order to distinguish clearly the lower level of instruction to be provided in the new institutions.

Nevertheless, the Board of Control chose no particular model but let the organization of the State University System develop with experience. In effect, the state universities would form a network, not a pyramid.

COLLEGE OR UNIVERSITY?

Some advocates of the flagship model also wished to emphasize the limited role of the Tampa institution by naming it a college. But the same factors that led to locating the new institution in Tampa argued for making it a full university in fact and in name. If the state was committed to bringing lifelong educational opportunity to more than a million people within commuting range, the Tampa institution would have to provide for the full scope of expectations including the highest graduate and professional degrees. The Board of Control and President Allen agreed on the evidence in the council's report to open at least three colleges (Liberal Arts, Business Administration, and Education) in the beginning and to start planning a College of Engineering. If the institution was to include several colleges, in keeping with customary usage it should be called a university.

Thus the Board of Control finally christened the University of South Florida officially, setting a precedent for naming the other new institutions. The meaning of the term *university,* its reference to variety, scope, and level of programs, and the precise role and scope of each old and new university in the state system have not yet been fully settled. But the board clearly established the principle of organizing a set of autonomous universities. Each would be responsible for developing programs to serve a regional constituency and for supporting the state's overall plans for social and economic development in cooperative effort through the State University System and its governing board.

Serving a rapidly growing urban population, the University of South Florida expanded beyond expectations and soon matched or surpassed older universities in size and scope. By 1975 USF had added Colleges of Engineering, Medicine, and Nursing; it had established 62 graduate programs leading to a master's degree and 7 leading to the doctorate, in which nearly 3,000 candidates were enrolled. Its constituency's expectations of a multiplicity of offerings and the undeniable need of the urban population for strong educational resources prevailed over the modest assumptions of its founders.

IVORY OR URBAN?

The Tampa campus today is nearly centered in its population area, as the board had planned when it chose the site. But in 1956 it seemed paradoxical that the board had located a university in Tampa to meet the needs of a growing urban area and then decided to build it in open country ten miles from the inner city. At that time only two sandy roads led to the campus although plans were ready for constructing the present network of arterial roads and an interstate highway. Its isolation aroused fresh controversy over the University's mission. If its program was to address directly the socioeconomic concerns of the inner city, it should have been located downtown. In its rural location, USF might provide a campus-centered program characteristic of older universities, distanced from city affairs.

With the equalitarian thrust of the fifties came a movement to break out of the ivory tower and engage higher education actively in community affairs. The University of Illinois was developing its Chicago Circle Branch in a 27-story building five minutes from the Loop, there to concentrate on urban aspects of the social and behavioral sciences and to duplicate only a few of the programs offered at Champaign-Urbana. Lewis Mayhew, hailing that development, urged that universities bring opportunities as close as possible to the ghetto, where educationally disadvantaged students face prohibitive costs in commuting to a distant campus.[7] Seymour Harris also advocated inner-city locations, noting that "students living within 25 miles of a college are twice as likely to go to college as those living beyond 25 miles."[8]

Others wanted campuses close to the business and industrial communities, which needed university resources for career advancement and effectiveness in economic enterprise. Clark Kerr saw universities as "bait" to be dangled before industry and considered higher education to be intimately related to "the rise and fall of industrial areas."[9]

An artistic community in the Tampa Bay area offered special prospects for university-community cooperation. Hundreds of distinguished artists, writers, and other intellectuals had settled on or retired to the Gulf coast. Four symphony orchestras and several theater and dance groups offered opportunities for collaborative work and cultural enrichment. And people in all walks of life looked for a full spectrum of educational, economic, and cultural resources in the University.

Considering this rising tide of expectations, President Allen and the planning staff decided that location was a minor factor. The University must work effectively with people in many settings in the community. First it would have to educate the thousands regularly enrolled; community concerns and university services would converge most significantly in the lives of students and faculty. Out of this primary interaction, a variety of collaborative activities could develop to enrich the quality of life in the seven-county service area.

The University would value community support. President Allen actively enlisted local political, cultural, educational, and business leaders, indefatigable in their efforts to bring USF into the Tampa area, to serve as consultants in planning and development. By 1959 the planning staff was assembled and members went into the community to discuss the University's plans and to solicit information and advice in schools, clubs, churches, and private homes. This outreach stimulated enthusiasm and gave the planners insight into community expectations for USF. For example, the College of Education would design its program to focus on urban public schools as the center of change and development in the whole educational system, and programs in the College of Business Administration would emphasize corporate enterprise and the concerns of management.

COMMUTER OR RESIDENTIAL?

The planners found that they had to consider statewide as well as local expectations. Into the temporary offices in downtown Tampa came inquiries from many students who, contrary to the council's assumptions, wished to attend from outside commuting range. President Allen and the planning staff wished to serve them even though no housing was planned on campus and next to nothing was available nearby. Students from the rest of Florida, other states, and other countries would provide a more cosmopolitan campus, in keeping with historic traditions of universities. But the legislature had not appropriated funds for residence halls. In the established universities, housing and food service functioned as auxiliary enterprises, generating reserves for capital outlay from charges for service. The University of South Florida had neither appropriations nor capital reserves, but the planners wanted to meet this new opportunity.

For the first year, 47 women could be housed in quarters designed for visitors and offices on the top floor of the University Center. For the future, USF could secure federal loans from the Housing and Home Finance Agency. A low-interest loan of $2.5 million for a residence hall would require $55,000 of USF money. President Allen appealed to the community for "Dollars for Dorms." Businesses, families, civic groups, and school children contributed more than $80,000 before the campaign got fully started, giving a remarkable demonstration of community support regarded as a happy harbinger for future town-and-gown relations.

MONOLITH OR CLUSTER?

The addition of residence halls presented the possibility of developing the "cluster-college" concept replicating in a large "multiversity" the close relationships, warmth, intellectual climate, and personalized learning that small colleges have traditionally prized. President Allen and the four deans had all attended or taught in small colleges. Wishing to avoid the depersonalizing "assembly-line" so roundly deplored, they considered the "cluster-college" model to preserve *smallness* as a necessary condition for personalized teaching and learning within a university that would enroll 10,000 students or more by 1970.

It was too late to modify the plan for the University of South Florida. None of the buildings under construction and none of the specifications for the first residence hall could be changed to fit the cluster-college concept. The first Dean of Students, Howard Johnshoy, urged that other residence halls be designed as living-learning centers, providing commuter-resident interaction and bringing some classroom instruction into the residence areas. Rooms for two residents might be enlarged slightly to accommodate a study center for a commuting student, or each unit of 40–50 residents might include a study hall for 10–20 commuters and perhaps a classroom.

Residence hall financing took almost all of the rental income; costs of nonremunerative social or instructional space would have to be met out of other university funds, which were nonexistent, or out of service charges. Charges to commuters using a study center would almost equal costs to residents—square footage costs are the same, regardless of use. So plans went no further than to provide a few lounges and conference rooms for residents and commuters to share.

But the cluster-college concept persisted. Plans for the second residence complex included a classroom-office building—on the theory that residents would schedule most of their classes there and thus interact closely with a small group of faculty. This experiment did not work; planners failed to consider students' highly diversified academic programs, which dispersed their classes all across the campus.

Advocates of cluster-college organization tended to assume that *smallness* was the determining factor in personalizing education. But their concern for the *process* of teaching and learning, with close personal interaction among students and faculty, turned out actually to be the significant factor. President Allen and the deans had to look for other ways to cultivate active personal involvement in teaching and learning, and some of them proved successful even on a large scale.

The University Center was designed for all faculty, staff, and students to use its food service, offices for organizations, lounges, conference and recreation rooms. All buildings had several conference rooms and most had a snack bar–lounge. Small-group interaction, the goal of the cluster-college concept, became a criterion for all facilities design. In each building, the majority of classrooms were designed for small configurations of 25–30 students, with a few seating 50, and one large auditorium or lecture hall.

The classroom became the actual social center of usf. The mixture of resident and commuting students made the classroom encounter the focal point of campus life and work, open to all faculty and students. The president and planning staff realized their commitment in the *process* of personalized learning at the center of the academic enterprise.

COMMUNITY PARTICIPATION

The system of higher education has always been regarded as a national asset, a source of professional manpower, research, and consultation related to national and international affairs. A new dimension appearing with the rising tide of expectations called for colleges and universities to provide similar resources for their local communities. How this new responsibility would develop was not clear, and its form has not yet crystallized fully. But the planners gave high priority to campus–community collaboration at the University of South Florida.

President Allen knew that community contributions would bring to USF not only financial strength but also commitment and friendship such as alumni would provide—when the University had any. In 1958 he incorporated the University of South Florida Foundation, opening membership to any friend and supporter. The Chamber of Commerce, public officials, and local civic groups actively supported the foundation. Its members participated in activities as "instant alumni," contributed regular gifts and pledges, and sponsored campaigns for "Dollars for Dorms" and for scholarship and loan funds. Through this organization large numbers of people in the community could actively continue their participation and support many projects not covered under general appropriations.

Prospective students participated in preparation for the University's opening. On September 5, 1958, President Allen invited juniors from local high schools to join in the first ground-breaking ceremony; some would be USF freshmen in 1960. Chamberlain High School, a brand-new school itself, sent its band, and school classes, troops of Scouts and other youth groups planted thousands of trees provided by the state forestry service. (One of the Girl Scouts, when she enrolled some years later, found the tree she had planted and sat under it with great pride.)

Community participation would center primarily in the educational program. Instead of having a separate adult and evening school, the staff decided to operate a full schedule of afternoon and evening classes taught by a cross section of the faculty, so that working adults could take advantage of the full scope of offerings. Pat Beecher, Director of the Division of Fine Arts, capitalized on resources in the artistic community, exhibiting works of art and inviting townspeople to participate in musical ensembles, concerts, and theatrical performances; they would fill in the ranks until the number of students increased and thereafter would strengthen the quality of campus productions by providing some high-performance models. Virtually all special events, and many other campus activities, would be open to community participation in some way.

"BIG TEN" OR "IVY LEAGUE"?

People throughout the area looked forward eagerly to supporting the USF football team. Hardly more than ten years had passed since the legislature, converting the Florida State College for Women into the coeducational Florida State University, stipulated that FSU have a football team to contend annually with the team of the University of Florida, similarly converted to coeducation from an all-male institution.

No such legislative mandate accompanied the establishment of the University of South Florida. President Allen announced that USF would not have a football team now or for a long time—if ever. First, it did not have enough money to implement fully its plans for physical education, recreational sports, and athletics. A carefully designed timetable gave first priority to instruction, second to recreational sports and intramurals, and third to intercollegiate athletics—to the extent that funds might be found in the future for these activities. Second, USF was engaged in higher education and would not become a hostage to commercial enterprise—as the intercollegiate conferences had been captured by professional teams to serve as "the bush leagues."

Protests erupted and sportswriters indefatigably castigated John Allen—even though Gilman Hertz, the first director of the physical education program, and many other USF people worked on plans for a professional football team in the area and even dreamed of a training center for the U.S. Olympic team. Almost everybody but Allen insisted that only football could give USF any school spirit. And the high schools from which students came actually had little support in their communities for activities other than football around which spirit and pride could develop.

Observing the numbers turned away from plays, concerts, and other events, one faculty member remarked that art and music seemed to have become USF's substitute for football. The fine arts actually became a focus of spirited community and student participation. Reservation of funds for more urgent needs than football opened the way for spirit and morale to develop in a great variety of other university-community activities and services.

By 1965 modest sums had become available for intercollegiate athletics, and USF joined the NCAA, fielding teams in soccer, tennis, golf, swimming, and basketball. Both men's and women's athletics were organized, and the women's tennis team made USF's earliest mark in national intercollegiate competition. The soccer team became popular, paving the way for a professional team in the area. Basketball also became a major intercollegiate sport. But all these activities developed in the context of a comprehensive program providing instruction, recreation, and intramural competition in a diversified array of athletic and recreational activities.

The University would be "Ivy League" rather than "Big Ten." It would have to husband its meagre funds in order to achieve the high quality of education that President Allen and the community leaders desired—if, indeed, it had any chance to become "a university of the first class."

2
The Accent on Learning

Rising Expectations

In October 1957 a startling event shocked the nation into a fresh appraisal of expectations for education: the Soviet Union scored a "first" by placing in Earth orbit a man-made satellite, Sputnik. In a field where people had assumed the United States always took the lead, the U.S.S.R. demonstrated to the world that it had come of age in science and technology. Consternation spread throughout the United States. Editors, politicians, and educators discovered that nothing in their education had prepared them for any such event. Therefore, the entire educational system had to be upgraded rapidly—national security was at stake.

President Allen summed up the reaction in a speech a year later: "Sputnik sent radio beeps to Earth with coded messages. We Americans were embarrassed and annoyed by this, because we like to be first. A lot of people who had never been very much concerned about schools went into orbit and started beeping. They now want better schools. For this I say, 'Thanks for the Sputniks'."[1]

Coinciding with this surge in public concern, the 1957 report from President Eisenhower's Commission on Education beyond the High School recommended stronger national commitment to more diversified educational programs and large increases in financial support both public and private. Reinforcing the principle of a birthright in learning, the report urged the nation to remove financial barriers for students through grants, loans, and tax incentives. It recommended an all-out effort to recruit the most competent teachers available for higher education by doubling salaries over the next five to ten years. In order to maintain quality in a period of expansion, research would have to be emphasized; the pendulum swung back from the 1947 emphasis on teaching.[2]

16

For the University of South Florida, John Allen had already prepared an approach to program planning consistent with community concerns for scientific and technological advancement. In 1958 he appointed Sidney French to develop a philosophy and an outline for the academic program in keeping with the Florida Plan and its focus on values inherited from centuries of humanistic education.

The University's Mission

French set two clear criteria for creating or selecting major components of the University's organization and program: the "Accent on Learning" and the "All-University Approach." These were not mere clichés but design principles that summed up the whole mission of universities in the modern world.

THE ADVANCEMENT OF KNOWLEDGE

French and Allen appreciated the scope of the "knowledge explosion." The volume of knowledge, according to some analysts,[3] was doubling every ten or twenty years. Growth in knowledge was steadily accelerating in the twentieth century, bursting out of specialties into interdisciplinary dimensions and expanding beyond any configuration ever considered to serve as the core of a university education. Containing the knowledge explosion and managing diversified ways to learn had become formidable tasks.

The philosophy and program for USF stood within the traditional commitment of universities to advance and share knowledge. Disregarding equalitarian access models and meritocratic ladders of achievement, French and Allen fixed the University's integrative center in the *process* of learning.

Sidney French wrote most of the first catalog for the University of South Florida. It is really an extended essay on shared values and visions in the commitment to advance and share learning. Its title, "Accent on Learning," continues in use today.

THE WHOLENESS OF LEARNING

French insisted that the University emphasize learning rather than training and personalized rather than specialized academic programs. The linkage of higher education to specialized occupations had split universities and had set their commitment to advance and share learning at cross-purposes with student and faculty concerns for

competitive advancement on a career ladder. He insisted in the 1960
Accent on Learning (pp. 29ff.) that the University must reconcile and
harmonize liberal and professional education:

> Recent studies indicate a strong trend in American liberal arts col-
> leges toward the inclusion of more professional preparation in their
> programs and, conversely, for the professional colleges to include
> more general and liberal studies in theirs. Thus, the professional and
> the liberal arts colleges are coming closer together in the effort to
> provide a continuum of studies which includes the general, the liberal,
> and the professional in the same program. . . .
>
> The University of South Florida intends to bring together general,
> liberal and professional studies in a way that provides unity to the
> whole program.
>
> For each student the educational program will combine work in
> basic studies with those of the liberal arts and the sciences and, where
> indicated, with professional studies. Ideally, a student's program will
> be devoted one-third to basic studies, one-third to professional studies,
> and one-third to elective choices.

The University's founders were so determined to maintain the unity
of liberal and professional studies and to reinforce intellectual effort
of high quality that they actually discouraged applicants who did not
share this vision—even though they feared that too few students
would enroll for the University to get off the ground. The catalog
called for strong student commitment:

> A university is a place for those who seek sincerely to develop those
> intellectual qualities, interests, concerns, and skills which characterize
> the educated person. In no sense should a college education be re-
> garded merely as preparation for a job. Nor is it merely a collection of
> courses or the amassing of credits. . . .
>
> A good college education has unity and balance which, on the one
> hand, assures breadth and knowledge in those areas of human culture
> and intellectual skill characteristic of the best in our heritage, and, on
> the other hand, promotes competence in some field of personal choice.
> This competence may be in professional, vocational, or career fields,
> or, more broadly, in the competence of better living. . . .
>
> Those concerned only with specialized job training should consider
> carefully whether this kind of an education would serve them best or
> whether they should seek their training in some institution more
> nearly meeting their needs.
>
> It cannot be over-emphasized that a university is a place for those

who seek to develop intellectual qualities, interests, concerns, and skills. Those who find no challenge in this; those who found high school work in the so-called academic fields—English, foreign languages, mathematics, history, natural science and social science—difficult or uninteresting should consider carefully whether they should apply to the University, where such fields are emphasized to an even greater extent than in high school.

When President Allen was asked what he considered the University's most significant policies, he replied:

First, our commitment to educate the whole man. Second, our emphasis on a faculty dedicated to the importance of good teaching. Then, our all-University approach—the insistence that everything we do contributes to education, in and out of the classroom. And finally, our encouragement of individual effort, setting a pace, faster or slower, as the individual requires.

These principles were not new. They simply placed the University squarely in the mainstream of liberal thought espoused by generations of educators. The distinctive feature was the planners' earnest commitment to implement its philosophy in governance and administration as well as academic programs. The University was also committed to community service, especially through urban social systems. Its program was designed to provide effective education for students who would enter these systems in the future and to open up lifelong learning for professional people.

These tasks clearly required both liberal and professional education. The University's constituency was sadly undernourished in both respects, and new designs were required to meet its expectations. Educational planning would have to be oriented to the future; liberal arts and professional colleges would share responsibility for analyzing community expectations in relation to resources needed for expansion and development of major social systems. Academic programs must be designed to anticipate and perhaps to shape changes in these patterns of urban life and work.

The comment that the "liberal" in liberal arts means freedom from intervention by the professional establishment may be partly true. Professional associations often monitor educational programs closely and take a direct part in their design and accreditation, so that professional education often tends to focus narrowly on competences presently required by practitioners. Liberal arts colleges try to cultivate the whole "state of the art" in the sciences and humanities, with much less emphasis on occupational configurations outside of teaching and research and much less influence from professionals in the field in designing their courses and programs.

At USF the deans responsible for planning both liberal and professional education made a commitment to keep pace with developments in major social systems. They worked together on program design and developed a general format that would apply to all degrees granted by the University. Within this framework, deans and faculties of each college and students planning their own courses of study could produce highly diversified programs supporting the purposes of the University.

The Design of Academic Programs

There are many ways to harmonize liberal and professional studies. The deans' approach was to personalize academic programs so that each student could integrate studies around personal expectations in a way consistent with USF's own mission. Each student had primary responsibility for planning an academic program tailored to personal needs and talents. Therefore, the faculties had to provide a wide range of courses and diversified methods of learning adaptable to many individual plans for completing a degree.

In academic work the deans emphasized for students a broad general education as the foundation for professional study and occupational entry; for faculty, effective teaching and the development of a strong intellectual community; for administrators, equal reinforcement of each college and department on the all-University principle; for the world beyond the campus, a concern for the culture of cities and for national and international affairs.

A BALANCE OF GENERAL AND SPECIALIZED EDUCATION

• Some students would major in a professional college and others in a special field of liberal arts and sciences, but all would share a common background in general education.

• Each student would choose at least six of eight full-year courses, interdisciplinary in design, assuring familiarity with the full range of methods used in any specialized study.

• For seniors from all colleges, a Seminar on Freedom and Responsibility would be required as a capstone for the entire degree program, putting shared values to the test in analyzing contemporary issues.

• A limit of 40 (semester) credits was placed on each major; students would have to distribute other courses among a broad range of collateral fields and free electives.

• Interdisciplinary methods were emphasized in teaching, and all colleges developed interdisciplinary courses and majors.

• To link the general education program to the many special disciplines of the Liberal Arts College, its faculty joined that of the College of Basic Studies to form one body for curriculum and faculty development. The two deans presided jointly over the planning process. In the beginning, almost all instructors taught both Basic Studies and Liberal Arts courses.

TEACHING AND INTELLECTUAL COMMUNITY

The accent on learning called for active participation by students in academic work with a faculty highly skilled in teaching. Sixty-five percent of the charter faculty held a doctor's degree, compared to a national proportion of 36 percent in 1960. In selecting faculty, deans aimed for a diversified "mix" providing nationwide experience in the academic disciplines and employment in fields other than teaching, interdisciplinary study and experience, and productive activity in publication, research, and the arts. But the main requirement was evidence of active, provocative engagement with students in the process of learning.

• The most important criterion for advancement in faculty rank and salary was effective teaching, followed by research and scholarly publication, then by contributions to the profession and the community.

• Quality of education depends on continuing development of skill by the faculty, sharing their experience with other scholars and other institutions. Accordingly, each member annually received funds for attendance at a regional or national professional meeting in order to counteract provincialism and to contribute to general development of effective teaching and research in the whole academic enterprise.

• For faculty members new to teaching, the deans set up a special seminar on the psychology of learning at the college level, demonstrating the instructional techniques and resources freely provided for students and faculty: a network of closed-circuit television; many other types of audiovisual material and equipment; facilities for computer-assisted instruction and research.

• The classroom became the primary center of close personal interaction. Sections were kept as small as practicable for the particular modes of instruction. Every available dollar was spent on faculty salaries and instructional expense. Minimum feasible funding went to administrative services, but deans, directors, program chairmen, and many of their counterparts in nonacademic administration also had some teaching assignments.

• Students were encouraged to do as much self-directed academic work as possible. The University's accent was on learning, not on the mechanics of classroom instruction. In addition to regular classroom activities students could take courses by independent study or design a project for credit beyond the usual offerings; and they could waive degree requirements or secure credit for advanced studies or life experience by examination.

• In each Basic Studies course, a uniform final examination was given to all sections, determining 40 percent of the course grade. One faculty member in each course worked half-time as examiner; section instructors evaluated personalized work and classroom participation. This approach emphasized the instructor's role of mentor for the students as responsible participants and directors of their own academic work.

• Most degree programs included a senior seminar integrating the whole student experience and orienting career plans toward emergent concerns and opportunities in the community. Scholarly writing was particularly stressed as an essential requirement in vocational responsibilities, graduate and professional study. In some degree programs, a senior thesis, a research project, or comprehensive examination, or all three, were also required.

• Practical experience, combining work and study, could be gained in Cooperative Education, in field studies, in laboratory and studio work, and in performance and production in the arts and mass media. Instruction laid particular emphasis on collaboration with faculty members (e.g., in research or artistic performance) and with people in the community.

THE ALL-UNIVERSITY APPROACH

The all-University principle rested on the assumption that all members shared equal responsibility, though necessarily in different forms. Students designed their own academic work and degree programs in keeping with this general diffusion of equal responsibility. But the University had to have a clear identity as a cohesive intellectual community. It needed a strong network for planning and governance to provide mutual reinforcement of shared values and visions.

• There would be one undergraduate degree, the Bachelor of Arts, awarded by the University in all fields of study. Requirements for academic standards and distribution of courses would be common to all majors. Of the minimum 120 (semester) credits required, one-third covered general education, at least one-third represented upper-level courses and at least one-half extended outside the student's college or liberal arts division. A grade average of C was required overall and in the major.

• Thus students were enabled—and required—to develop a diversified repertory for study and practice. Academic policy and procedure let them transfer easily from one college or major to another as their educational and vocational interests crystallized.

• Students were relied upon to initiate voluntary organizations and activities. One hour each day was left free from scheduled classes, so that students and faculty were free to participate in voluntary activities and in University governance and planning.

• The library had open stacks and both faculty and students could request book orders. Art galleries in the library, University Center, theater foyers, and Fine Arts building held monthly exhibits of local and traveling collections. The bookstore stocked several thousand paperback titles—the largest such collection in the area—to encourage students to read outside their field of study.

• An "All-University Book" was chosen each term by a faculty-student committee for all members of the University to read and discuss in classes, carpools, dormitories, and lunchrooms. Titles such as *The American Presidency, Platero y Yo,* and *Member of the Wedding* were chosen for entertainment or for pertinence to some aspect of public, community, or personal experience. Each term at least one general forum or debate was held on the book, with the author participating when possible. The popular practice was abandoned after three years for lack of time and space on campus to accommodate the large numbers who wanted to attend the special forums.

• The council of each college brought together faculty representatives from its several programs and at least one representative from each of the other colleges. This assembly provided multidisciplinary planning for faculty development and facilitated the articulation of new and modified courses, programs, and techniques of instruction within and between colleges. The lending and borrowing of faculty members was encouraged, and the "roving ambassadors" helped to cement faculty relations across disciplinary lines.

• In the belief that traditional departments tended to fragment a university, the academic organization within colleges formed instead around programs, the degree sequences that had multidisciplinary form.

• Deans lunched together weekly, occasionally to discuss business but mostly to discuss almost anything else. They wished to perpetuate the camaraderie enjoyed during the planning period. Similar formal and informal groups developed, including a Secretaries Hour and Career Service Luncheon.

• The University Senate and standing committees had all-University membership, including students, faculty, and staff. These groups developed program and policy proposals for approval by the President.

COMMUNITY INVOLVEMENT

In developing its identity and welding its members into a community of mind and spirit, the University sought to strengthen its linkages with the entire system of higher education and with the wider community, especially in its urban enterprises. Throughout Florida people supported USF; in Tampa they welcomed its faculty and staff, involving them in local cultural, religious, and public affairs, just as USF welcomed them to campus activities.

• Participation in fine arts, lectures, forums, and other voluntary activities was open to the local community. Many community people contributed to instruction out of special experience or expertise in many fields. In return, faculty and staff participated in many community undertakings: health and mental health programs, libraries, schools, orchestras, drug and crisis intervention, new community colleges, environmental protection, local and regional planning councils.

• President Allen offered a long-term lease for religious bodies to construct facilities in keeping with campus design. Baptists, Episcopalians, and a "Chapel Fellowship" combining several other Protestant faiths established such centers, and a Catholic center was constructed nearby on diocesan land. The University also recognized groups from Jewish, Greek Orthodox, independent Protestant, non-ecclesiastical, and non-Western traditions as voluntary associations, and all belonged to a cooperative Religious Council.

• Special seminars, conferences, and workshops for civic and professional associations, managers and employees of businesses and industries were provided generously by the University. The faculty provided many leaders of national professional associations, other local, state, and national societies, and public and private agencies of all sorts.

• Thousands of students gave volunteer service to community agencies in education, recreation, human services, planning, environmental protection and government and economic development. In 1963 Sargent Shriver, the director, visited the campus to find out how USF came to produce the largest number of volunteers for the Peace Corps, in proportion to enrollment, of any institution in the country.

• Students developed thousands of individual and group field studies in response to community and agency needs. In its first year the University planned a Center of International Studies, concentrating initially on relations with Central and South America; it introduced a program for students undertaking field studies in foreign countries and special services for foreign students at USF.

Academic Leadership

John Allen demonstrated his commitment to this integrative approach in his appointment of principal administrators and planners. Each one was experienced in and committed to general and liberal education, interdisciplinary method, and integrating liberal and professional studies.

Dean Sidney J. French, a chemistry professor, had been a liberal arts dean at Colgate University and Rollins College. Shortly after coming to USF, he founded the National Association for General and Liberal Studies. He was to head the College of Basic Studies and then become the first Vice-President for Academic Affairs. The chairman who developed the Biological Sciences program, Edwin P. Martin, succeeded him as Dean of Basic Studies.

Russell M. Cooper, Dean of the College of Liberal Arts, came from the University of Minnesota where he had headed an interdisciplinary program. He had been Chairman of the Committee on General Education and President of the American Association for Higher Education. Cooper was particularly concerned with personalized learning in a large university setting and with academic freedom for students and faculty.

Lewis B. Mayhew, Director of Evaluation Services and Institutional Research, had been active in general education at Michigan State University and in the Committee on Liberal Arts Education of the North Central Association of Colleges and Schools. His incisive research designs for performance evaluation gave evidence of high educational effectiveness, consistent with the University's concern for student development over and above access models for equal educational opportunity.

In Elliott Hardaway, from the University of Florida, the president found a librarian who combined the parsimony and interdisciplinary learning characterizing his profession with comprehensive administrative skills and an irrepressible conviction that higher education was great fun. He was knowledgeable about new media and technologies as well as books, and his grasp of general university operations led President Allen later to appoint him Vice-President for Administrative Affairs to succeed Robert Dennard.

Jean Battle, Dean of the College of Education, had been Dean of Liberal Arts at Florida Southern College in Lakeland. Over the South he had helped many colleges and schools confront problems of racial integration. In his concern for improvement in elementary and secondary education, Battle was committed to the principle of engaging children as active participants, and he believed that teachers needed a strong general education to provide the variety and enrichment necessary for children to enjoy learning and develop strong skills and interests.

Charles A. Millican, Dean of the College of Business Administration, had a similar concern for enlarging the capabilities of managers and executives in corporate enterprise and for personalizing professional education. He had attended and taught in liberal arts colleges and wanted to retain the values of small-college experience in a large university. He later became the first President of Florida Technological University in Orlando (now the University of Central Florida).

Designing Professional Education

In determining an effective approach to community service for each professional college, the dean considered the prospective needs of related social systems and chose to focus instruction on a broad or narrow range of activities within them. All of the deans together developed some shared values on which programs must converge. They should be designed for continuous updating to prefigure social change; they must share resources for maximum economy and effectiveness in learning. Programs should converge on the human encounter where high standards of performance make an essential contribution to personal and public welfare.

EDUCATION

Jean Battle, the first Dean of Education, liked to think of learning as "the opening of worlds." Considering education to represent *organized teaching and learning,* he centered teacher education programs on the process of learning. He outlined threefold configurations for major fields of study, integrating study of the learning process and the developmental tasks across the stages of human life with the professional roles of teaching, counseling, and administration in schools and other institutional settings.

Students have many options in designing their programs, including choice of the subject-matter component in the learning process. With the other deans, Battle designed secondary and postsecondary programs to draw subject-matter courses from other colleges. Because of the consistency in content of learning for young people and adults from high school forward, other colleges could provide content while the College of Education concentrated particularly on the repertory of *techniques* for teaching and learning. The deans underlined the all-University commitment to teacher education by giving these students dual membership in Education and the college providing the subject-matter courses.

Content and technique interact in any event; but the ways children learn and what they learn will differ distinctly from the ways of young people and adults. The same conditions apply to special education where both content and technique must fit unusual developmental tasks of gifted, retarded, and handicapped people of all ages. Students in early childhood, elementary, and special education, therefore, must rely on the College of Education for both content and technique.

Battle strongly emphasized urban education, in which the greatest variety of institutional settings appears and the most distinctive changes develop in the responsibilities of educators. With the inte- gration of American schools and the expansion of education in developing nations, program design also emphasized cross-cultural interaction. The cosmopolitan constituency offered ample resources. For example, in the Ybor City neighborhood, a historic center of Spanish and Italian cultural and business activity, a community commission was undertaking historic preservation and neighbor- hood development for an area that now included a growing black population.

Planning began in 1960 for urban, intercultural programs. One of the first was an accelerated graduate program, Training Teachers of Teachers, TTT, designed for those wishing to teach other teachers, counselors, and administrators preparing to facilitate the develop- ment of unitary school systems. Workshops and conferences for school board members and educators laid much of the groundwork for TTT, and its studies included a period of "cultural immersion" by working and living in a community new to each student's experi- ence.

In 1962 planning began for a Peace Corps–Teacher Corps training program, conducted from 1968 to 1972. The first to combine train- ing for overseas and stateside volunteers, it centered on urban de- velopment in newly industrialized and Third World nations, offering field studies in local schools and Ybor City and overseas training in Ghana. For the governments and universities of Honduras and Gua- temala, the college designed teacher education programs similarly focusing on the rise of cities and urban education.

ENGINEERING

Dean Edgar Kopp centered the Engineering program on the general system of technology and emphasized its effects on the quality of community and national life. The approach followed systems the- ory, an interdisciplinary development maturing in the early 1950s and integrating concepts related to such phenomena as the workings of a digestive system, a river, a railroad, telephone system, or school system.

In the College of Engineering, each major covers a distinctive technological system: Electric and Electronic Systems, Energy Conversion and Mechanical Design, Industrial Systems, and Structures, Materials, and Fluids. Each major requires basic work in all four areas, undergirding specialized studies; a major in General Engineering provides for personalized design with a comprehensive view of the entire system of technology. Courses in each field incorporate economic and ecological concerns which faculty research has also emphasized. For example, studies of tidal flow affecting the dispersion of effluent from power plants and sewage systems have used computer models refined by field studies.

BUSINESS ADMINISTRATION

Charles Millican gave the College of Business Administration a "stereoscopic" view. An intensive focus on the structure and function of corporate organization applied to programs in management, marketing, and accounting. An extensive view of the whole economic system applied to programs in economics and finance. The major in General Business Administration provided for other perspectives in a personalized design.

The approach seems to have been influenced by Floyd Reeves, one of the members of the Council for the Study of Higher Education. He was particularly concerned with faculty development and suggested among other things that USF locate a liberal arts department in each professional college. He did not wish to see the whole liberal arts program diffused across a university but he thought that a college of liberal arts could share some "outposts" with other colleges to mutual advantage. Reeves had concluded that scholars in liberal arts need to help "certified practitioners" break out of "establishment thinking" and keep professional education advancing across the frontiers of knowledge.[4]

The location of the economics faculty in the College of Business Administration was consistent with Reeves' suggestion. The College of Social and Behavioral Sciences also offers an economics major; students can choose either college, according to their career plans.

Programs with a corporate orientation have diversified and include other perspectives and other types of enterprise: small business, public and private nonprofit sectors of the economy, consumer-provider relations, risk-taking, planning and information systems.

An M.S. degree in Management introduced in 1972 particularly addresses the public and private nonprofit sectors, and prefigures the integration of business administration programs into comprehensive studies of the entire economic system, which the faculty began to plan in 1970. The cross-fertilization that Reeves recommended has enlarged the original design, strongly integrating professional and liberal arts study and research.

MEDICINE AND NURSING

Opening in 1971, the Colleges of Medicine and Nursing have centered their programs on the one constant in the changing system of health care: the professional responsibility for the health of all participants—clients, patients, families, the whole community. The colleges seem to be converging on other shared responsibilities: as medicine moves toward traditional concerns of nursing for people as participants rather than objects of treatment, nursing is moving toward concerns of medical education for scientific expertise in the process of maintaining and restoring health.

Plans for medical education took the classic approach exemplified at Johns Hopkins—"the whole-patient" approach recognizing health, illness, and recovery as functions involving all of a person's lifeways and interactions over an entire community. The programs center in clinical instruction as the source of both scientific and practical expertise and employ interdisciplinary methods extensively.

Dr. Alfred Lawton began the planning for the College of Medicine, Dr. Donn Smith succeeding him as dean in 1969. With Dr. Alice Keefe, first Dean of the College of Nursing, they decided to conduct clinical instruction in local hospitals under cooperative agreements. Recently a University teaching hospital has been considered, a modification of philosophy and design occasioned primarily by continuing difficulty with the divergence of patient-oriented instruction from technology-oriented predilections in the local medical community. This difficulty reflects some trends and issues which national planning has sought to answer, especially through community-based networks for health care. It also suggests that something more than better training and planning—perhaps the creation of a new system—may sometimes be required in order to keep any major social system centered in concerns of the people it serves over generations of cultural change and community development.

The College of Nursing includes in its programs a strong foundation in the health sciences and interdisciplinary studies related to leadership, problem-solving, and decision-making in the treatment process and the system of health care. New configurations of instruction cover a variety of settings for nursing practice such as schools and industry, and a variety of roles for nurses outside of treatment and patient care, such as research, health education, counseling, planning, and administration. Both medical and nursing education at USF emphasize the essential responsibility of students and practitioners for self-directed, lifelong learning.

Designing General and Liberal Education

To serve the distinctive purposes of general and liberal education, Sidney French and John Allen established two separate colleges. On the all-University principle, the entire planning group set objectives for both types of programs.

First, general education, centered in the College of Basic Studies, must develop shared values that integrate learning, and commonalities in knowledge and practice that sustain community life and the culture of cities. Second, the College of Liberal Arts must advance "the state of the art" in science and humanities in order to sustain the educational enterprise itself and to provide the knowledge required in all social systems as people learn to cope with future concerns and opportunities.

The liberal arts programs would cover specialized fields in both new and traditional domains of science and humanities. But the deans and President Allen emphasized interdisciplinary studies in all colleges for a number of reasons. Parsimony and integration of learning worked together. Wherever instruction could capitalize effectively on commonalities in content and technique, it was clearly to the advantage of a university limited in funds and faculty to design fewer but broader courses and programs around a common focus.

The interdisciplinary approach also facilitates personalized learning. Students need not be rigidly confined within a special field but should freely cross territorial lines in designing their degree programs and develop independent study, reading, and research for their work in regularly scheduled or self-directed courses. The deans particularly wished to capitalize on student experience in independent studies, especially those of interdisciplinary design. For the most challenging problems and opportunities for advancing knowledge often emerge outside of established disciplines, and cross-fertilization seems to produce creative teaching and research of high quality.

The capabilities of interdisciplinary method for modifying content, technique, and environment of learning while sustaining coherence and thrust were also considered an asset in cultivating University-community interaction and containing "the knowledge explosion." The concern of the planners for effective education of high quality called for capitalizing on such capabilities for instruction, research, and community service and also for the all-University approach to organization and governance.

From the outset President Allen established the University's strong foundation in general and liberal studies. Addressing a community group in 1957, two months after assuming the presidency, he spoke of the value of this essential foundation for vocational development:

> Our colleges should insist on every student taking a course in American institutions which would give the political, economic and sociological history of our way of life. . . . Every student should know something of science and mathematics, should study literature, philosophy and fine arts, should have education in effective thinking. We want everyone to be well trained in effective writing, speaking and reading. After such an education for citizenship and personal living responsibilities, then we would expect each student to specialize in depth in one of the many fields open to him in a modern American college or university.[5]

Administrative Organization

President Allen adopted a fairly standard model for organizing the University around three areas for academic, student, and administrative affairs, headed by deans (the title was later changed to vice-president, the term generally used here).

Allen functioned initially as Vice-President for Academic Affairs, and Sidney French assumed that position after the College of Basic Studies consolidated. Robert Dennard, Vice-President for Administrative Affairs, and Business Manager Andrew Carroll Rodgers joined the planning staff from the University of Florida, both well versed in policies and practices of the Board of Control, Cabinet, and Budget Commission. Also in Administrative Affairs, Clyde Hill, a civil engineer, was responsible for planning facilities and campus development in concert with the Board of Control architect in residence. Student Affairs was the last area to be staffed, by Howard Johnshoy from Ball State University, a rapidly growing Indiana university developed out of a teachers college.

One application of the all-University approach which Sidney French and John Allen particularly favored was to include in each administrative area some functions closely related to other areas and involving all members of the University.

Academic Affairs included the colleges, the Office of Records and Admissions under the registrar, the library, and after 1962 the Office of Institutional Research and Evaluation Services.

Administrative Affairs included Educational Resources, which provided universitywide support for both instruction and administration including the closed-circuit TV network, broadcasting stations WUSF-FM and WUSF-TV, and multimedia services. This arrangement gave some academic responsibilities to Administrative Affairs along with the traditional responsibilities for physical plant, financial planning and management, finance and accounting, and auxiliary services. Its Personnel Services division included personnel records, retirement, and fringe benefits for the faculty as well as general personnel management for nonacademic staff.

Personnel Services also handled Cooperative Education, graduate placement services, student employment, and career planning. This arrangement did not please Howard Johnshoy, the Vice-President for Student Affairs. He envisioned a single center in Student Affairs for an array of developmental services tailored to students' changing needs from admission to placement.

Within an hour after Margaret Fisher arrived in 1960 to serve as Director of Student Personnel, Johnshoy sat her down to design a proposal for such coordinated services. The plan covered resources and activities of faculty, administrators, the library, health, counseling and other Student Affairs programs, and community agencies. But Johnshoy's centralized concept was not to be fully implemented until the third vice-president, Joe Howell, organized the Personal Resource Center in 1972. The Student Affairs area actually was too short-handed to carry career development services in 1960. The University and the students got maximum mileage out of Personnel Services under its director, Jack Chambers, an industrial psychologist also skilled in computer services.

Administrative Affairs also administered housing as an auxiliary service. Johnshoy was not happy to have this responsibility also located outside of Student Affairs. Residential staffing was not pro-

vided beyond supervision of construction and business management
for the first year, so he and Bob Dennard worked out a plan for
Student Affairs thereafter to assume responsibility for staffing and
organizing programs of residence life and activities, standards and
discipline, while Administrative Affairs continued to handle financial
and facilities management. Robert James Decker, assistant director
of Student Personnel, assumed responsibility for residence hall planning and program development in 1961.

Student Affairs covered other responsibilities for orientation, financial aid, health, counseling and developmental services, student
standards and disciplinary systems, and voluntary associations, activities, and events. The University Center, directed by Duane Lake,
a leader in the National Association of College Unions, served
faculty, staff, and students as an all-University activity center.

Other Student Affairs functions also involved interaction with
almost the entire membership of USF. Academic advising was initially coordinated in Student Affairs and all faculty members had
some students to advise. Both instruction and advising benefited
from the faculty's close connection with orientation, counseling, and
developmental instruction. In 1964 when enrollment became almost
equally divided between lower- and upper-level programs, a corps
of advisors was organized and the coordinator, Henry Robertson,
moved into Academic Affairs to work more closely with the college
deans and the advisors designated for each major.

Developmental services in reading and writing, speech and hearing, and personal and career counseling—often provided by related
academic units—were administered in Student Affairs at USF. These
services were also closely linked with programs in English, mathematics, speech, and education, and gave general support for educational and career planning in all the colleges.

Dual assignments were the rule in Functional Physical Education.
For the first few years, degree requirements stipulated by statute or
State University System policy included two years of instruction in
health and physical education. The USF planners separated required
programs from the professional program to be developed in the
College of Education. Functional Physical Education courses became
part of the College of Basic Studies, and the staff had dual appointments in Student Affairs, developing the tripartite program of instruction, recreation, and intercollegiate competition.

Location of Functional Physical Education in Basic Studies and Student Affairs left the professional program free to develop without the burden of general education. The College of Education has developed an exemplary major focusing on public school teaching in the areas of health, physical development, and recreation.

In general, the plan for University organization called for such sharing of responsibilities and resources by faculty, staff, and students, all contributing equally to its programs and activities.

ADMINISTRATIVE APPROACH

In planning and budgeting, USF administrators gave first priority to instruction and second to academic support services, including those activities developed by students. Third-priority allocations to general administration were kept to a minimum through ingenuity, resource-sharing among colleges and administrative units, and "pooling" duplicative functions. In recruiting, the president and the deans looked for staff having both academic and administrative experience. Many versatile people were attracted to USF by the opportunity to combine administration with teaching and research.

The University was also committed to student participation in governance, relying on students especially to initiate voluntary associations and activities expanding academic work beyond the classroom and giving all University members an opportunity to share common interests. For this reason, providing professional Student Affairs staff to support student-directed activities was a general administrative principle.

For example, the 47 women living in the University Center in 1960–61 were given staff leadership. Margaret Fisher wanted them to organize independently and manage their own regulations and activities with some part-time staff and faculty advice. President Allen and Howard Johnshoy, however, pointed out that initial decisions would set patterns for future residence halls. Staff support would be very important in laying the groundwork and linking residence programs to academic programs. Johnshoy was still hoping also for a cluster-college program or some other type of living-learning center.

Accepting these arguments, Dean Fisher found Phyllis Marshall, who had been Dean of Women in a small, residential liberal arts college. Marshall arrived just behind a hurricane and just ahead of the students to assume dual responsibilities for program development in the residence halls and the University Center.

Accordingly, the development of administration and governance must be viewed from an all-University perspective. The organizational chart (Figure 2.1) prepared in early 1960 shows the three areas of administration and the distinction between academic and administrative functions in governance. It does not do justice, however, to the integration of all parts of the University into a network of teaching and learning, providing a system of governance rather than a government.

A Faculty of High Quality

Recruiting faculty was extremely difficult because of a nationwide shortage of Ph.D.'s and a noncompetitive salary scale in the Florida universities. In 1958 President Allen and the planning staff outlined some questions to be resolved in securing faculty members of high quality and developing their roles and responsibilities.[6] Three questions seemed especially significant:

> What, if any, should be the differential characteristics of day and evening school teachers?
>
> How can prospective faculty be interested in dual or multiple appointments in the several colleges in the University of South Florida?
>
> How can faculty, specializing in the several fields, be organized so as to avoid the dangers of departmentalization without jeopardizing the scholarship and security which comes from close working relationships with others in the same disciplines?

Floyd Reeves met with the planners in February 1959 and approached these questions from a different standpoint. First of all, he wanted the faculty to participate in all aspects of University and community activity with no reference to rank and no distinction for teaching day or evening classes, part-time or full-time, or involvement in research, administration, or community services. The all-University approach implied a whole-faculty approach to governance.

Second, the University must simply find venturesome people, competent to take on dual appointments and multiple functions, not those who wanted a traditional academic setting. Reeves recommended recruiting from the military and other public service, from business and industry, high schools and community colleges, as well

Fig. 2.1. Temporary Organization of the University

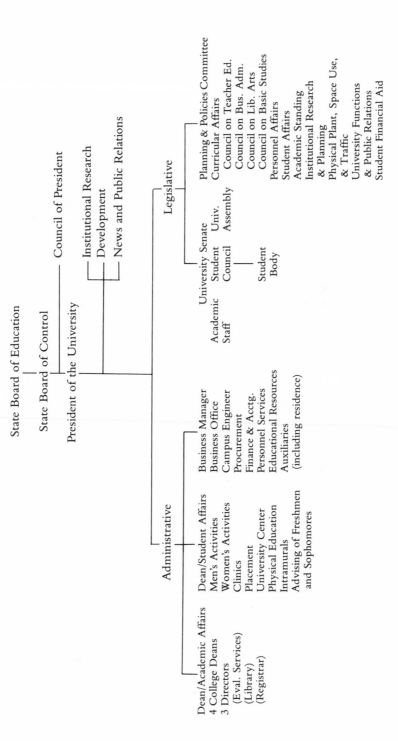

as graduate schools, in order to secure a strong infusion of experience from many enterprises and social systems.

President Allen wanted a young faculty, so that a small cadre of charter members would give continuity for ten or twenty years of growth and development. Reeves suggested that the deans seek younger faculty fresh from graduate schools "whose degrees come from two or three different universities, with at least one degree from a public university." For all faculty, degrees in more than one field and teaching experience in two or more geographic regions or types of colleges would be desirable. Reeves suggested aligning the percentage of Ph.D.'s from Florida and southern universities with the percentage of the U.S. population in Florida and the South.

Stressing quality rather than quantity of scholarship, Reeves insisted that "productivity in scholarship seldom if ever interferes with effective teaching." Two or three peers should evaluate a candidate's published work; and the best evidence of effective teaching would come from a visit to the campus with participation in a class or seminar.[7]

Reeves' recommendations were not carried out precisely, but their spirit was reflected in the characteristics of the faculty. Over the first five years, the 1965 Self-Study showed a high percentage of doctorates (62 percent), with annual figures varying from 58 to 65 percent. Ph.D.'s were well distributed: 37 percent from colleges and universities in the North-Central Association, 33 percent Southern, 16 percent Middle States, 5 percent Western, 4 percent New England, 2 percent Northwest, and 3 percent from foreign institutions. The percentage from the South was higher, the percentage from Florida lower, than the proportionate population. In recent years the proportion from the South has increased to around half.

The faculty actually brought a great variety of experience to USF in everything from agriculture to zoology. The average age was under 40. Most appointments (43 percent) were at the rank of assistant professor. In a highly competitive market, the low turnover rate in 1960–65, below 14 percent for all faculty and staff, was a welcome surprise.

The Best Students Ever to Attend the University

Students began to contribute to the planning for the University almost as soon as they were formally admitted. Beginning in June

1960, the charter students came in groups of fifty for orientation and registration, selected from a number of different high schools in order to avoid perpetuating traditional rivalries at USF. These registration groups would form the base for student participation in University governance and for generating activities, organizations, and services outside the classroom. Each group elected a convener and continued to meet as long as members considered it worthwhile. Some groups met several times on their own before the first day of classes. There was a good deal of politicking for leadership positions in the prospective student government and other activities.

After completing the tests for advising and developmental instruction, each group discussed the students' role in the University, career expectations, and ways of planning academic programs and class schedules; they registered for courses in conferences with faculty advisors.

Dean Johnshoy presented three tasks for the student body to accomplish during the first term: organizing a coordinating and planning council for the University Center; developing a system for initiating, regulating, and scheduling activities outside the classroom; and forming an association of students, or adopting some other procedure to secure student participation in planning and administration, including student representation in the University Senate.

In these group discussions, deans and advisors encountered many misperceptions about student and faculty participation in a university. They had worked out a general approach to counter fallacious folklore such as "Universities educate more effectively by selecting a better quality of students," and the concept of an academic assembly line with freshmen going in one end, graduates coming out the other, and dropouts representing "poor college material." Lew Mayhew incorporated much of their thinking in the 1961 Faculty, Staff, and Advisor Handbook.

• Academic work is real work. (People often set up a false choice between going to college or going to work, which is really a choice to work in college or somewhere else. The choice is not exclusive, since students often work in a household or business at the same time.)

• Students do academic work. (People often misperceive faculty as doing all the work in advancing knowledge, while students take courses as if they were dishes at a dinner, or doses of medicine. In customary practice, students contract with the university to do work in a degree program, each course being one task in the program. Work on their classroom assignments must contribute also to their teachers' responsibility to advance knowledge, and develop the students' own capabilities to continue independently in that responsibility throughout their careers.)

• Instructors grade academic work—not students. (Students must produce papers, lectures, experiments, works of art which instructors evaluate. Students use the evaluation to improve their capabilities and produce still better work. Examinations do not test quality of work, except in terms of performance under pressure of time. Instructors should, therefore, do much more than design and score examinations. They must assign and evaluate the variety of work necessary for students to master techniques in a broad field of scholarly work, and help them contribute to the advancement of knowledge.)

• Grades should be read as direction indicators for improvement in quality of work. (Students should take the initiative to confer with instructors about points to improve, errors to correct, or strengths to capitalize upon in the future. The grade report gives a general indicator; students have the responsibility to follow through, improve their work, and manage their plan for education and career development.)

Student tradition held that universities are set up to flunk people out as often as possible. The proposition that USF was set up to help students succeed, and faculty and staff would help students do good academic work, did not fit the folklore. Many students took the orientation program skeptically; they were not prepared to believe that USF really wanted everyone to do good work.

The idea that students must contribute to USF through voluntary organizations and activities was more enthusiastically received. Registration groups went to work to generate all kinds of associations and special events; they formed committees to work on the three administrative systems outlined by Dean Johnshoy. Asking students to build up the new University appealed to the spirit of voluntary association, strong in the family and community experience of most students. The idea that students contribute to the advancement of knowledge also stirred the imagination. But these "nontraditional" students were still skeptical about the all-University approach and their shared responsibility for the mission of higher education.

3
Governance

Scalar Principles

Analogies to scalar configurations (ladders and pyramids, thermometers and yardsticks) express a commonplace concept of social organization as a process of stratification according to caste and class. In scalar analogies, it is commonplace to speak of "higher education," to certify "according to degrees," to locate jobs at some "level" on a bureaucratic pyramid or make plans to advance on a "career ladder." It is commonplace understanding that "the higher, the better" applies to position or level in a scalar configuration, and "the higher, the fewer" applies to any reward such as an A on an examination or any status such as full professorial rank.[1]

Among these analogies, the scalar principle of organization is recognized by the practice of locating responsibility, not according to distinctive functions in a process of concerted study and action, but at graduated levels or degrees on a scale of authority, descending from the highest sovereign center.[2]

Analogies involve differences that are as important as similarities. Both common sense and the laws of physics affirm a simple fact of life: you cannot do two different things at the same time with the same set of concepts, tools, and techniques. As everyone who sews knows, a tape measure will not hold a garment together. Yet the scalar principle of organization has often been applied by an unexamined analogy, on the implicit assumption that the same configuration used to place people in proper categories or positions will also hold them together in common enterprise.

This error has many ramifications, and many difficulties in American education seem to arise from the mingling of scalar concepts in the meritocratic tradition with equalitarian themes and principles.

Models for University Governance

At the end of the 1950s the Carnegie Corporation commissioned a study of college and university governance, on which the 1947 President's Commission had made major recommendations. John J. Corson, a management consultant and experienced university trustee, conducted an extensive survey and found manifest unrest among trustees, presidents, administrators, faculty, and students.[3] Many felt equally frustrated over their formally documented organization, typically based on some governmental-legislative or managerial-bureaucratic model, and over the informal network or "grapevine" often used when formal apparatus failed.

The scalar principle typically shaped formal organization but tended to bend its operations out of shape and misplace authority and responsiblity. Often it fragmented a university, and made it harder to bring people together for learning. Decisions "from on high" often would not fit actual conditions on the scene of the action in a classroom or administrative office. On this distortion of the process of organization, Professor Earl Latham of Amherst College wrote to Corson, "Administrative absurdity increases directly as the square of the distance between context and process."[4]

Such dissatisfying effects of the scalar principle of organization are to be expected. In universities, each configuration of people-process-resources for instruction or governance forms in a unique way. Specific to each setting and task for study and action, it will rarely duplicate any other configuration anywhere. Having few if any matching parts, an organization for teaching and learning simply does not have enough commensurable elements to be laid out on a scale.

Consequently, Corson advised everyone concerned for governance in higher education to recognize "the fact that the *scalar principle,* so firmly embedded in the minds of those acquainted with business, governmental and military organizations, has no duplicate in the academic enterprise." Colleges and universities have to integrate into well-orchestrated governance four types of operations, each involving many unique elements.[5]

   • Multiple purposes, to meet diversified needs for lifelong learning by people in all walks of life.
   • Multiple programs and activities, specific to each purpose, dif-

fused over many fields of study and dispersed to many geographic locations on and off the campus.

• Diversified configurations of people-process-resources, each specific to a unique activity and usually subject to periodic changes in participants, process, or subject-matter—to the extent that a particular configuration could not be replicated even if anyone wanted to do so.

• A unique configuration of capabilities and expectations, functions and responsibilities, requiring commensurate authority, for each and every person involved.

Corson found that colleges and universities had usually developed the most satisfactory ways of governance around processes of planning, applying principles and techniques closely related to the process of teaching and learning. He suggested that faculties should organize around educational planning and center their responsibility in functions of teaching, research, and service rather than in a representative body with legislative authority. Administrators should center on their functions in support of the academic program, facilitating the provision of resources for teaching and learning. Presidents and trustees should organize their functions to facilitate a university's connections with the whole educational system, with governments, and with other institutions in the community, across the nation, and around the world.

An effective approach to governance should apply other principles operating effectively in many institutions, regardless of the scalar principle reflected in their organizational charts. These principles are nonscalar, and related to functions or processes. They call for authorization through procedural guidelines for discretionary, on-the-spot study and action. They function most effectively through a network for information flow and feedback so that members can learn from each other how developments over the entire organization can keep in tune with a well-orchestrated institutional plan for instruction and administration.

In many respects Corson's work matches the "all-University approach" at the University of South Florida. The study was published after USF was ready to open, but many features of its governance exemplify principles and processes that Corson recommended.

Organizing the Faculty

The all-University approach to governance clearly centered on the process of teaching and learning. Sidney French wrote in the first

Accent on Learning (p. 51), "A University is composed of a group of colleges under a central administration." But the temporary organizational chart, other documents, and the best recollection of participants, indicate that the planning staff had initially been thinking in terms of a governmental model with an administrative bureaucracy and a legislative body for the faculty alone.

On February 26, 1959, the president and deans discussed with Floyd Reeves a preliminary plan for faculty organization, included in the working paper on faculty development.[6] The copy of this paper in the Archives includes notations by Elliott Hardaway, librarian, that appear to indicate significant changes by the planners in this meeting or subsequent sessions. For the design for governance that was presented to the charter members in 1960 took a different approach, applying the all-University principle and centering governance in the planning process. It diffused responsibility and authority throughout the systems for participation by students, staff, and faculty. The preliminary plan proposed:

1. An all-University assembly of faculty above the rank of instructor, to be responsible for curricular and educational matters. (Comment: "Disfranchising 20 percent of faculty.")

2. To meet monthly, the agenda prepared by an executive committee (president, deans, directors of administrative areas, six faculty). New business open to proposal from any faculty member. (Comment: "Why college reps? Deans rep[resent] colleges.")

3. Its decisions to be final, subject to veto by the president under unusual circumstances. (Comment: Query "?" as to "circumstances." Query as to veto: "Is it true? Where does the control come in?" [SUS policy contemplated no such process of presidential veto or legislative override.]

4. To establish committees for each administrative area, with elective membership:
   • Faculty Affairs (handling grievances, promotion, and employment standards)
   • Student Affairs (handling grievances, voluntary activities, standards and discipline)
   • Summer and Evening Sessions
   • Admissions and Orientation
   • Institutional Planning (including support of research)
   • Physical Plant
   • Administrative officers to serve *ex officio* on related committees.
   • The colleges to organize *ad libitum*.

(Comment: Query on the *ex officio* position of administrative officers, apparently relating to duplication of their responsibility for managing the work of administrative units by also designating committee chairmen. Query on absence of any committee concerned for nonteaching staff, and their exclusion from the organization as a whole. Query on the responsibilities within the colleges for deans and faculty. Query on the grievance procedure—bypassing the instructor or dean who could act in the first instance, and leaving no place for appeal except to the president.)

All-University Governance

The planning staff carried the design for governance beyond the working paper and dealt with two dimensions of organization: the University's internal system for planning (going beyond the organization of the faculty) and the external connections to the State University System, linked to the state government through the Board of Control. These two dimensions converged on the office of the president.

The University's internal organization was designed on the stages in the planning process rather on than the scalar principle and employed conciliar rather than legislative bodies. All faculty and staff were included without distinctions of rank and student participation was anticipated. Authority and responsibility were located on the scene of the action, each faculty member being responsible for action in the classroom, in research, and in advising students.

Matters affecting a particular course or program involved its faculty and their program chairman. Deans were responsible for all-college matters, acting on cumulative information delivered by the chairman from each faculty unit. Each vice-president was responsible for coordination of all-University functions in an assigned area, supported by a committee with all-University membership. The vice-presidents advised the president, who had final responsiblity for internal policy and program development and for making all appointments to positions in teaching, administration, and universitywide committees. In turn he was fully responsible for forwarding proposals that required action by the Board of Control and for developing internal plans and decisions consonant with sus plans, policies, and pertinent statutes.

Proposals usually came to the president through two advisory bodies. The Executive Committee included the vice-presidents, the librarian, the business manager, and two college deans serving for one semester on a rotating schedule. The University Senate included 40 faculty, 5 nonacademic staff, and 5 student representatives.

Proposals proceeded by consensus from stage to stage, coming to closure on the final action by the president. Chairmen, directors, deans, vice-presidents, and the president functioned as facilitators of planning and feedback from classroom experience and the work of each college and administrative area into the all-University context.

A Planning Approach

The assignments for each committee outlined the steps for planning and decision-making and the linkages with other stages and other systems in the process of governance. If any existed, no general flow chart from this period has come to light, but Figures 3.1, 3.2, and 3.3 roughly outline the systems decribed in committee documents. These provided three channels for educational, administrative, and all-University planning. Like systems that Corson found effective and economical, each provided a two-stage developmental process from initiation to closure on a policy or other action.

Educational and administrative channels provided for development of plans and policies preliminary to introducing them into long-range, all-University deliberations, and also for operational decisions within established guidelines. Program (departmental) or college faculty worked out preliminary plans for academic programs and policies that went through the dean and college council into the all-University process. Operational matters were typically settled in a program or college faculty. The channels were open for exchange of information and advice on any decision, action, or grievance, by anyone concerned, from any place in the organization and in any direction. Any formal or informal group could propose a policy change or a new program. Any grievance went first to the scene of the action, to the teacher or officer responsible for redress, and then could be appealed to the dean and finally to the president.

On administrative matters anyone—faculty, staff, or student— could forward requests for advice and decisions or suggest proposals for new policy and program. A signal might go directly to a committee, but action was usually more effective when a recommendation or question was forwarded through the director of a particular unit or the vice-president.

Fig. 3.1. The Educational Channel

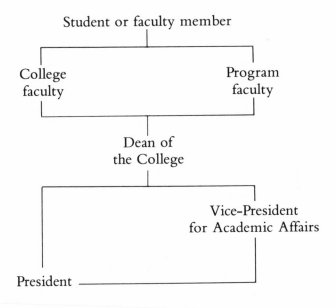

Fig. 3.2. The Administrative Channel

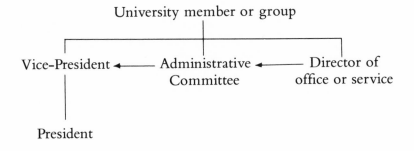

Fig. 3.3. The All-University Planning Channel

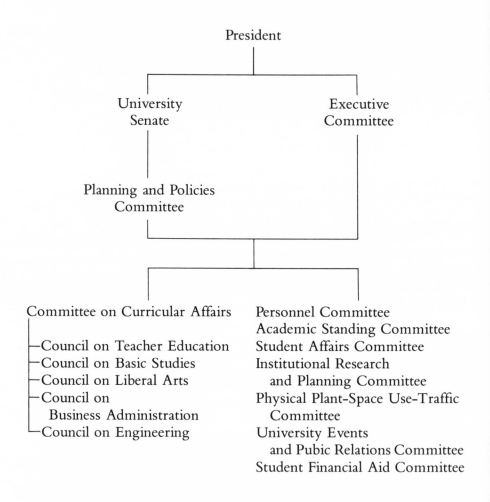

President

University Senate

Executive Committee

Planning and Policies Committee

Committee on Curricular Affairs

─Council on Teacher Education
─Council on Basic Studies
─Council on Liberal Arts
─Council on Business Administration
─Council on Engineering

Personnel Committee
Academic Standing Committee
Student Affairs Committee
Institutional Research and Planning Committee
Physical Plant-Space Use-Traffic Committee
University Events and Pubic Relations Committee
Student Financial Aid Committee

In each administrative area, directors met with staff in their units (such as the Health Center or Personnel Services) and the vice-president with the heads of all offices, services, and units on operational matters and forward planning. Administrative committees worked on two sorts of matters: long-range policy and program development and discretionary judgments such as waivers, appeals from staff decisions, and exceptions to some policy and practice (e.g., petitions to the Committee on Academic Standards for waivers of particular requirements).

Any proposal affecting the entire University linked into a third system, particularly designed for long-range planning and all-University development. For example, new degree programs or changes in student standards and discipline went through this channel since their adoption would affect the entire University's program, budget, and academic and administrative support systems.

College councils and administrative committees sent proposals into the Planning and Policies Committee, which checked them for any missing links and scheduled final review by the University Senate. Each college had a multidisciplinary, all-University council. Administrative committees had multidisciplinary membership from colleges and administrative offices with which they coordinated operations. In the planning process, these groups included ad hoc any other people concerned in a proposal and checked with related councils and committees, before a recommendation went to the Planning and Policies Committee and the Senate.

Any member of the University, any informal group or formal unit within it, could initiate the planning process on an issue or proposal. New ideas often developed in workshops or retreats.

The timetable was flexible; councils and committees typically set the sequence of study and action tasks early in their deliberations. Tasks in the first stage of study and design were usually scheduled concurrently in several different agencies. For instance, the design of a new academic program typically started with a task force from related fields of study whose members would immediately get in touch with administrative and student affairs units to begin related planning. As the proposal took shape, more formal, systematic exchange of information and advice would be arranged to complete the plan and carry it through channels to the college council, senate, and president.

Student membership on councils, committees, and task forces, proposals from the Student Association or other organizations, and periodic surveys provided extensive student participation and feedback. Individual or group proposals from students could go through any Student Affairs office or go directly to the particular academic or administrative office concerned.

COORDINATING FUNCTIONS

All three systems were designed to keep advice and counsel, study, and decision-making as close as possible to the scene of the action. The president consulted the Executive Committee weekly; with any officer only two stages removed, at most, from classroom or administrative units, the president could keep in close touch with the process of growth and development and feed back systemwide developments quickly to the whole University.

The University Senate kept future-oriented plans and current developments in order and also facilitated organization of the whole network of councils and committees. It elected three student and four faculty representatives from its membership to the Planning and Policies Committee, which secured nominations for councils and committees and advised the president on appointments.

PRESIDENTIAL RESPONSIBILITY

There was little point in going first to President Allen for action; even in critical circumstances, he typically sent internal matters back to the scene of the action or into the planning process. Many people were firmly convinced that authority and responsibility always go with rank and took questions or complaints "straight to the top." Allen would listen attentively, then say, "You really should do something about that and this person will help you."

This approach—especially the idea of a mere student doing something about the whole University—was mind-boggling to some people. But Allen was rarely disposed to do what someone else could do effectively; neither was he inclined to intervene in responsibility he had delegated. Frank Spain relates how he told Allen just before opening day that some room numbers had been mixed up and did not match the class schedule. "Allen said, 'What do you plan to do?' I said a notice might be handed out at convocation, and he replied, 'You may have just enough time to print it'."

Some people felt that John Allen did not care much about students and faculty because he usually passed along requests and made referrals. In fact he cared a great deal, particularly about not interfering in their responsibility. There was nothing cool and aloof about his approach to the complex tasks involved in the University's relations to the state's educational system and government.

Allen had compelling reason to concentrate on work with the Board of Control, Cabinet, and legislature. USF was the first university created under the plan for expansion. Feedback from its experience would affect prospects for implementing the Florida Plan and determine substantially the identity, autonomy, and scope of programs for USF and other new universities. The Board of Control, the Cabinet, and the legislature were learning to understand a university new to their experience. A diversified network for the State University System was developing, equally new to their experience. Together, they were conducting "action research," in which John Allen provided essential information from experience at USF.

Engagement with the State University System substantially influenced the decision of the planning staff to shift from a governmental to a process model for governance. Under Board of Control policies, the president had final administrative responsiblity in a university. Lengthy legislative proceedings, especially adversary proceedings entailed in any veto, would be counterproductive to understanding and support both inside and outside the University. A straightforward planning process, steadily developing consensus from the initial study to closure on the president's action, would facilitate growth and development. This process of developing consensus was consistent with Allen's style and his background in the Quaker tradition. But USF could not really afford any other approach to governance.

PERSONALIZING ADMINISTRATION

The diffusion of authority and responsibility meant that administration as well as instruction became more personalized. With responsibility went degrees of discretion, facilitating personalized decisions in keeping with the setting, the contingencies and alternatives presented on the spot. Within the guidelines something a little different, a little more fitting, could usually be done.

Almost all policies included procedures for discretionary judgment. Academic areas provided waivers of degree requirements on the basis of special experience in school or employment. Mature students could earn credit at USF for life experience some years before the standardized CLEP instruments came into use. In administrative areas, procedures could speed up action or accommodate unforeseen circumstances by very simple arrangements. Personalized arrangements often eased the time constraints that bring hardship to so many commuting students who have multiple responsibilities to family, community, and employment.

In keeping with this personalized approach, Frank Spain and the registrar's staff displayed a poster bearing the University seal with the legend "Accent on Lagniappe."

Student Participation

The planners did not specify a form of organization for the student body but viewed student participation from the all-University perspective, considering all members as adults equally responsible for planning and risk-taking in educational and career development, equally contributing to the University's development. During the late 1950s, student personnel associations had worked out some basic concepts and principles for student participation in teaching and learning, planning and governance. Their professional approach centered on the process of adult development and the developmental tasks involved in lifelong careers. They emphasized student rights and responsibilities consistent with constitutional guarantees for every person. The approach was generally equalitarian and recognized that the tradition of common law, with faculty and administration standing in loco parentis to students, failed to describe adequately the manifold relationships between students and universities.

For example, Student Personnel Work as Deeper Teaching emphasized the interaction of classroom instruction, counseling, student services, and governance, making voluntary associations and activities an integral part of the whole institution. The authors viewed participation in the governance of academic life and work as an important dimension of general education. [7]

In 1953–54 a joint commission of student personnel associations worked out a developmental approach to student standards and discipline, departing from the doctrine in loco parentis and the habit of defining standards in terms of violations with fixed penalties. Developmental standards should be "educative and preventive," describing the *right* way to do things and the process of making positive, effective decisions and correcting errors. Disciplinary procedures should aim at "re-education and action" and provide for joint planning by a counselor and student to develop a course of action that the student could carry out, incorporating any corrective action or compensatory penalty, and keeping the student in the university whenever this was feasible.[8]

At USF, a 1959 Conference on Intellectual Tone[9] particularly emphasized these principles. The planning staff and five consultants, including Philip Jacob, author of *Changing Values in College,*[10] were studying the implications of the accent on learning and the all-University approach for the roles and responsibilities of students. These principles converged on the students' responsibility for planning their own education and career and their important initiative in enriching learning through activities and services outside the classroom.

The conference report emphasized the adventure of learning that students and teachers share. An effective university should have the true spirit of the frontier, "the acceptance of uncertainty with confidence." In this spirit, the planners left to students the design for organizing the USF student body.

According to tradition, USF would probably have a student government. Sidney French wrote in the first *Accent on Learning* (p. 51), "It is anticipated that students will wish to organize a student government and perhaps elect class officers. They will probably decide to publish a student newspaper and establish men's and women's government organizations."

Charter students also presumed they would have a student government, being influenced by academic tradition and encouraged by advice from the faculty and from friends at the University of Florida and Florida State University. Both universities had a strong tradition of highly independent student government, strongly oriented toward state government and politics, only marginally toward the academic enterprise. Its leadership positions had often been used as springboards to elective office in local, state, and national government.

The U.S. National Student Association often advocated such a political orientation, reinforced by experience in international conferences and student exchange. The autonomy of student organizations in the universities, and their activity as a political power bloc in many other countries, more often followed syndicalist rather than democratic principles. Yet many student government leaders considered this "activist" approach to be a desirable model for students in America.

NSA leaders also wanted to involve all students more fully in the whole academic enterprise. In 1955 an NSA survey[11] identified many contributions that student government could make to a university and found substantial consensus between students and administrators on such functions as activity coordination, planning student programs and services, and evaluating instruction.

Perhaps the most important consensus concerned the role of student government in attempting to counteract the pervasive sense of apathy, alienation, and helplessness under arbitrary authority, apparent in "The Silent Generation" of the 1950s. This was a far cry from the almost habitual outbursts of violent rebellion against administrative autocracy and the rigid "academic lockstep" on American campuses from colonial times to the early 1900s. Many were alarmed over the tendency of students of the 50s to turn away from learning altogether and to put up passive resistance to arbitrary, insensitive authority.

STUDENT-BODY ORGANIZATION

After the staff decided on a planning model for governance of USF, expectations of a student government also changed. President Allen stated clearly that the University would operate under the Constitution of the State of Florida. The campus was not a political jurisdiction entitled to a constitution and government of its own, for students or any other members.

Allen and the deans were deeply concerned with bringing people together for effective action in the University and across the community. Student participation was essential in many different ways of work; diversification might be impeded by setting up any single agency for the entire student body. The planners also resisted strongly a syndicalist approach; separating student, faculty, and administrative jurisdictions would simply make it harder to bring people together on all-University matters.

Howard Johnshoy and Herbert Wunderlich, his successor as Vice-President for Student Affairs, were strong proponents of the all-University approach, cultivating student contributions throughout the University. Johnshoy insisted that governance meant bringing people together, not putting them into membership categories or boxes on a chart. Wunderlich emphasized "self-responsibility" and "self-governance" as fundamental democratic principles. Both objected to the exercise of arbitrary authority by any student agency as vigorously as they supported students against any arbitrary action on administrative or faculty authority.

President Allen concurred with Dean Johnshoy on developing a student association rather than a student government. Its responsibility should include coordinating activities, recruiting and training students for various all-University committees, campus and community services, and national and international undertakings. It seemed clear that a legislative body and a bureaucracy could not work very effectively on such a diversified program. Accordingly, as the registration groups formed, Johnshoy outlined a network of activity councils to be coordinated by a general council of the Student Association.

ACTIVITIES SYSTEMS

Volunteers or elected representatives from all registration groups formed task forces to develop systems for participation in governance. With the task force on the University Center, Duane Lake and Phyllis Marshall developed its council and program committees, planned the program for the year, and designed the procedure for scheduling events and activities that the center's staff would coordinate with the class schedule for facilities use. Another group worked with Gilman Hertz and the Physical Education faculty, planning a full-scale Functional Physical Education Program of recreation, intramurals, instruction, and sports. A Coordinating Council of registration-group conveners worked with Margaret Fisher to design procedures for voluntary associations and special-interest activities. With Howard Johnshoy an elected Provisional Committee worked on the design for the Student Association.

By November 1960, the student-staff task forces had laid the foundation for many long-term developments.

 • Leadership training for students volunteering to serve as officers or representatives in activity, academic, and administrative councils.
 • A network of councils and procedures for organizing, recognizing, coordinating, and promoting organizations and special programs: academic, fine arts, recreational, religious, residential, publications, political, honorary, and fraternal.
 • State approval for the University's financial office to handle accounts for voluntary associations.

• Staffing and publication of a student newspaper, originally as a campus edition of the *Tampa Times,* then as an independent publication, the *Oracle.*

• Revision of the president's preliminary decision to permit no fraternity organization until the University was accredited and eligible for chapters of national societies, so that social clubs and fraternal societies could organize; after USF accreditation, as they became eligible, they could petition for a national charter.

• A plan for residence hall life, adopted by the 47 women living in the University Center. (Their parietal rules discomforted the Student Affairs deans and later occasioned considerable protest).

• Completion of an interest survey and distribution of listings of interested persons to organizers of clubs and activities, University committees and councils.

• Publication of a *Guide to the Development of Student Activities* covering all the policies, procedures, standards, and guidelines developed to November 1960. (This stands today in much of its original form.)

Focusing on process rather than on structure often seemed difficult. For all of their objections to bureaucratic authority, students typically started out to write a constitution and determine "who was over whom," on the scalar principle of organization. The process of diffusing authority and responsibility according to function seemed hard to grasp. But they were eager to set a good record for the charter class, and when immediate action was in sight, they could bring the process sharply into focus.

For example, with perhaps a hundred groups getting started at once, the system of recognition and standards for organizations had to focus on process. Rules were limited to the need to know the purpose, who was responsible, whether they belonged to the University, and how members would conduct their affairs. The emphasis on student contributions to academic work called for procedures facilitating exercise of the rights of free speech, assembly, and publication. Adopted by the Coordinating Council and approved by the Committee on Student Affairs, the University Senate, and the president early in 1961, these guidelines retain much of their original form.

• Recognition procedures called for a letter of request stating purposes, leaders, program plans, and any proposed affiliation with national or community organizations. (Such affiliates must be able to conduct their own affairs and must initiate the relationship to off-campus organizations, rather than having local or national societies "colonize.") The letters were reviewed by the Director of Student Activities (advised by a Student Activities council) and by the Vice-President (advised by the Committee on Student Affairs) for final approval by the president. Organizations filing a letter continued to meet with provisional recognition; and because many organizations were ephemeral, permanent recognition was considered on the basis of the first year's results.

• Standards called for open membership (conditional only on commitment to the purposes of an organization, without discrimination on personal or group characteristics); open meetings and conduct of business; open records; annual financial and program reports to the members and the Office of Student Organizations; and operation in accordance with public law and University and Board of Regents regulations.

• Organizations could use the University's name, facilities, and services; schedule events on the University's calendar, on and off campus; and provide activities open to the whole University and the general public (subject only to coordinated scheduling of time and space, which imposed severe physical constraints for the first two or three years).

STUDENT STANDARDS AND DISCIPLINE

Registration groups usually advocated an honor code with stated offenses having fixed penalties, to be administered by student government under an honor court. Traditionally such a judicial branch handled hearings in the first instance on any violation of standards and regulations, with appeal to administrative officers.

The typical honor system did not seem to fit the University very well. First, referral to a central honor court would slow the process of handling offenses and would not even touch errors and minor problems of scholarship and behavior that could and should be corrected on the spot. Second, the developmental approach to standards and discipline called for effective action from the outset. Positive standards were needed, showing the right way to do things and including a way to amend errors and shortcomings immediately. Third, the administration was responsible for guaranteeing due process in hearings on violations of regulations, in keeping with constitutional principles. This responsibility did not require a court with adversary proceedings but called for participation by students with full information about the situation. The University could follow a counseling, problem-solving approach consistent with its educational role and avoid the misleading analogy to trial and punishment by a court.

Accordingly, President Allen decided that the Vice-President for Student Affairs would handle standards of conduct in academic, interpersonal, and intergroup relations. Responsibilities would be delegated to faculty for classroom matters and to self-governing councils in activity areas, with appeal to the vice-president and the president. Especially where misconduct might lead to denial of enrollment or admission (just about the only penalty available to a university), the vice-president might conduct the hearing in the first instance on his or the student's choice.

In any hearing, surveying the error or violation, the circumstances, and the consequences followed counseling procedure and aimed to develop some way to correct errors and improve performance and habits. The resulting plan often involved further work with a counselor or advisor. Only where no feasible plan could be worked out with tolerable costs and risks to the student and the University was separation or denial of admission considered.

Howard Johnshoy insisted on documenting positive standards stating procedures to realize desired outcomes. He often said his aim was to promote higher education, not misconduct. He had considerable support from studies of the learning process for his conviction that punitive approaches tend to exacerbate "failure anxiety" and to invite misconduct and underachievement.

In keeping with these principles, faculty and students had to share responsibility for academic standards. The deans advised that any error merits a failing grade on that part of the work. If cheating occurs, the whole work deserves a failing grade, and action to break the habit of cheating is imperative. Teachers sometimes find that they cannot work further with some students who have deliberately done mischief or done no work at all. Procedures allowed a teacher to drop a student just as a student can drop a course (the original USF grading system included a Y grade for this purpose), or to give a failing grade in the entire course. The general approach assumed that scholarly integrity involves continuing cooperative effort to avoid and correct error, which punishment alone will not accomplish.

The same principle applied to other standards which usually included procedures for dealing with situations that typically interfere with orderly conduct of shared responsibilities. For instance, the policy on class attendance simply stated, "Students are expected to attend all sessions of any class for which they are enrolled." Knowing that illness and other difficulties will occur, President Allen also set up an attendance office, making it more convenient for students to notify instructors about an absence as a matter of courtesy and also to make arrangements for team or group projects. The Attendance Office checked on prolonged absence and helped students make special arrangements if they wished to continue study.

Johnshoy explained to the registration groups how the interests of students and University converge on the practice of scholarly integrity. Unless students reported misadventures, errors, and violations of law or regulations, faculty and staff could not help them develop high performance. Students had to decide what was more important: to give oneself or another student a chance to do better work or to let an error or a bad habit continue and mislead many other people. Johnshoy's suggested approach followed the counseling technique of early intervention in problems and crises.

The message that students had to take action apparently registered. The charter students apparently set up an informal group standard. They decided that USF had to be first class. That meant high standards of conduct and no cheating. They did in fact report themselves and others, sometimes to instructors, sometimes to counselors and advisors, on all sorts of mishaps and offenses.

But the prohibition-penalty tradition was strongly entrenched. Students and faculty repeatedly pressed for lists of offenses with fixed penalties. Diffusing responsibility was one thing, having people accept it was quite another matter. Students and faculty were often persuaded that "automatic penalties" are more convenient and more equitable than dealing with each distinctive matter of personal right and responsibility on its own merit.

THE STUDENT ASSOCIATION

Difficulty in dealing with process surfaced in organizing the Student Association. The Provisional Committee fixed on a constitutional model with legislative, executive, and judicial branches when it drafted bylaws in November 1960 for student-body vote to create the Student Association, elect officers and student senators.

Dean Johnshoy objected to the governmental model; but the committee could think of no other way to organize except to write a constitution like the federal document. At the same time, however, the Coordinating Council put forward its conciliar system for activity areas, which members considered a superior model for the Student Association. Inevitably the two groups collided. Some members of each task force, aspiring to work in any student-body organization toward a political career, felt their whole professional career was at stake. Neither group would at first entertain the idea of setting up both a Student Association and a number of other self-governing bodies.

This uproar arose primarily out of difficulty in finding a base for representation in the various organs of the Student Association. The immediate base, the registration group, was a transient form; the colleges would provide a base for representation of their majors, but only after three or four years. The Provisional Committee proposed to take over the Coordinating Council's base in the voluntary associations but not its plan of work. This move was not satisfactory because not all students took part in activities.

Eventually, the issue was resolved by adopting both plans for different purposes and setting up a network of coordinating bodies, rather than bringing all voluntary associations under a single agency. Activity councils were separated from the Student Association and directly linked to the Student Affairs office for planning and policy matters and to the University Center for scheduling and other procedural matters. The Student Association would draw representation from "civic groups" organized as electoral bodies at each year's orientation; after 1964 the colleges would provide the base. Electing student senators and securing other representation in governance would be a major task for the Student Association, along with participation in general planning, and programing all-University events such as parents' day, major speakers, and political gatherings.

The judicial branch of the Student Association provoked acrimonious debate with Johnshoy and with some irate students over its claim to manage the whole system of standards and discipline as an "honor court." Allen and Johnshoy would not budge from their decision to follow a counseling process for hearings on offenses and grievances or change the positive standards and procedures already established. Johnshoy and the Provisional Committee finally agreed to limit jurisdiction of the judicial branch to such affairs as elections, management of funds, and discharge of assigned duties in the Student Association.

Any alternative to governmental models with centralized control seemed hard for student committees to grasp. For instance, the

Provisional Committee, in keeping with USNSA recommendations, wrote into its bylaws that the student legislature must approve all outside speakers invited by any campus group. The Coordinating Council's guidelines required clearance with the Student Affairs office only when a meeting was to be open to the general membership of the University or the general public; this procedure was a temporary measure required by severe space-time constraints.

Johnshoy turned down the Student Association rule as an arbitrary exercise of power, verging on unwarranted interference with academic freedom and freedom of speech and assembly. The Provisional Committee protested that his decision was autocratic, undemocratic, and authoritarian, and represented one more instance of tyrannical administrative interference with student rights and civil liberties.

Johnshoy on several occasions confided that he found himself at a loss in trying to understand the students' approach and philosophy in trying to set up a central authority, a bureaucracy empowered to tell them what they could and could not do in every conceivable situation. He would say, mournfully, "What ever became of the Bill of Rights?"

As Johnshoy and Fisher saw it, much of the difficulty arose from general dissonance between political folklore and educational processes. Governmental models, almost reflexively applied to any sort of organization, were not consonant with the planning model adopted in University governance. Furthermore, the short orientation sessions gave neither students nor faculty time enough to work through some of the ways that rights and freedoms, participation and responsibility actually work in higher education. More study was needed on the application of the teaching-learning process to organization and governance. A full-term orientation course was proposed by several faculty and encouraged by Johnshoy, Fisher, and other Student Affairs people.[12] But funds and staff were not available for this way of working through the implications of the accent on learning and the all-University approach for student's roles and responsibilities as contributors to higher education. Classroom instructors were very helpful in explaining these matters, pertinent to such courses as Human Behavior and The American Idea. But understanding made headway very slowly against scalar analogies, meritocratic assumptions, and traditions deeply embedded in academic and community folklore.

Life on the Academic Frontier

Coming Alive

People who go into teaching usually enjoy learning, even though professors often forget that they are also students. Assembling for the first orientation session at USF on September 6, 1960, the charter faculty and staff, however, felt very much like freshmen getting ready for the first day of classes—apprehensive but eager to get acquainted and start a new adventure.

They followed a rigorous daily schedule for three weeks of preparation. Each morning in general session President Allen, the deans, and outside consultants took the staff through the evolution of the University and the developmental process for the future. Each afternoon program faculties worked on course outlines and materials and spent part of the time in advising entering students. On some afternoons councils and committees planned immediate and long-range developments in academic programs and University governance. Most people had a good deal of homework every night. And the schedule was interrupted by a rather nasty hurricane. It left comparatively little damage on campus but gave the charter members the special sense of cohesiveness that so often comes from going through a bad time together and emerging unscathed.

Consultants underlined public matters having particular import for the University's future development. For instance, A.J. Brumbaugh traced the process of designing the Florida Plan for higher education. He emphasized the continuing responsibility of university faculties for updating its projections and programs, especially for graduate education. He stressed the autonomy of each university as an important factor in keeping the state's educational resources abreast of actual experience and expectations in the course of growth and development. Sound plans for higher education could come only "from the grass roots," from university faculties closely in touch with regional constituencies.

Representative Sam Gibbons played a major role in legislative action on the plan for higher education and the establishment of the new university in Tampa. He gave a short course in Florida government. The cabinet system, unfamiliar to many of the charter faculty, locates many responsibilities in this body of elected officers, including functions of the State Board of Education. The governor acts more as a moderator than a chief executive in a conciliar process for coordinating departments headed by officers equally accountable to the electorate.

In the legislature both rural-oriented "porkchoppers" and urban-oriented "lambchoppers," often at odds on other issues, joined in the commitment to the plan for higher education. With redistricting imminent, representation from urban centers would increase, with a change in the political climate very likely to become increasingly evident. Legislative action was steadily shifting from biennial "horse-trading" sessions and episodic decisions toward more orderly planning for statewide development. The universities must provide special resources in statewide planning, and well-designed proposals from university faculties would be essential to continue the orderly development of higher education.

Braulio Alonso, Principal of Tampa's Jefferson High School, was president-elect of the National Education Association. He considered urban areas such as Tampa to be undernourished in higher education but rich in opportunities for cultural development. People in all walks of life were eager to learn. Alonso described the social, recreational, cultural, and health services offered by centers in Cuban, Spanish, and Italian neighborhoods and similar resources of other neighborhoods and ethnic groups. These could be more freely shared across lines of color and language that still fragmented the city. The cosmopolitan population presented a mixture of values and expectations ranging from ideologically rigid, authoritarian, and ritualistic, to liberal-minded, humane, and public-spirited.

The schools were struggling to integrate, to expand and to enrich learning. Alonso described USF's charter students as eager to learn and independent-minded, naïve to higher education but often worldly-wise about neighborhood and community affairs. Many would have both volunteer and employed experience to contribute to academic work. He urged the faculty to capitalize upon student contributions in the classroom and to cultivate community service that would strengthen cohesive spirit and intercultural values.

The staff orientation period was unique. President Allen and the planning team capitalized effectively upon the strong frontier spirit of camaraderie they had shared as they brought new members into the University. They had by no means done everything in advance, but they had established the minimum "falsework" around which all charter members had constructive work to do from the moment they arrived. Large-minded, friendly, and generous toward one another, charter faculty and staff worked with challenge, skepticism, and criticism, remarkably creative and free from any disposition simply to replicate some hallowed tradition of another Alma Mater.

Their spirits rose to a climax in a grand celebration at the first convocation, September 26, 1960, at 10:00 A.M. Thousands of dignitaries, parents, children and spouses, friends, neighbors, and tourists filled the boulevard in front of the Administration Building. The faculty and charter class marched in the traditional academic procession, colorful, untidy, dignified, to music by the Chamberlain High School Band, which also played for the first time the USF Alma Mater, written by Wayne Hugoboom of the Music faculty. The chain of office and medallion were bestowed for the first time on a president of the University of South Florida, and each charter student received a miniature medallion. USF's own green-and-gold hood was bestowed on George Cooley, awarded the first honorary degree for his contribution to a magnificent botanical collection already in use. Governor LeRoy Collins and other dignitaries spoke; there were congratulations and gifts all round, red roses from the governor to Grace Allen.

As the academic procession unwound, ushers distributed notices correcting classroom numbers. Eventually finding their first classes, instructors turned to the blackboard. There was no chalk in the trays. There was no chalk anywhere on campus and none on order. Neither were any test tubes in the laboratories or anywhere else on campus. (Chamberlain High School obliged.) In the new and unsettled University, it was a comfort to find that at least one law of nature held: Murphy's Law, "If anything can go wrong, it will."

Creating an Environment for Learning

The campus clearly declares the identity and mission of the University of South Florida. This visual statement represents a signal achievement by some gifted and determined people: President Allen, Bill Breidenbach and other state architects, the several architects of its buildings and artists who embellished them, and Clyde Hill and the Physical Plant staff. The buildings blend into one another and into the landscape in manifold patterns of sand-toned brick and white sunscreens.

The state Department of Agriculture found most of the campus to have "the second-worst soil in Florida." On this rather forbidding landscape, Roxy Neal and the groundskeepers within the year worked a kind of magic with trees and shrubs from their own nursery, palms transplanted from other construction sites, and drought-resistant plantings. Some of the students and faculty helped; about sixty spent a wind-swept weekend planting oak and elm trees on the mall, literally up to their necks in sand. Sand was a shared nightmare for charter members of USF. Out of sand and other shared visions the University of South Florida began to develop identity.

A SENSE OF PLACE

People sometimes forget the importance of a sense of place in establishing the identity of an institution and the roles of people in it. Lyn H. Lofland, studying the city as "a world of strangers," found that the sense of place orders almost exclusively the conduct of both individual and concerted action. "In the modern city, a man is where he stands."[1]

The USF campus declared "Here stands a university" from the very beginning. But the sense of place did not declare its urban identity clearly until the city began to grow around the campus about 1965. There were egrets, owls, squirrels, and opossums in profusion on campus, and an occasional deer; sightings of bear and puma were reported. Out in the sand and swamps, people often felt lonely and isolated—none more so than the 47 women housed in the University Center in 1960.

The rural surroundings, the long daily trek to campus, and the pervasive sand sharpened the frontier spirit. The sense of being out on the growing edge of civilization and the frontiers of knowledge had strong physical reinforcement. The sense of bringing a university to life was intensified by the day-to-day experience of making things grow on campus. From this pioneer experience came a powerful vision of an environment created for learning.

A SENSE OF CARING

Shared visions and shared experience build shared concern, and today the campus looks well worn but well cared for. Carelessness and vandalism have left remarkably few traces despite their inevitable occurrence. Destructive acts were openly resented and protested from the very beginning.

Violence, vandalism, and malicious mischief have accompanied universities and students throughout their history. In the United States, as Jacques Barzun once remarked, the first half of the twentieth century was an unusual period of fairly quiet, peaceable campuses. He attributed this phenomenon to the younger age of admission and the elective system.[2] Other observers consider the transfer of disciplinary authority from the president to student personnel specialists and the development of new approaches to organization and governance also to have had calming effects.[3]

Beneficiaries of this period of the quiet campus, USF students were, nevertheless, determined to uphold the noble tradition of protest against an autocratic administration. In October 1960, they mounted the first demonstration, "The Great Bermuda Shorts Riot"—an assembly of about 50 students peacefully protesting "the rigid dress code" (which did not exist in policy).

Under the rules for scheduling activities, the Mall and Crescent Hill, on opposite sides of the University Center, were open for free speech and assembly; demonstrations and protests took place there as well as concerts, fairs, and forums. A free speech board in the University Center and letters to the *Oracle* provided public comment on any issue or concern. All of these arrangements were extensively used during the years of nationwide student protest, 1964–70.

One contractor surrounded a building site with a handsome board fence, promptly appropriated as a "graffiti fence." It blossomed each morning into a fresh array of cartoons, slogans, and epithets, even excoriating graffiti and once declaring in royal purple and shocking pink, "Anthropology Lives!" Considering that the contribution to free speech from this fence had helped to get USF through a very bad time with little of the violence worked in other places, many people regretted the removal of this serendipity.

Protests and demonstrations at USF did little irreparable harm to persons and property, and many were conducted in high comic style. A certain degree of care to avoid disruptive or destructive results seemed to characterize most demonstrations and confrontations.

A SENSE OF TRADITION: "THE GREEK WAY"

Having no traditions, members of the University could create and choose dreams and themes as they pleased. President Allen and Dean Johnshoy wanted to infuse traditions valued in the scholarly enterprise, especially the classic Greek vision of freedom and love of learning. Until USF became fully accredited, no "Greek" national fraternities could organize. Few faculty and students would study classic cultures. But somehow the intellectual tone should express the Greek spirit.

Students responded positively. Social clubs, instructed not to use Greek letters, combed dictionaries and conferred with Greek friends and families to choose suitable names: Arete, Paideia, Delphi, Enotas, Talos, Kio. Others chose Latin, Spanish, or acrostic names: Fides and Siges, Verdandi and Tri-sis. By student vote, Greek names were chosen for campus publications: *Oracle* (the newspaper) and *Aegean* (the yearbook).

President Allen protected against infelicitous nomenclature by laying down the rule that all buildings would be named according to function and memorialize no person living or dead. He laughed when reminded that more than one building might have the same function, as the time came to open the first residence hall. After his fashion, he asked Student Affairs to suggest a way to name the halls. Fisher and Johnshoy decided that this was an ideal occasion for invoking the Greek spirit. The problem was to avoid "the 'orrible dooble ongtong" in Greek as in English. The *Pseudepigraphica Academica*[4] gave clues to many things to avoid. Dean Fisher finally offered some alternatives: a list of stars and constellations, a list of cities, regions, and islands noted in Hellenic civilization, and names of noted Greek astronomers—or else, "just number 'em in order of construction."

John Allen chose to give place names to residential areas: Argos in the spirit of the Argonauts' voyage, then Andros noted for its beautiful women, Samos for the fleets' winged victory for freedom, and Melos for the honey island. Each building would be numbered in the astronomical fashion by letters in the order of the Greek alphabet. So Alpha was the first hall in the Argos complex, and others followed, down to Mu Hall in Andros.

Diffusing the Vision

Almost as soon as the University had established its sense of place and affirmed its identity, its spirit and vision were to be diffused. Planning for regional centers began in 1958. Beginning in 1965 the University moved into other cities. USF in St. Petersburg occupies a massive, hurricane-proof building originally used for maritime training, where submarines, other Navy and Coast Guard vessels, and Jacques Cousteau's *Calypso* have docked along its bulkhead. The Sarasota center combines the opulent, Italianate Ringling mansion with the clean-cut modern halls of New College. The Fort Myers center reflects Edwardian, public-edifice, "red-brick" urbanity.

The University's learning network runs through all sorts of other places across the service area. The seconding of faculty to regional centers assures a quality of outreach instruction in keeping with that on the Tampa campus. To some extent, this practice works against any coherent physical and social sense of place. Still USF is moving with the mainstream of higher education toward greater diversification and dispersion of teaching and learning, toward people in homes and workplaces as well as multiple campuses. Rising costs and rising expectations make still further diffusion likely. Having become a network for learning, USF also has to learn how to make a network sustain identity and cohesiveness, going beyond the physical environment that so visibly and palpably shaped its experience.

Realizing Identity

The University had few unique features, yet it had a unique identity. People were proud to be members of the University of South Florida. They could cite no particular aspect that was distinctive, but in the totality of its experience they recognized shared values and visions that gave the University its identity and distinction.

Variety and freshness were the rule. Anyone could contribute to plans incorporating things old and new that added coherence and excitement to the intellectual enterprise. Members did well by each other, each in a unique task with unique contributions, bringing the University to life.

There was good reason for pride. Before USF opened, people had many misgivings about the quality of the faculty and students. Representatives from other institutions competing for top-ranking faculty and students sometimes described USF as likely to become merely "a second-class university on the second-worst soil in a second-rate town in the second-worst state in the Union." In off moments, even some of USF's members perceived it to be a stepchild in the family of universities, little higher than the two-year colleges in the meritocratic rankings.

Nevertheless, students and faculty members achieved distinction individually and for the University. Overall academic performance of students regularly topped the results on standard measures from a comparison group of institutions selected for their general excellence or special distinction. The record of community service by all members was particularly outstanding. Self-esteem and high morale were attributed to the University's clear mission, purpose, and philosophy and to the involvement of all members equally in responsibility for its growth and development.

GROWTH

Scheduled according to 1956 projections to level off at 10,000 students in 1970, the University of South Florida passed that mark in 1967 and continued past 20,000 by 1975 to vie with Florida State as Florida's second largest university. The faculty increased from 109 (FTE) in 1960 to 338 in 1965, 834 in 1970, and 966 in 1975. Buildings mushroomed from 5 in 1960 to 100 or more in 1975; the value of facilities exceeded $100 million. Symbolizing this enormous expansion, a new library opened in 1975 to house over a million volumes, replacing the original one designed for 250,000.

The University's rapid growth in enrollment, facilities, and programs was so extensive that it was almost an entirely different institution every year. This was not forced growth, early to bloom and quick to wither. By careful planning, attentive to individual and community development, sturdy, mature growth continued.

ACCREDITATION

In 1963 President Allen invited the Southern Association of Colleges and Schools to send an advisory committee to determine whether USF was developing toward worthy candidacy for full accreditation. Committee members expressed pleasure at the progress made so quickly. They found that the University had a clearly defined philosophy and explicit statements of purpose consistent with its mission and its responsibility to students, to the state and its people, and to the traditional work of universities in advancing and sharing knowledge. The University had developed academic programs, governance, student and administrative services in line with its philosophy. They felt that USF was well on its way to full accreditation as soon as it met the requirement to graduate at least three classes.

This accolade was welcome as an affirmation of effective planning, realistic aims and standards. With the first full class due to graduate in a few months, the SACS report smoothed the way for charter members to present their candidacy for entry to employment and to graduate and professional schools of high quality.

The first graduating class was very self-important, very proud of themselves for having done first-rate academic work, for being first to graduate, and for their contributions in bringing the University to life. And in due course, after the second official self-study and site visit in 1965, the University of South Florida became a fully accredited member of the Southern Association.

During its first years, progress was remarkably smooth. Students were eager to learn, faculty dedicated, administrators in tune—all worked together to make the great venture succeed. Everyone was aware that each action established a precedent, each new organization and activity became a tradition; and everyone wanted everything to be done well.

Euphoria pervaded the charter faculty and student body. A dean remarked in 1961, "It seems almost too good to be true. We can hardly do anything wrong. I wonder how long the honeymoon can last."

Somebody Misplaced the Horizon

Twenty years after the Cabinet established the University of South Florida and fifteen years after its classes opened, inward, disquieting signs of disorientation belied outward, visible signs of success. Early goals were scarcely mentioned except to wonder whatever became of the all-University approach. People strove mightily toward efficiency and productivity; every administrator, professor, and student was expected to produce quantifiable results. Some remarked cynically that productivity had displaced academic work, and accountability the accent on learning. To others, the assembly-line model of freshmen-in/graduates-out seemed to have displaced participation in learning and community service.

People still worked to clarify values and project a course of development for the University. But the process did not seem to work. Neither its past course, its present position, nor any future goals seemed to fit together or stay fixed long enough to set a new course. A program chairman said, "We are like a big ship all steamed up with a crew busy at their posts, but with no destination." Nothing seemed to be wrong with the compass, charts, or navigation. Somebody must have misplaced the horizon.

POLITICAL SHOCK AND STRESS

The first and most disorienting shock came in 1962. A legislative investigating committee, called the "Johns Committee" after its chairman, state Senator Charley Johns, a leading "porkchopper," set up shop in a resort motel. Members were quietly interviewing University and community people to ferret out suspected communists, homosexuals, and immoral persons.

Several concerned persons disclosed its activities to USF staff. President Allen took counsel with the deans and general faculty; the USF chapter of the American Association of University Professors also concurred in his proposal to invite the Johns Committee to work openly on campus. The committee agreed, and many students and faculty went in voluntarily to give positive testimony on the University's commitment to intellectual and moral values. Others were called in connection with investigations of various complaints.

After several weeks, the committee issued a lengthy report. Admitting that it found little evidence of ideological and moral aberrations, it nevertheless expounded at length on readings, speakers, personal and group activities, and free-wheeling classroom discussion, considered socially, politically, or morally objectionable. In the absence of President Allen and Dean French, Dean Russell Cooper made immediate reply to these loose, unsubstantiated allegations, showing the many fallacies and lack of evidence in the report and affirming the University's commitment to academic freedom and scholarly integrity.

AAUP chapters, the American Association of University Women, and many other organizations in the community and the professions gave strong support to the University. The state's leading newspapers deplored the committee's "McCarthy tactics." In 1963 President Allen told a joint meeting of the Florida House and Senate that the University was sound and mature. He insisted that modern universities cannot conform to a political power structure, a spoils system, or any ideological model for personal and social values. All material, all experience, and all perspectives must be considered and tested in the search for truth.

Not long thereafter, the legislature terminated the Johns Committee's appropriation, following its publication of an explicitly illustrated report of sexual aberrations—a "purple pamphlet" that became a prized item for collectors of pornography.

AAUP CENSURE

For several months the committee's activity kept the campus in ferment. The Johns Committee disrupted the fragile falsework sustaining the right to due process in handling grievances and accusations against students and faculty. A necessary keystone, the Board of Control's systemwide set of policies and procedural guarantees, was undergoing study and had not yet been firmly set in place. Many feared that these rules might become highly restrictive in response to overt political pressure. The unsettled political climate had made the University's officers exceedingly cautious and the Board of Control very slow and careful in bringing to closure the systemwide safeguards for academic freedom.

Then President Allen suspended an assistant professor of English prior to hearings on a complaint about his classroom use of a highly critical review of "beat" literature. There being no cause for any charge whatever, he was quickly reinstated and offered promotion but elected to accept a better position elsewhere. The president next canceled an agreement to employ for one term a distinguished political scientist recently retired from a prestigious university. This action was prompted by protests that proved to arise from unsubstantiated accusations that were apparently laid in the first place against another professor with a similar name.

Complaints having been filed with its Committee on Tenure and Academic Freedom, the AAUP censured the University of South Florida in 1964, and noted systemwide as well as internal shortcomings. "The Board of Control was particularly culpable in its failure to stand between this new institution and its critics. The president likewise failed, at least during the period specifically involved in this report, to respond with the proper vigor to the forces of ignorance, prejudice, and repression."

The retired professor was invited to lecture at USF in order to redress the grievance. After lengthy study of further developments in Board of Control policy and USF practices, the AAUP removed its censure in 1968.[5]

These events shook profoundly the spirit of solidarity. As the AAUP noted, unwarranted interference had come from both private persons and public bodies who disregarded orderly procedures for handling complaints and criticisms. The Johns Committee fostered mistrust and the very misperceptions and misleading folklore that people in the State University System were trying hard to counteract. Some community leaders, friends, and members of USF had preferred to use undercover investigations rather than orderly and open dealings. The experience undermined much of the congenial, collaborative spirit in University and community undertakings.

Faculty members were divided on administrative decisions made under pressure. Even prudent souls considered some actions to be excessively cautious, some too hasty, poorly planned, and verging on arbitrary intervention. There were ample causes for criticism and ample reasons for caution. In the absence of firm systemwide policy, USF administrators had to make hard decisions with inadequate assurance of support on both internal and external matters. Critics considered that the president had acted arbitrarily, and the whole administration had acted irresolutely. To a considerable extent, these feelings rang true to experience: it is hard to act resolutely and reasonably in a highly fluid situation.

Teaching and learning proceed by "the spirit of things that *work*" in a developmental process. Some ways of work succeed, some fall short, and all have to be tested repeatedly against shared experience.[6] Its founders and planners followed a developmental process for USF and set up the minimum falsework to sustain durable ways of work that were consolidating block by block out of shared experience. Arbitrary political intervention caught the university and the community unprepared and off guard. To a considerable extent, people were euphoric and complacent over highly gratifying achievements from five years of hard, challenging work. Universities usually have well-tested procedures for coping with interference; but USF's "crisis drill" had been neither fully designed nor adequately rehearsed. With little more than a year of full-scale operation, safeguards were just beginning to consolidate and could not protect fully against any external or internal shock.

A number of faculty members committed to stimulating and provocative teaching concluded that the president and central administration would not and could not support open, candid study of pertinent issues. Some bolder spirits and some highly productive scholars left. Those who remained grew cautious and inclined to keep their own counsel. The unity of the faculty and the tradition of free inquiry, indeed the very "frontier spirit" that held the University together, had been disrupted.

ADMINISTRATIVE CHANGE

With growth in enrollment came stress that brought about changes in organization of the colleges. In 1964 the Basic Studies and Liberal Arts faculties formally separated. Each member selected the preferred college according to teaching responsibilities, research opportunities, and peer relations; both colleges continued in their designated roles and responsibilities. Then in 1966 Liberal Arts established departments to replace the original organization around degree programs.

Each change gave faculty a home with a smaller group of colleagues and fewer students to advise. It relieved the burden on chairmen, who had found it difficult to hold together the growing number of specialized and interdisciplinary courses in the program configurations. Some faculty, equally committed to interdisciplinary and specialized studies, had to make a difficult choice; others welcomed identification with a smaller group of like-minded colleagues.

The exchange of teaching assignments across the disciplines and the interdisciplinary design of research and academic programs did not come to an end but tended to diminish in frequency as enrollment pressure on all units increased. Condescension and disparagement often surfaced between specialists and generalists. In some cases Basic Studies faculty found that customary opportunities to teach also in a specialized field were closing. Their competence for advanced instruction in any field was often unjustly denigrated in general.

The change reinforced territorial claims and rivalries. Faculty unity seemed to diminish in the face of departmental contentions. Advances in some highly productive research areas seemed to be blunted by lack of support for interdisciplinary collaboration. The gains in a home base sustaining faculty development seemed offset by losses in all-University spirit and cohesiveness.

NEW STUDENTS, NEW PROGRAMS

Additional stress came from the change in student mix. The advent of graduate studies in 1964 opened a period of rapid growth in their enrollment and curriculum. The proportion (but not the numbers) of lower-division students decreased while the number and proportion of upper-division undergraduates and graduate students increased. Many faculty members, especially in the sciences with their tradition of research apprenticeship, derived considerable satisfaction and self-esteem from graduate instruction and devoted increasing time to graduate students and research.

The change in student mix and curriculum caused budgetary strains. An increased proportion of capital outlay and expenses for research and graduate instruction meant a diminished share for materials, equipment, and facilities serving undergraduates. Always confronted with personnel budgets out of fit with total enrollment and student mix, deans and chairmen consistently (but not always successfully) resisted the tendency to increase the size of undergraduate classes, a typical device to provide faculty time for graduate studies.

In fields where small sections were essential (e.g., English and mathematics), graduate assistants began to teach introductory courses in the traditional way of apprenticeship and financial aid, thus releasing more professors for advanced instruction. Graduate assistants were competent teachers, some highly stimulating and helpful. All suffered equally from invidious distinctions of rank that led some of their students to feel cheated on their investment when a teaching assistant instead of a "regular professor" conducted a class.

Earl McGrath, a member of Florida's Council for the Study of Higher Education, underlined the grave danger that swelling graduate enrollment will thus undermine the quality of undergraduate education.[7] The planners of the University had prepared for this eventuality but had few well-tested ways to cope with it. USF's experience may not have been as painful and imbalanced as that of other institutions; still, strain and ambiguity beclouded the University's purposes and identity. Only one clear purpose guided this development: graduate education at USF was an imperative response to urgent community needs and expectations.

Under New Management

The State of Florida went into a steady-state approach to planning after 1970, while USF steadily grew. Statewide planning now aimed to maintain equilibrium rather than to meet future goals. Committed under the statewide plan to develop regional centers within its organization and instructional program, the University was not adequately funded under steady-state principles. Development of its future-oriented plan often seemed an exercise in futility, a disruptive experience for the administration and faculty. Heavy, persistent stress caused acute fatigue, often manifest in outbreaks of cynicism, impatience, and bad temper.

This strain coincided with a second reorganization of the Colleges of Basic Studies and Liberal Arts into four new colleges: Language and Literature (later named Arts and Letters), Fine Arts, Natural Sciences, and Social and Behavioral Sciences. The change accommodated the steadily swelling numbers of students, faculty, and academic programs more comfortably but fragmented the University still further. Additional trends toward fragmentation came when the Board of Regents adopted systemwide ways of work that fixed specific areas of responsibility for faculty, administrative, professional, and career service personnel. All of these changes came under a new administration.

John Allen retired on July 1, 1970, to be followed by Harris Dean as acting president until Cecil Mackey took office in February 1971. Dr. Mackey, an economist and lawyer, had been a U.S. Assistant Secretary of Transportation and for two years Executive Vice-President of Florida State University before his appointment to the University of South Florida. He replaced all the vice-presidents, the business manager, and several deans. He brought a different administrative style, organizing the new group of young, energetic administrators as a central management team. President Allen delegated responsibility for planning; President Mackey assigned responsibility to execute plans that his team designed.

At the same time, planning capabilities were being enhanced in the state government. A restructured Department of Administration was trying to strengthen and centralize program and budget controls. The Board of Regents, successor to the Board of Control, and the Chancellor's staff were developing the planning process and management information support for the State University System.

The trend toward centralized authority left many deans, department chairmen, middle-level administrators and Career Service directors feeling that they no longer were responsible contributors to the University but mere instruments of administrative control. The faculty, even more disaffected, felt they had become mere hired hands turning over classroom machinery, with no personal contributions and no responsibility that would affect the University's mission and future development. The team spirit that President Mackey tried hard to cultivate, and the sense of shared values and shared responsibility which so many members of the university had actually enjoyed, now seemed to dissipate. "Latham's principle of administrative absurdity" seemed to prevail, taking decisions away from the scene of the action to remote administrative and governmental levels.

People felt that the University of South Florida was bound to become distinguished, but the spirit and style would differ distinctly from those envisioned in 1960. The University was visibly maturing in its commitment to advance and share knowledge, but its course of development and its new horizons could not be established clearly, whether by deliberations among its members or by presidential directive.

BLURRED VISION

Universities across the country confronted similar problems and developmental tasks. The reaction to Sputnik may have seemed irrational, but the consequent increase in public support for higher education was neither inopportune nor foolish. Prompt improvement was badly needed.

For example, a distinguished financier had told the Commission on Financing Higher Education early in the 1950s that the largest single financial contribution to higher education came from the salaries not paid to faculty members. In many institutions, pay scales from the 1920s and 1930s still prevailed. The shortage of faculty was understandable, especially the shortage of well-educated, challenging teachers with initiative and vision.

Even the simplest, most obvious standards of quality and safety seemed to be neglected. An advisory commission reviewing applications to the U.S. Office of Education for facilities grants found evidence of appalling, sometimes hazardous conditions even in some highly prestigious centers for graduate study and research.

Between 1960 and 1973, federal investment in higher education grew from $732 million to $5.8 billion. Allocated by program category, Congressional appropriations earmarked a substantial proportion for medical education and health-related research and for defense-related research and development, often requiring high costs for hardware and specialized personnel. Categorical appropriation tended to make subventions for medicine, science, and engineering out of proportion to the support for other disciplines using other technologies. General facilities grants and other program support in many instances fell short of funding levels originally authorized, especially for graduate education. The pattern of federal investment made it difficult for cooperating universities to maintain well-balanced internal organization and development.

In keeping with trends in federal planning, specialized research institutes had been established in many universities, following a pattern familiar to science, technology, and medicine in developing sponsored research in other fields, such as education, business administration, and the humanities. Financed primarily by external subventions, professors in research institutes tended to become more and more detached from the general life and work of a university as well as from its general administration and budget, less and less involved in teaching and mutual concerns of faculty and student colleagues.

The University of South Florida felt this surge of investment and the press to make itself in a modern image celebrated by Clark Kerr as a "multiversity."[8] It established research institutes, graduate programs, and Colleges of Engineering, Medicine, and Nursing with strong research components. But the developmental process to which its members were primarily committed moderated some pressures, imbalance, and divisive or dissonant strains that often created problems elsewhere.

DISRUPTION AND REVOLT

Suddenly the extraordinary student revolt of the mid-sixties erupted, surfacing first at the University of California at Berkeley, then sweeping across the nation. Students demonstrated against racism, sexism, the Vietnam War, military research, and the whole educational system. Protests were accompanied often by acts of disruption, vandalism, violence, and terrorism. Activists denounced "the Establishment" and demanded justice and peace in society and a more decisive voice for students.[9]

Protests appeared particularly to attack autocracy in university administration, an archaic curriculum irrelevant to student needs, pedestrian teaching by professors more interested in their own research and professional advancement than in students and their learning, and obsolete parietal rules that seemed to demean students in their adult rights and identity. At the University of South Florida, student protest caused comparatively little disruption of teaching, learning, and governance; it was attended by very few instances of vandalism or violence. There was a running battle over the county's outdoor noise ordinance, affecting amplified speeches and rock festivals. And a highly critical protest developed against the administration, demanding change in parietal rules and disciplinary regulations and more student voice in governance.

Student unrest and growing faculty disaffection probably contributed to President Allen's decision to retire in 1970, two years before the mandatory age. The work of maintaining the University on course, in line with its goals and visions, had lost much of its enjoyment and reward. The stress was more than doubled by efforts to maintain communication with protestors who often seemed to prefer antic dramatization to constructive dialogue.

The protest movement seemed to dissipate by late 1971, and universities settled down to take up some unfinished developmental tasks. Yet educational effectiveness and innovation seemed less important than before at USF. The focus was still on process, but an emphasis on efficiency in operating the machinery of classroom and campus prevailed over effectiveness in facilitating teaching and learning.

Accent on Efficiency

Even the prestigious Carnegie Commission reinforced the preoccupations of the authorities in Tallahassee. Its monumental studies on higher education (twelve general reports plus some sixty special studies) during the 1960s made almost no mention of goals, the integrative design of academic programs, or effective instructional methods. The studies seemed preoccupied with questions of who should go to college and where, how universities should be governed, and how higher education should be financed.

This preoccupation with operational efficiency converged with the style of President Mackey's administration. But the difficulty with principles of efficiency was to find any evidence of their constructive effects upon teaching and learning. At USF the effects often seemed to be adverse; in many other universities, similar indications appeared of dispiriting anxiety, disorientation, and dissipation of energies for teaching and learning.

After 1971 the University's emphasis upon integrating general, liberal, and professional education dissipated with the creation of four colleges out of Basic Studies and Liberal Arts. The vision of a teaching-learning community was obscured by departmental fragmentation and the priority on research and publications. The all-University approach no longer tied the colleges together; each began to develop its own goals, programs, and regulations.

Horizontal communication in the University, both formal and informal, gave way to official, vertical channels. The concern for urban and international problems continued, but objectives and approaches were still poorly defined. Members of USF continued in active community service; but little reinforcement seemed to come from colleagues or administration, and the community began to show signs of disillusion and disaffection instead of congenial, collaborative spirit.

Members of many universities realized that mission, goals, and purposes had to be clarified in order to keep higher education on course. Yet the focus on efficiency tended to blur shared visions that would help to chart a course.

The ten-year self-study and site visit for SACS accreditation in 1973 focused on this task. The visiting team recommended thorough study of the statement of purpose and present stage of program development, in terms of the responsibilities of USF as an urban university. President Mackey replied that he would appoint a faculty-student-alumni-community committee "directed to examine the University's responsibilities in relation to its urban and metropolitan environment," clarify and update its purposes, and recommend changes in undergraduate and graduate programs in line with revised purposes. This Task Force on Mission and Goals was asked to report in 1976 at the end of the University's second decade.[10]

Survival on the Frontier

The experience of USF may suggest some of the reasons for the durability of the traditional American model for residential education in a rural or small-town setting. The small, ivory-tower academy, aloof from community concerns, has protected scholars to some degree in their freedom to teach and learn. An urban university, open to the world and involved in community development, foregoes both geographic and social distancing as a protection against disruptive pressures. Members of an urban university can and do capitalize on other features of the residential model. They create on campus and in other settings an environment conducive to learning. They develop mutual support and safeguards for academic freedom around the sense of place, the sense of belonging, the spirit of shared responsibility for academic freedom and scholarly integrity.

Such an environment and such a spirit of mutuality and integrity can develop also in patterns of urban life. Moving out of the ivory tower puts universities alongside their constituencies in common concern for sharing these values in a vital community. Universities will often have to tolerate stress and interference in both academic and community affairs. But no university has to tolerate ignorance. It can serve community concerns for learning to face the future with understanding and confidence.

The University of South Florida withstood more shock and stress than a fledgling institution could expect to endure without forfeiting some important values. It did not fall apart, forfeit its values, or stray very far off course, despite dispiriting pressures. Its experience suggests that universities may have great inner strength to share with the community and nation. Planning, mutual responsibility, integrity in coping with error and misadventure, all have survival values that community and university can share in "the spirit of things that *work.*"

5
General Education

The General Education Movement

The term "general education" came into use in American higher education late in the nineteenth century. It aptly described the collegiate education of the pre–Civil War period: a uniform liberal arts curriculum without specialized branches or vocational orientations. In the last half of the century, many factors—the war, the women's movement, advances in agriculture, industry, research, and exploration—produced scores of new studies in the arts and sciences which no uniform curriculum could possibly incorporate.

The free elective system was introduced so that students could select courses from this burgeoning array according to personal experience and expectations. Faculties required only a minimum number of courses equivalent to four years of full-time study for a degree. At the turn of the century, the elective system prevailed in American higher education; but by World War I, it clearly showed shortcomings of its own—in specialization too narrowly conceived or in idiosyncratic choices too scattered to make sense.

Faculties adopted standard requirements for a major field of concentration as an integrative foundation for a vocation. Concurrently, the modern movement for general education developed out of faculty concerns for some foundation in shared values and knowledge common to all students and adult citizens.

The modern movement for general education can probably best be dated from 1919 when Professor John Erskine introduced the "Contemporary Civilization" course at Columbia University, designed and taught by a group of its most distinguished faculty. The course began with great social and philosophical documents embodying shared values underlying contemporary civilization. In this context, students and instructors confronted challenging contemporary issues; sharing their independent studies in small discussion sections, they worked together in the dual task of threshing out answers to issues and developing personal value systems.

Erskine's course quickly became a model for other universities. About 1925 H. H. Newman formed a faculty committee at the University of Chicago which developed a survey course, "The Nature of the World of Man," that traced basic theories of the sciences, particularly evolution, with the aim of opening the world of science to ordinary students and citizens. At the University of Iowa, Professor Shambaugh's "Campus Course" similarly opened the worlds of philosophy and the arts.

Many universities began to open the whole intellectual enterprise for all students by designing sets of broad, interdisciplinary courses, sometimes paralleling introductory courses in related major fields, sometimes meeting the requirements of a strong foundation for both majors and nonmajors. The latter approach—designing a common core of general education—was more economical than the "cafeteria" system from which students selected as they pleased. It also assured a well-balanced, integrative center shared by specialized programs in all of the arts and sciences. General education courses could be designed to open up connections to other fields (e.g., the influence of evolutionary thought on literature) and also give some penetration into fundamental content and technique for prospective majors (e.g., laboratory and field studies in the social sciences).

Such a thrifty, effective core curriculum could not be realized in many universities without redesigning the whole academic system. Not just one set of courses but also the major sequences, academic standards and degree requirements, faculty organization and development, and teaching assignments often had to be restructured to center in general education.

During the 1930s more and more universities took this parsimonious approach to academic planning, and four distinctive models for course and program design began to crystallize.

Models for General Education

• *Survey methods* provided a series of one-year offerings covering the humanities and the natural and social sciences. These "block-and-gap" courses penetrated deeply the most fruitful blocks of integrative concepts, and skimmed over connections to other topics and fields of study. They gave comprehensive scope with ample opportunity for exploration of fundamental principles. Eventually, survey courses began to founder in the expansion of knowledge because they had to undertake more than could be covered in a year without having more gaps than blocks.

• *Great Issues or Great Ideas courses,* similar to Erskine's Contemporary Civilization, made no attempt at comprehensive survey but explored a few vital questions intensively from many different perspectives. One desired outcome was to develop a repertory of methods of inquiry by engaging students in systematic analysis of substantive issues. Solutions were not expected: issues were usually chosen because they were puzzling, so that students would have to try several methods and learn to avoid premature closure and hasty judgments. For example, Colgate organized its Natural Science course around phenomena, such as the Carolina Bays, that can be only partly understood, even by interdisciplinary analysis. Professors having the necessary interdisciplinary background were in short supply, so that a succession of specialists frequently taught these courses. Students were often dissatisfied with the use of a specialized "vaudeville team," which tended to fragment the course. Interaction with a single instructor who could keep track of their work and help them integrate their mastery of the repertory was preferred and was usually more effective.

• *Instrumental design* organized general education around practical concerns, following John Dewey's commonsense assumption that personal, practical interests will open the way into any field of learning. In order to gain an empirical base for instrumental design, graduates of Stephens College kept a journal of activities and concerns for Dr. W. W. Charters; at the University of Minnesota, a series of "adolescent studies" surveyed needs of pre-college youth. On the basis of such estimates from shared experience, faculty teams designed sets of instrumental courses that would deal systematically with developmental tasks from humanistic and scientific perspectives and help students make the transition from adolescent to adult roles and responsibilities.

Many students and faculty warmly welcomed instrumental approaches because of their timeliness and pertinence; and, just as often, established departments criticized them as thin and superficial, inadequate as a foundation for the content and technique required for advanced academic work, uneven and unpredictable in quality. Nevertheless, instrumental courses began to spread through the system of higher education, primarily because of the positive results from methods that focused on the process of intellectual development and opened up broad fields of study to many different techniques and perspectives.

• *The Great Books of Western Thought* provided the center for the entire curriculum of St. Johns College, Annapolis. In 1937 President Stringfellow Barr and Dean Scott Buchanan reorganized the college to form seminars where students read the great works of the past and wrestled with ancient and perennial problems—especially the problem of creating a general synthesis of knowledge. They also studied foreign languages and mathematics for four years, on the rationalist principle that the purpose of education is to cultivate logical thought. There was virtually no direct attention to contemporary social concerns or personal needs; concentrated practice in rational analysis was expected to prepare students to tackle virtually any issue systematically, with firmly established values. This approach assumed that general intellectual power will readily transfer from one field to another. Many educators question the validity of this assumption.

Hundreds of colleges developed many variations on these four models. General education broadened from courses to sets of degree requirements and to interdisciplinary degree programs (such as the University of Texas introduced in 1935.) Some universities organized separate colleges for general and interdisciplinary education, as USF did in 1960; others had a department or division for general education in the college of liberal arts; and some diffused responsibility for general education across the several colleges as USF has done since 1971.

NATIONAL CONCERNS

During World War II, three developments gave special impetus to the general education movement. First, President Conant prodded Harvard University to confront the equalitarian thrust for lifelong educational opportunities and the rising expectations of higher education as a national asset. A faculty committee published a landmark report in 1945, committing Harvard to general education as the foundation of its entire curriculum.

> The primary concern of American education today is not the development of the appreciation of the "good life" in young gentlemen born to the purple. It is the infusion of the liberal and humane tradition into our entire educational system. Our purpose is to cultivate in the largest possible number of our future citizens an appreciation of both the responsibilities and the benefits which come to them because they are Americans and free.
>
> Such a concept of general education is the imperative need of the American educational system. It alone can give cohesion to our efforts and guide the contribution of our youth to the nation's future.[1]

Second, a national committee published *A Design for General Education for Men in the Armed Services,* which formed the basis for the organization of the U.S. Armed Forces Institute (USAFI). The institute began by recommending a series of textbooks to help military people broaden their education in their off-duty time; it went on to develop a continuing education program of formal studies for college credit.

Third, the 1947 President's Commission on Higher Education incorporated many ideas from the *Design* for USAFI in its recommendations for general and continuing education. Avoiding the survey, Great Books, and Great Issues approaches, the commission proposed integrated, instrumental programs designed for students to develop as effective human beings and citizens: "The crucial task of higher education today, therefore, is to provide a unified general education for American youth." The commission listed eleven goals of general education, which came to influence many new programs including those of the University of South Florida.[2]

As Hefferlin pointed out, the general education movement has tended to gather momentum following any national crisis such as World War I, the Great Depression, and World War II.[3] In these traumatic periods, people seem to examine their own education and seek to reconstruct personal and social values. Then they begin to urge schools and colleges to provide the next generation with a strong core of shared values that will undergird their education and careers and prepare them better to cope with crisis. The general education movement in the U.S. has developed out of this conviction that education is meant to bring people together in shared values and shared responsibilities sustaining personal and national life.

The Basic Studies College

John Allen and Sidney French organized the College of Basic Studies and built the general education program on year-long courses in the humanities and the natural and social sciences, as a standard requirement for all B.A. degrees at USF. The college was given separate identity and distinctive responsibility to administer the Basic Studies requirements; to develop additional experimental and interdisciplinary instruction, including the courses and programs for the Advanced Basic Studies major and for intercollegiate majors combining liberal and professional studies; to provide a home base for students in these interdisciplinary majors and for all entering students until they declared a major; to provide a home for faculty committed primarily to general education and advance their interdisciplinary studies and research.

With general education centered in the liberal arts, the University would in effect have two types of liberal arts college; and, consequently, a close, almost symbiotic relationship was established between the two faculties. Since the College of Basic Studies was the first that would come into full-scale operation, Allen and French selected the deans of all four colleges, and the deans selected the charter faculty, primarily for their experience and interest in general education and interdisciplinary studies. This common concern contributed to the frontier spirit of adventure and camaraderie and enriched all the colleges.

BASIC STUDIES REQUIREMENTS

The three areas of the humanities and the natural and social sciences were too broad to fit conveniently into one-year modules. Accordingly, the deans agreed on seven modules covering these areas, a Senior Seminar bringing all-University groups together for final integrative work, and Functional Physical Education closely integrated with voluntary activities. The design gave students the choice of a foreign language, the choice between a language and mathematics, the selection of physical or biological sciences, and the choice of political or behavioral approaches to the social sciences.

Thus, the general education program included nine modules: Functional English, Human Behavior, Science (biological or physical), Functional Mathematics, Functional Foreign Languages (German, French, Spanish, Italian, Russian), The American Idea, Humanities, Senior Seminar, and Functional Physical Education.

The program had a clearly defined pattern but avoided "the academic lockstep" of uniform, linear sequences of courses that so often forces students to undertake work in some area of comparative weakness before they have a chance to balance and consolidate their skills and study habits. To reduce recalcitrance and capitalize on students' ingenuity in making the most of their strengths while cutting their losses in areas of weakness, the deans and program designers provided options in both content and timing, and allowed the full four years for completion of the Basic Studies requirements.

Six required modules plus the Senior Seminar covered 39 of the 120 semester hours required for the B.A. degree. All students had to complete Functional English; typically they took this and another module in the first year, two in the second, one in the third, and two in the fourth—including the Senior Seminar, also required of all students. Sometime during the first two years most people completed any Physical Education requirements that were in effect on a credit or noncredit basis. Students also had options to waive a requirement by advanced studies in high school or on the basis of standardized test scores, and to earn credit by examination on the basis of special experience or independent study.

The design for each module began with laboratory sections for practicing skills and techniques, offering tutorial assistance in evaluating individual work, correcting errors, and improving quality. Then students would contribute from their individual work to discussion sessions integrating their reading and practical experience. A mass lecture would integrate the theoretical and historical context of the course and open up the major issues addressed by students.

The planning group knew that many students perceive academic work to be much like schooling: a dull round of routine tasks, the same for everyone. They wished instead to share with students their enjoyment of learning as a delightful risk and adventure, as the vocation and recreation of adults. With this purpose in mind, they designed many optional topics and ways of work into each module so that students would virtually be forced to plan a personalized course of study.

The General Education Courses

FUNCTIONAL ENGLISH

Truman's Commission on Higher Education recommended a broader scope of studies in English to cover the fourfold art of communication—reading and writing, speaking and listening. Functional English added the art of thought and included studies of all five cognitive arts as they vary according to subject matter and technique in different scholarly disciplines.

Chairman Robert Zetler and the faculty assumed that students would learn to communicate better if they were given something of value about which to think and communicate. They presented, instead of a standard textbook, six or seven paperbacks each term, each related to the distinctive content of one of the Basic Studies courses. For example, Physical Science shared George Gamow, *The Birth and Death of the Sun,* as a textbook. The "All-University Book" was required reading.

Reading provided the basis for the weekly lecture where students sharpened listening and recording skills. Lectures were taped so that students could review or keep up with the class despite an absence. Two hours of forums and panel and group discussions sharpened skills in listening, thinking, and speaking; biweekly papers sharpened writing skills. An hour of laboratory work, with tutorial assistance ad lib, dealt with all communication skills.

The faculty of Functional English made an agreement with faculty in other courses that all would evaluate students' writing for clarity and style and refer students to the English laboratory for any needed help. Faculty in general tend to complain about the quality of student writing, and the USF faculty agreed to do something about it.

Skills in speaking and listening were not always strongly emphasized except in a set of laboratories specially designed for practice in oral communication. Most college teachers have minimal training in these skills, which are often slighted in their graduate education. The Functional English course called for faculty with an understanding of the process of learning and human development, a broad general education, and some linguistic knowledge—an unusual combination for English teachers in the 1950s and 1960s. So the spoken and written forms of communication tended to gravitate toward distinctive sets of laboratories and discussion sections.

This course was a rich diet for students and faculty. However, it had to be trimmed down, and with changes to the trimester and quarter calendars it had to be cut back. First the faculty reduced the number of paperbacks, and in 1966 they chose an anthology having much the same content. In the 1970s the course has concentrated on developing a personal style of writing and then learning to communicate clearly in different fields of study by different forms of writing. Using a basic rhetoric text with optional readings, students work on the construction of sentences, paragraphs, and longer essays or fiction, and finally write at least three papers of a thousand words or more, dealing with different fields of study.

This change was prompted by several factors. The general faculty, insisting that students write good English, had to refer students needing improvement to the English teachers, who took this responsibility seriously under the agreement; but other faculties began to lay more and more responsibility on the English Department, and to give less and less help on the spot. When graduate studies began in 1965, teaching assistants were given some sections, and criticism began to increase. Other departments began to complain that these inexperienced people interpreted material from other disciplines too superficially—notwithstanding the intent of the Functional English faculty to deal with the influence of other disciplines on English literature, rather than to interpret science and humanities. Nationwide, interest in integrated communications courses diminished; teachers everywhere became increasingly concerned with student writing—and with the public outcry over "Why Johnny can't read!"

At present, no clear evidence indicates any change in communications skills on the part of current students compared with their predecessors. About one-fourth of entering freshmen waive the requirement through advanced studies in high school or the College Level Examination Program. Consequently, complaints about English usage now fall on CLEP too.

HUMAN BEHAVIOR

Conceived in the spirit of the Truman Commission's recommendations on self-understanding and social responsibility, the course in Human Behavior went considerably further as it sought to explain how people behave like human beings. The faculty had the advantage of a unified interdisciplinary theory: Leslie Malpass, the chairman, centered the design on social learning theory, and the course moved from the dynamics of personal behavior into organizational development and the dynamics of collective behavior. It dealt with philosophy in terms of logical methods and basic concepts of human nature. It presented the repertory of research methods in biological and social sciences for analyzing evidence about human behavior and its determinants.

The faculty incorporated laboratory and field studies into the discussion sections of 25 to 30 students. In 1965 enrollment grew too large for the 500-seat Teaching Auditorium-Theatre, and time for additional mass lectures was not available. The faculty tried multiple showings of videotaped lectures, but students complained that these were boring. The general lecture was dropped completely, and instruction proceeded wholly in discussion sections. Trying to replicate the lecture content even with videotapes and films, visiting experts, or "swaps" among the faculty, aggravated many teachers who were uneasy about going beyond their primary specialty.

In 1967 the course was redesigned and rechristened Behavioral Science to emphasize its stronger concentration on scientific method. The first term became physiological-psychological and the second anthropological-sociological; the third term applied the methods presented in the first two terms to in-depth analysis of institutions and patterns of culture. More and more instructors insisted on limiting their assignments to one of these segments, and the course lost some of its integrative strength. The expanding Liberal Arts programs drew many experienced professors into their advanced courses; with the shortage of faculty having interdisciplinary background, Behavioral Science frequently had to settle for one-term specialists and younger instructors with a rather limited repertory.

Behavioral Science remained popular with students who desired a broad, behavioral orientation to the social sciences. It had a remarkable number of spinoffs into advanced study in leisure, aging, criminal justice, women's studies, and a set of advanced courses in Interdisciplinary Social Science. It continued into the 1970s, but the number of sections fell from 65 at its height to 18 after the course became optional in the distributional requirements for general education.

BIOLOGICAL SCIENCE

The planning team felt that a single one-year course could not cover both biological and physical science and separated these modules so that either one would fill the degree requirement. Some students took both, counting one as an elective. The majority selected Biological Science for several reasons: the quantitative techniques of physical science were too much to attempt for students shaky in mathematics; most students had taken biology, and only a few had studied physics in high school; some just preferred a course related to people among other living things.

The faculty designed the course around problems, particularly those concerning interaction of organisms and environment as the most vital issues confronting scientists. The lecture-discussion format had to be altered as advanced courses and research took up more of the scarce laboratory time. Field studies and demonstrations were included in discussion sessions, but students missed the "hands-on" learning.

Under the quarter system the module was divided into six one-term courses from which students chose three to fit the science requirement. Instruction remains pertinent to contemporary problems; interest and enrollment remain high.

PHYSICAL SCIENCE

The range of subject matter in physical science makes course design difficult. Clarence Clark, the chairman, avoided the survey method and elected to present problems that had to be approached from many different perspectives and to integrate astronomy, chemistry, physics, and geology in the process.

The objective was to teach students how scientists go about solving problems by gathering, organizing, and analyzing data, then drawing strong inferences on the evidence. There was no attempt to prepare for advanced and specialized study. Instead, the faculty wanted to introduce students to the principles and methods that have proved useful in understanding the universe and to the history and philosophy of science bearing on contemporary problems of theory and practice.

Because its enrollment was smaller than that in Biological Science, the Physical Science sequence could reorganize in 1971–72 around one-term courses, maintain much the same enrollment, and retain the laboratory schedule of two hours a week.

FUNCTIONAL MATHEMATICS

The original design for Functional Mathematics aimed to explore the variety and beauty of abstract constructs and systems. Assuming considerable high school background, including concepts of functions and irrationals, the chairman, Donald Rose, and the faculty planned to begin with number theory and proceed to the basic concepts employed in calculus. Very soon it became clear that most students could not even cope with algebra and the concept of number. The content was modified to start with finite mathematics, resting upon arithmetic, and proceed into logic, set theory, finite linear analysis, and programing. Like the "new math" of the lower schools, Functional Mathematics emphasized the reasons for mathematical concepts and operations rather than routine practice in calculations on formulae. This approach helped the first classes of students, who fell between the declining "old math" and the advent of the "new math" in the schools. The faculty also helped to develop in-service training for teachers and programs for advanced instruction in high-school mathematics.

The professors' experience of students' strengths and weaknesses proved very helpful in designing the rest of the mathematics program; as the original group moved into advanced courses, graduate assistants filled in. With the revised content manageable by students of adequate skill in arithmetic and with tutorial assistance always available, the course maintained good enrollment despite an initial decline when distributional requirements made courses in logic and statistics equivalent options.

FUNCTIONAL FOREIGN LANGUAGE

After Sputnik, American universities revamped foreign language programs, giving particular attention to the spoken word used by travelers, statesmen, and businessmen with secondary emphasis on simple reading knowledge suitable for graduate study. Functional Foreign Languages developed the four functions of listening, speaking, reading, and writing—in that order. The faculty aimed for students to gain enough competence to proceed to advanced literature and composition courses or to study abroad. Students could select a language in which they were proficient and start with the segment of a basic or advanced course that would best challenge them to new learning.

USF used electronic technology extensively for programed instruction. In Functional Foreign Languages, laboratory work enabled students to advance independently using taped materials in a self-directed program, as rapidly as time and talent allowed and as far as they wanted to go. Lectures and discussions dealt with fundamental linguistics and the cultural context of each language, giving the course both functional and humanistic dimensions.

Instruction gradually reverted to more traditional techniques. Distinction among the four functions and the emphasis on the listening-speaking laboratory programs seemed artificial and hard to integrate. Classroom work now blends the four language functions and emphasizes history and culture more strongly. The courses now stress reading more than speaking; but the cosmopolitan character of Tampa encourages continued emphasis on the spoken language, as many students have two or three "mother tongues." Still, the program in general seems fairly pedestrian and appears to have lost much of its original style.

Since Functional Foreign Languages have always been partially elective and included advanced studies, student morale has been good and achievement strong. In keeping with a national trend, however, the University's students and constituency generally show diminishing interest in foreign languages today.

THE AMERICAN IDEA

Focusing on the Americas and their role in the world, this course complemented Human Behavior with studies of social systems and international and cross-cultural relations. The chairman, Robert Warner, and the faculty discarded the problems approach as frustrating and superficial; problem after problem was analyzed but left dangling. The survey, Great Issues, and Great Books approaches seemed equally objectionable.

The American Idea took an instrumental approach to the study of public policy, using basic documents and critical works (in paperback) that analyzed the developmental process of organization and policy-making and identified and proposed alternative approaches to matters of policy and practice. The course was avowedly oriented toward shared values of democracy: freedom, equality, and justice, constitutional principles of the grant of governmental powers, reserved powers, and guarantees of civil rights. It aimed at sharpening capabilities for participation in institutional, economic, and political decision-making. Faculty and students developed a civic practicum, giving one credit for voluntary service in a public office or social agency or in tutoring inner-city children. This was eye-opening experience, translating social problems into the life and work of real people. In the hemispheric and worldwide dimensions of The American Idea, analysis and reduction of parochialism, provincialism, and chauvinism presented particularly important tasks.

Gradually the course settled into a sequence covering the American experience in one term, international relations in the second term, practicum and independent study in the third term. Inevitably, faculty tended to gravitate toward one or another segment according to their special interests. The American Studies program spun off into the College of Arts and Letters; it deals with the culture, arts, and literature of the many peoples of the United States. The International Studies program grew out of the second part of the course. Programs in Women's Studies, Afro-American Studies, Criminal Justice, and projects in the Off-Campus Term also had roots in The American Idea. Morale and enrollment remained high until the introduction of distributional requirements.

THE HUMANITIES

Humanities courses can generally be divided into two types, emphasizing appreciation and understanding of the arts, or emphasizing the purpose and values of man's existence. The USF course stood in the first category but also included creative experience. The chairman, John Hicks, and the faculty considered the best approach to offer not a survey but as deep an induction as possible into a few representative art forms and historical periods, emphasizing sensitivity, taste, and creative experience rather than forms and facts. Works of art, architecture, and literature were studied in the lecture-discussion format. The weekly laboratory offered a variety of forms in which students created their own works; the faculty required the choice of a form and medium *least* familiar to the student in order to provide new experience rather than demonstrate established proficiency. Students confronted their work as artists and as audience, making their experience part of the course content. The artists were all amateurs, but performances, publications, and exhibits revealed much talent.

The faculty chose works from rich historical periods: non-Western, Classical, Renaissance, and Modern. They sketched in but did not elaborate the cultural background. When the major program in Humanities had consolidated in 1965, the faculty designed a set of one-term basic courses dealing more strictly with works and art forms themselves, emphasizing their aesthetic concepts and values more than their cultural context. The laboratory was dropped in 1974, when problems of sharing studio and workshop time with growing Fine Arts programs became acute. Then the design shifted back to studies of rich historical periods, considering all of the arts as examples of different cultural and philosophical orientations.

Throughout these design changes, Humanities retained an excellent faculty. Around 90 percent have the doctorate, and they have considerable artistic talent that is often drawn upon as a special resource for many related fields in the arts and literature. Students have high regard for the course, even though it has lost some of the original scope and flavor and now capitalizes on philosophical concepts rather than creative work.

FUNCTIONAL PHYSICAL EDUCATION

Gilman Hertz, the first director, and the faculty in Functional Physical Eduction designed the two required years of instruction and activity for maximum breadth and variety: a basic course in health and the psychophysical aspects of behavior and human development; a sampling of all types of physical activity; and demonstrated proficiency in swimming or another aquatic activity, in one team and one individual sport or recreational activity. Students could choose class participation or individual, programed instruction. Proficiency was demonstrated by written and performance tests or by evidence such as "letters" earned in high school or another college and records of ranking performance in some recognized competition.

The emphasis on variety was prompted partly by the community's fixation on football as the only important student activity. The staff introduced a whole array of other sports and recreational activities for learning as well as enjoyment. For instance, scuba diving served people in marine sciences, and mountaineering served geologists and other natural scientists. They introduced soccer, rugby, fencing, archery, lacrosse, and several other sports that were new to the experience of most people in the area.

The program included individually designed conditioning courses which could be selected to meet the individual activity requirement; the Health Center staff collaborated in programs for health maintenance or improvement, and a physical therapist soon joined the faculty. These provisions made it possible to include handicapped or temporarily disabled students in physical education; they could choose from a number of activities that the faculty could adapt to individual capability and regimen. In only a few cases were handicapped students released from requirements; they typically entered the "mainstream" and took the basic course and as many other activities as faculty could design for them. Requirements could be waived on the basis of age or military service; some who secured waivers chose to participate in instruction and voluntary activities anyway.

SENIOR SEMINAR

Every candidate for the B.A. degree had to complete this multi-disciplinary, one-term, capstone seminar, as close as possible to graduation. The faculty chose to center on freedom and responsibility as shared values integrating general, liberal, and professional studies. Students read a series of paperbacks dealing with freedom and responsibility in society, the arts, science, personal behavior, major institutions, and social systems. On the basis of shared readings, they presented work of their own—papers, works of art, games, experiments, filmed documentaries—and directed class discussion.

The chairman, Edgar Stanton, and the coordinating committee confronted an unusual staffing problem in offering the two hundred or more sections required to serve the whole graduating class each year and restricting each to twenty students, the maximum number for effective use of seminar method. No faculty were seconded to the course; all teachers were borrowed, and they came from all departments and colleges. It was something of an honor to be chosen, as the committee looked for teachers with interdisciplinary experience, highly skilled in facilitating self-directed student work, and prepared for a large-minded approach to wide worlds of knowledge and practice. The recruits included a number of librarians, counselors, and administrators who brought fresh perspectives and profited from interaction with students.

Instructors were learning as much as the students; they could not look upon themselves as "authorities" but functioned as facilitators of a completely idiosyncratic course. Textbooks were dropped. The members of each section designed the work and gave unique content and value to each seminar. Many students reported a marvelous sense of freedom and heightened enjoyment, especially after the comparative constraints of their major. Course and instructor ratings were always near the top of the scale. Added comments attested to the intense pleasure in integrating and using mature intellectual powers in multidisciplinary encounter. Many underlined specific elements of the course as pertinent to immediate concerns and future expectations in personal life and a career—even if it was a uniform degree requirement!

Despite this record of positive, creative work by more than 20,000 students in a unique, exceptionally effective course, President Mackey attacked it. He decided that it was too superficial, unstructured, and idiosyncratic to have the predictable form necessary for any standard requirement. The Faculty Senate voted, almost unanimously, to retain the Senior Seminar as a uniform degree requirement on the basis of its unique and effective integrative quality. Mackey rejected this proposal and ordered the colleges to make the course optional.

About 20 percent of the seniors continued to enroll in much the same all-University configurations as before. The small percentage reflects in part a forced choice inherent in the change to tuition based on a fee per credit hour: to pay for credits above the 180 required for the degree or to choose within the standard 180 credits between an integrative Senior Seminar or another elective that enlarges the options for career opportunities. A good many students on a tight budget say they do not even have a choice but must select a career-related option because of known requirements for a graduate program or job to which they have applied or already made a commitment. One senior wistfully suggested that Senior Seminar would make a nice "graduation present" from the University to all of its seniors—and added, "Or let us pay with green stamps, or put it on Master Charge!"

Whatever Happened to General Education?

The Basic Studies program was highly diversified and well integrated. Each course was designed to link the experience of students as human beings and as citizens into the systematic study of several broad disciplines—and to engage students as contributors so provocatively that their learning would make a difference in their values and their personal and career development. Teachers and teaching methods were all chosen to buttress this philosophy.

The program went forward successfully; students participated with growing understanding and enthusiasm. Faculty members often enjoyed learning along with students, spreading their wings into broader issues and fields of study. Designers of the program were invited to speak to many regional and national associations and professional societies. A steady stream of American and foreign visitors came to see the program in action and gain ideas for other universities. The 1963 SACS team commended its broad scope and integrative design.[4]

By 1973 the general education program was in shambles, the College of Basic Studies had been abolished, and the integrative model for general education had been replaced with distributive requirements, going back fifty years to the pre–World War I free elective system.

What influences were at work? Was the original concept flawed? Did other interests supplant it? Did someone sabotage it? Was it the victim of unforeseeable circumstances?

DESIGN

Sidney French and the program chairmen took full advantage of models for general education that had crystallized over many years out of many studies, both national and institutional, down to the recommendation in the Brumbaugh Report for a strong, integrative general education core in all of Florida's new universities and community colleges. They took full advantage of interdisciplinary design for both its elegance and its parsimony.

The design was bold and challenging, calling forth positive effort by faculty and students to link immediate experience to future expectations, to share responsibility and contribute positively to the mission of advancing and sharing knowledge. Personalized design enabled students to fit their studies to their strengths and into their off-campus conditions of work and other responsibilities.

Continuous feedback from student work and a uniform final examination enabled instructors to fine-tune the plan for each section and to update each course between terms. Producing their own work facilitated the development of students' capabilities for self-direction and self-evaluation.

Changes in calendar were unexpected; and each change added to the cost of offering all segments each term in order to prevent "swinging door" enrollment from making too many students fall a year or more behind in their passage to a degree. Other errors were relatively minor and were quickly corrected with feedback from experience: overestimating volume of work in relation to other commitments; underestimating "math anxiety" and overestimating the strength of high school studies in mathematics.

Each change disrupted the integrative design more and more. But this fragmentation primarily came from a foreseeable flaw. Modular programing is often the method of choice for personalized courses designed to integrate learning over broad and diversified fields. In order for students to round off each block of studies instead of having to leave the last few pieces missing or half-finished, flexible timing is considered optimum if not essential to modular design. The schedule should leave reasonable limits for extending deadlines at the discretion of students and teachers. But the only way to capitalize fully on the elegant design of year-long modules at USF was to take an incomplete grade. Students often used this option, and carrying the loose ends forward to the next term soon began to overload and disrupt carefully planned programs, imposing a growing burden on students, teachers, advisors, and the Records office.

From the outset, year-long modules were simply split in half; in due course some became fixed, linear sequences of Course I, II, III. The faculties who shifted instead to one-term modules did not suffer as much damage or enrollment loss from changes in calendar or adoption of distributional requirements as did those committed by choice or necessity to maintain a fixed, year-long, linear sequence.

The fundamental flaw was the attempt to have it both ways: to apply year-long modular design in a semester calendar with fixed deadlines and short vacations. Its effects became worse as terms got shorter with the change to trimester and quarter calendars. But the original plan amounted to a distributive rather than an integrative design in actual practice, and the faculty eventually made this fact official. Another difficulty was the absolute constraint on adding any optional courses or any new or modified subject-matter that could not be designed into one or more of the original nine modules. In the change to a distributive design, the faculty also enlarged the scope and variety of options in the general education program.

STUDENTS

Students turned out to be eager, intelligent, and receptive. Not even the gaps in their high school background kept them from giving

Basic Studies "a good college try." Their most frequent complaint was that the program was required. End-of-term evaluation compared favorably with all-University results on criteria for quality of both content and teaching. The fact that each course was future-oriented and designed around student and community concerns probably facilitated the students' generally effective and sometimes highly enthusiastic involvement.

Most people indicated that they actually enjoyed Basic Studies—especially the Senior Seminar, which came when they were in top form. USF students held many demonstrations in the 1960s—but at no time did they attack the general education program. This phenomenon contrasted sharply with student protests in many other universities where general education requirements often came under heavy fire.

FACULTY

Developing the general education program was enjoyable and exhilarating for the faculty. General and interdisciplinary education presents an intellectual challenge of the highest order. Most of the charter members of all four colleges shared this challenge and the high morale generated out of the effective response.

The faculty in the College of Basic Studies effectively applied to undergraduate teaching many techniques traditionally reserved for graduate work. Their success in these and other experiments, and their creative design for advanced interdisciplinary courses and majors, facilitated the cross-fertilization vital to the liberal arts. Fusion with the Basic Studies faculty helped the College of Liberal Arts to counteract some proclivities to rigidity and territorial rivalries that are part of its heritage.

In fact, the College of Liberal Arts seemed to get the lion's share of benefits from both fusion and separation. The deans and faculties were highly sensitive to patent risks of encapsulating general education and experimental and interdisciplinary teaching and research in a separate college. Any rigid configuration, specialized or interdisciplinary, would be detrimental to student and faculty development. Accordingly, interdisciplinary design was extensively used for advanced Liberal Arts courses and programs. The faculty members who developed new courses in either college tended to gravitate before and after separation toward the seed-bed in the College of Liberal Arts, with its more diversified mixture of specialized and interdisciplinary studies.

Giving all freshmen their original home in the College of Basic Studies was a convenient administrative device intended to give them clear, positive identity as "Basic Studies majors." This made little difference to students, who typically declared themselves "undecided" anyway. It made a great deal of difference to the faculty.

The predominance of freshmen and sophomores in its student mix blurred the identity of Basic Studies as a college having its own courses and majors, its own faculty distinguished in research, publications, and community service. Basic Studies looked more like an administrative artifact than a college; and the predominance of lower-level students made it look like a community college, despite the four-year general education program and its offerings of advanced courses and majors. The fact that Basic Studies professors conducted courses and research at advanced levels was not highly visible, and their Liberal Arts colleagues tended to regard them as inexperienced and poorly qualified for advanced and graduate instruction. Faculty in other colleges often forgot or discounted the prolific work in experimental and interdisciplinary design for teaching and research in Basic Studies—or thought the work had come from people in Liberal Arts.

After separation of the two colleges, this tendency turned into open disparagement of Basic Studies faculty in general and in particular. The Liberal Arts faculty shared the credit for remarkable accomplishments in the first three years; afterward, they tended to claim the lion's share of prestige and reward because they were now progressing into advanced and graduate work after getting the "purely introductory" general education courses off on the right foot.

After separation, the College of Basic Studies continued to carry the major burden of advising all entering students. The introduction of an advising corps released more time for liberal arts faculty to develop rapidly growing advanced and graduate studies, and budget allocations also shifted in this direction. Faculty development in Basic Studies by comparison was undernourished. Shortages of funds, time for new instructional design and research, and leaves for postdoctoral study and writing brought counteractive pressures against an effective response to the high challenge of general and interdisciplinary education. Growing frustration steadily depressed faculty morale.

Both colleges for the liberal arts made a strong start in the three years of fusion. After that, the College of Liberal Arts continued to sustain cross-fertilization and nourishment for its faculty and its programs; the College of Basic Studies more or less had to "live on its fat."

ADMINISTRATION

President Allen set the role and scope of the College of Basic Studies as the center for general, experimental, and interdisciplinary teaching and research. He chose a close friend and colleague, Sidney French, one of the foremost national leaders in general and interdisciplinary education, to plan the entire educational program for the University and to administer first the College of Basic Studies and then the Academic Affairs area. He set the timetable for development and for separation; he fathered and nurtured Basic Studies with special care in both joint and separate operations.

In the late 1960s, however, Allen became rather disenchanted with Basic Studies leadership. Dean Edwin Martin and the course chairmen encouraged the faculty to study issues of student protest when pertinent to a course. Concerns over change, disparagement, and contentions in the University came into the classroom along with national and international issues. Faculty members who tried to deal fairly and candidly with underlying issues and values and to counteract rumors and folklore became mavericks almost by definition—perceived to foster in the classroom the disruptive behavior displayed on the Mall. Allen found the contentious atmosphere and free-wheeling discussion distasteful, especially when they compounded the heavy pressure he had to take from critics outside the University.

But the president's primary difficulties were administrative and financial rather than academic and political. If USF were to fulfil its responsibility for graduate education, these programs would have to have high quality and grow rapidly. He would have to give them high priority even if some equally essential, well-matured programs came under stress. Consequently, section size in both general education and advanced courses in Basic Studies crept upward from the initial average of 26 to 38 in 1971; the 1971 all-University average showed 30 in lower-level and 25 in advanced sections. More dispiriting was a salary differential, disadvantaging Basic Studies faculty by comparison with Liberal Arts counterparts, a gap that grew larger as section size and consequent work load increased.

Chairmen began to despair when their efforts proved futile to recruit, reward, and retain professors of strong interdisciplinary experience, who were ever in short supply. They turned to young instructors, graduate assistants, and adjuncts; but this alternative gave the more experienced professors an extra burden of helping transients and fledglings cope with the general education program, on top of the load they had to carry in advanced Basic Studies courses. Trying to compensate for this increasing load by securing adequate salaries for these experienced professors, the dean and chairmen had little choice except to increase the size of sections; but this practice required more fledgling teachers, overloaded the experienced cadre, reduced effectiveness, and reinforced the tendency to disparage Basic Studies courses and faculty in general. This regressive cycle rapidly used up the "fat" and brought the College of Basic Studies to the verge of starvation.

THE NEW REGIME

Harris Dean, who succeeded Sidney French as Vice-President for Academic Affairs, became acting president in July 1970. Acutely conscious of these difficulties, he appointed a special all-University committee to review the situation in Basic Studies in the context of growth and development in the whole University. The committee quickly agreed that the commitment to general education would best be served by recombining the two faculties and then reorganizing the College of Liberal Arts.

> We move that we agree in principle that the concept of general education as a requirement be retained by the University.
> The Committee recommends the fusion of the Basic College [sic] and the College of Liberal Arts, and the rearrangement of the totality into four colleges based substantially on the current divisional structure of the College of Liberal Arts.[5]

President Mackey took office in February 1971, and by the end of the academic year he had approved this preliminary recommendation and abolished the College of Basic Studies. He directed that the new budget correct salary inequities, and increases averaging $1,500 substantially improved the morale of Basic Studies professors as they moved into Liberal Arts departments.

Some teachers committed to interdisciplinary work, however, did not fare well. Some departments that strongly emphasized loyalty to the specialty found people with interdisciplinary experience uncongenial and hard to fit into their strong expectations for specialized teaching, research, and graduate instruction. The Basic Studies people had designed and conducted advanced courses and used experimental techniques. They had tolerated a steadily increasing salary gap and increasing student load. They had been assured fair treatment at the time of separation but got a regressive cycle of malnutrition. Now they were assured fair treatment in the time of reunion. Loss of support from their old college, at best a cool reception in their new home, and an uncertain job market over the country seemed like a poor way to fulfil this assurance. Some felt decidedly put upon by the whole experience.

The study committee, in recommending the distributive model for general education, matched the pattern typical of community colleges. Transfers with an A.A. degree received blanket credit for general education requirements under the articulation agreements going back to 1959. Now they outnumbered generic students in the upper division. The design for a four-year program now appeared unfair—both to generic students who had to spread Basic Studies over four years and to transfer students who had to finish similar general education requirements in two years. The inequity seemed particularly obvious when Basic Studies had lost its modular design and a distributive pattern fit the "swinging door" enrollment pattern in both types of urban institutions.

The distributive model made no difference in degree requirements for approximately equal blocks of general education, major, and elective courses. General education now required 60 out of 180 credits with a minimum of 8 credits in each of five basic fields: English communication, fine arts–humanities, mathematics and quantitative methods, social and behavioral science, and natural science. Out of hundreds of designated courses, students typically have five or more options for each requirement.

The current situation is similar to that in many other colleges and universities; the design for general education seems to have gone back fifty years to the "cafeteria" approach of the free elective system. The principal change appears in the balance of general education, major, and elective requirements. Hefferlin found many colleges adopting the same type of design that USF follows and suggested that it was best described as a "Chinese Restaurant" system: "Select two from Group A and two from Group B."[6]

The movement for general education still continues. Students still seek an education to meet their needs as human beings who are more than wage-earners. The concern for coherence in learning is so essential to personal and institutional identity that it can hardly be thwarted. For instance, Michigan State University has redesigned and re-emphasized its general education program. At Columbia University, Daniel Bell's proposal for a realignment in general education has not yet been accepted, but Vice-President de Bary has set up a major plan for interweaving general education with professional studies throughout the student's experience. [7]

Developments at USF and other universities appear to be consistent with certain changes in the style of cross-generational encounter and cultural inheritance which Margaret Mead observed and analyzed. [8] In "postfigurative" patterns of culture, the older generation builds shared values into the experience of rising generations. This style appears analogous to the nineteenth-century common curriculum and the twentieth-century general education movement; in each case the faculty identified commonalities and handed down the content of integrative studies required of all students. "Prefigurative" styles involve sharing between younger and older generations, each learning about dimensions of life and work new to the experience of one or the other or both. The trend toward shared responsibility of students and advisors for general education, with more options to consider in designing a well-integrated degree program, seems analogous to the prefigurative style. This way of work does not dwell on commonalities in content but concentrates on a common process for linking past experience to future expectations, out of which shared values develop for students and faculty, university and community.

6

The College of Liberal Arts

Sustaining Tradition

Plans for the University of South Florida embodied an American tradition of the liberal arts college as the core of a university. Elsewhere, this concept was coming under heavy attack. Treating the liberal arts as instrumental to professional education, a number of large universities were distributing all segments of their liberal arts program among the professional schools. In many universities, a European persuasion that higher education is characterized by specialization in progressively narrowing fields began to influence program design.

Jacques Barzun suggested that the liberal arts tradition, after dominating higher education for centuries, was obsolete. High schools and community colleges had taken over responsibility for a liberal education shared by all citizens. The professional schools had assumed responsibility for specialized study in the arts and sciences.[1]

Earl McGrath lamented the displacement of broad-based liberal arts studies as the core of the entire student experience by the "graduate-school mentality"—a single-minded preoccupation with the narrowest possible line of study and research.[2] Resisting this tendency, he and the entire Council recommended in the Brumbaugh Report a strong emphasis on general and liberal education as the center of all the new universities and community colleges in Florida.

Convinced that a university must organize around a strong center of values in liberal learning, President Allen and the first deans determined to preserve and extend the tradition of a unified liberal arts college, as the two President's Commissions on Higher Education had also recommended. The Liberal Arts College would lay the groundwork in the community for a lifetime of learning and would nourish and sustain growth in the whole University. The goals set forth in the 1961 catalog remained virtually unchanged for a decade.[3]

> The Liberal Arts College . . . continues the general and liberal educa-
> tion begun in the College of Basic Studies. Here the student may
> explore further vocational interests and develop breadth of knowledge
> and precision of intellect so necessary for responsible leadership in our
> society. More specifically, the College seeks:
>   1. To allow students to continue the exploration of new subjects
> affording fresh ideas and talents enriching to life.
>   2. To enable students to try out several subjects as a means of
> determining the wisest choice.
>   3. To give sufficient development within the chosen vocational field
> so that the student will be prepared to obtain a job upon graduation or
> move successfully into a graduate or professional school.
>   4. To collaborate with the other colleges of the University in
> providing liberal arts courses to balance required training in those
> professional schools.
>   5. To cultivate independent thinking, creative imagination, and
> value commitment to help students become constructive leaders in
> their chosen activities.

Organizing the College

Parsimony being a major consideration at USF, interdisciplinary de-sign was frequently the method of choice in planning for the College of Liberal Arts. Program committees tried to avoid highly spe-cialized offerings, especially "service courses" for professional col-leges. They identified core areas to be covered by courses of broad scope that could enroll enough students to be cost-effective. These could be continuously updated to keep a coherent focus on the heart of the discipline for the growing number of specialized courses around the periphery. Self-directed learning, characteristic of adult life and emphasized in graduate and professional study, was also economically desirable as a way to generate new courses while containing their proliferation.

Especially in the formative years of tight budgets and burgeoning enrollment, this approach proved highly effective. In 1964, when USF had about 6,500 students, the Liberal Arts College offered 30 pro-grams with 467 courses (89 at the lower level and 378 at the upper level). In 1973, when enrollment exceeded 15,000, a survey for the

USF application to Phi Beta Kappa found that almost all of the 1,148 liberal arts courses (83 lower level, 463 upper level, 602 graduate) were offered at least once a year. Almost all the omissions were designed for new major sequences and would be scheduled as soon as the first students were ready. Most of the liberal arts majors retained the small core of integrative courses adopted in 1960.

ADMINISTRATION

How can a dean ever preside effectively over a large number of faculty and students pursuing diversified personal interests in everything from art to zoology? Controversy over this question was one factor leading to dissolution of the liberal arts college in several major universities during the 1950s and 1960s; it repeatedly surfaced at USF.

The question seems specious—rather like asking how one person can possibly conduct a large symphony orchestra. President Allen and Dean French simply determined that the University must capitalize upon "orchestrated" liberal education, dealing with administrative burden in terms of development rather than dissolution of the College of Liberal Arts. Dean Russell Cooper organized four divisions: Fine Arts, Language and Literature, Natural Science and Social Science. Each had a broadly knowledgeable director who worked with six or eight program chairmen, each having a faculty of six or eight. Study and experience have found six or eight units to be optimum for coordination of effort; A.J. Brumbaugh found the model effective when he was a dean at the University of Chicago and recommended it to John Allen and Russell Cooper for its values in facilitating interdisciplinary collaboration and reducing the territorial rivalries plaguing many large universities.

Faculty members had a home base where they did most of their teaching and took multiple assignments in other divisions and colleges as needed. The program chairmen taught nearly full-time and worked with the division director on the development of faculty, program, and budget in a small council close to the action in the classroom. The dean and four directors were only one step further from the classroom in planning for the whole college; they also taught part-time, so that classroom experience actually had direct bearing on administration from beginning to end.

Divisions came under increasing strain as the enrollment and the number of programs increased. By 1965 directors began to flounder

under the increasing administrative load; and they began to rely on program chairmen for budget and personnel matters even more than they were authorized to do. In order to bring authorized responsibility into line with actual functions and work load, program faculties were reorganized into 26 departments, and directors delegated greater responsibilities to their chairmen for facilitating the flow of resources into the classroom. The chairman still had primary responsibility for faculty and program development. The leaders of USF wished to personalize the work of faculty as well as students; and the chairman in a small group of colleagues cultivated the frontier spirit of sharing responsibility for developing the field of study and the spirit of camaraderie in mutual support for professional development.

On the other hand, the enlargement of the chairman's responsibility made many faculty members nervous. Some chairmen did try to dominate the department and exercise power far beyond their actual authority. Resistance quickly mobilized and the Liberal Arts faculty adopted a policy for a standard three-year term as chairman with option for renewal.

Chairmanships were not related to rank but to availability and willingness to serve. Just before a term ended, the division director canvassed members on their willingness to serve as department chairman and the colleagues they would like to nominate. The director and dean conferred on the two or three most qualified and favored and recommended a final choice to the Vice-President for Academic Affairs for an appointment by the president. The process assured full participation by members without getting into a divisive contest for election.

Chairmanships changed readily. The policy reinforced the role of a chief among equals and left primary responsibility for initiating and implementing plans with the faculty. Thus, turnover entailed discontinuity only when a department desired some new departure; only in a few instances did a slump or standoff require a search for a new chairman outside the college.

At least twice a year the dean held meetings for the whole college faculty to discuss matters of general concern and directions for future planning. More informal and creative were quarterly retreats at Chinsegut, a nearby estate whose Eskimo name means "a place where values long lost may be found," where anyone was welcome to spend the day discussing any matter concerning the college and the University.

ADMINISTRATIVE STYLE

After one of these retreats a professor remarked, "Russ Cooper runs this college like a YMCA." This remark was both kindly and percipient, for Cooper had done both professional and volunteer work with the campus and community YMCA. He tried several times to organize a "Y" at USF and was a board member of the interdenominational University Chapel Fellowship. Out of this background he drew much of his administrative style: his distaste for rankings and territorial rivalries that impeded the sharing of resources and responsibilities; his concept of administrators as chiefs among equals; and his conviction that effective power came from reconciliation—from bringing people together to set goals and commit their resources to attain them.

Many people thought that Dean Cooper's style was equivocating and irresolute; some thought he never made up his mind at all. The impressions are understandable in terms of an academic folklore about deans making instant decisions and handing down arbitrary orders. Russell Cooper's manner did not fit this model. He did not waver when he had to assure fairness and due process in dealing with complaints against a faculty member. In planning and decision-making, his style was to bring people together, keep the process moving along as they made up their minds, and then facilitate the action to which they committed all their powers.

"A liberal arts faculty is like a bunch of mavericks—they can be loose-herded, but neither led nor driven," said Dean H. T. Parlin of the University of Texas. Cooper had a loose-herding style that was effective in moving the Liberal Arts faculty along together. And always he moved toward shared values and shared visions that would bring people together in the enjoyment and advancement of learning—not by power but by reconciliation, by the spirit of things that *work* for coherence and wholeness.

The Liberal Arts Program

Over and above the foundation in general education, the Liberal Arts faculty provided two-thirds of the B.A. degree program. For a well-balanced design the faculty decided to divide the requirements equally—half in the major field, half in optional studies fitting a personalized plan. They also counteracted narrow specialization by limiting students to a maximum of 40 credits in a single division.

Excess credits were allowable but were added to the minimum 120 required for graduation.

This concern for diversification and scope rested on knowledge of the stages of occupational development. Students could expect to make more than one shift of occupation as opportunities emerged in mid-career. They must capitalize on studies of broad scope in addition to specialized expertise. A broad, diversified foundation in the major as well as general education would facilitate career transitions; myopic expertise would tend to create problems and limit opportunities. Commitment to a specialty should proceed far enough for a graduate to find an entry job or continue in graduate study. But heavy investment in specialization should be left for commitments beyond the baccalaureate degree.

THE PLANNING PROCESS

In developing course offerings each program faculty followed roughly the same distribution applied to the major sequence: about half the courses were designed for diversified choices, and half for the core shared by all students. Linear sequences of prerequisite-and-course were minimized in order to open more personal choices for majors and nonmajors.

The faculty steadfastly resisted proposals for a "minor" field. This requirement would add to administrative operations and costs when everyone wanted to keep administration simple and inexpensive in order to put maximum investment into academic work. Moreover, the minor would give students only "two strings to their bow," while the faculty wanted to design electives that would give at least three or four configurations of skill and experience to strengthen the major and open up more options for career development.

Most majors required a culminating, integrative seminar (in addition to the Senior Seminar in Basic Studies); a few also required a senior thesis and comprehensive examination. The thesis-examination tended to become a work of supererogation, as so many other opportunities were open for self-directed, innovative work; this requirement gradually disappeared in most instances.

The faculty was also sensitive to the fact that truth cannot be confined within a single scholarly discipline; many potent facts and insights lodge in the interstices between specialties. In research as well as teaching, the dean and faculty of Liberal Arts tried to give ample opportunity for crossing artificial lines and cultivating interdisciplinary collaboration.

As a consequence, the Liberal Arts college provided a home for a number of interdisciplinary programs that grew into departments with their own faculty. For example, American Studies spun off from a team-teaching program in Basic Studies. Afro-American Studies focused upon the black experience in America from the perspectives of African heritage, liberation from slavery, the breakup of the caste system, and contemporary aspirations for identity and equality. Religious Studies organized around the development of personal values, ecclesiastical and communal polity in the process of man's search for wholeness and vitality.

Each division organized one or more interdisciplinary majors. This arrangement was especially helpful to students in secondary education and community college programs, who often wanted a foundation in many aspects of a field, not just a single specialty. A collegewide Liberal Arts major was offered, which each student could tailor to fit any combination of liberal and professional interests. The dean reviewed the student's purposes and plan of work; when he found the design sound, he assigned a faculty advisor who would facilitate progress toward the degree. Twenty or thirty students started such majors each year. For example, one of the first Liberal Arts majors was committed to the ministry and wanted a foundation in the liberal arts, education, and business management for his work as a teacher and administrator of a congregation—specialized religious studies would come in the seminary.

INTEGRATIVE FUNCTIONS

The scope of expectations, content, and techniques for learning in the liberal arts is as broad and diversified as society itself. Next to unifying the membership of the college, the development of close connections with each of the other colleges was a major concern of the dean and faculty of Liberal Arts in their responsibility as an integrative center for the University. Fusion of the Liberal Arts–Basic Studies faculties was the closest such linkage. This proved particularly valuable in interlocking general, liberal, and professional studies for students new to higher education. It strengthened interdisciplinary methods and cultivated a diversified repertory of techniques for teaching and learning.

Rather than joining the two faculties, linkage with the College of Education provided dual membership for students entering secondary and post-secondary teaching, counseling, and administration. Dean Battle and Dean Cooper wanted to counteract the tendency for

people to teach as they were taught and to encourage the development of a diversified repertory to fit differing subject matter and the
different ways people learn. So the colleges shared responsibility for
involving people in learning: Liberal Arts contributed diversified
content, Education contributed diversified techniques. The joint effort was cost-effective in avoiding duplication of courses, and it
capitalized upon feedback: students introduced Liberal Arts classes to
methods learned in education courses; the Education faculty and
classes profited from Liberal Arts instruction giving greater scope in
subject matter.

Resource-sharing was the approach to Business Administration,
where the Economics "outpost" was located, and to Engineering,
where the computer sciences served the whole University. All-
University membership in each college council also capitalized on
ways of sharing resources and responsibilities, an important part of
the heritage of the liberal arts, and cultivated intellectual community
across the University.

Reorganization of the Liberal Arts College

The College of Liberal Arts flourished like the green bay tree. It
enrolled at least 40 percent of USF students each term and had about
the same proportion of the general faculty. It steadily added new
courses and programs, including graduate work in nearly every
department and doctoral programs in five fields by 1972. Research
grants and scholarly publications of its faculty regularly exceeded
those of all other colleges combined; and the primary commitment
to teaching continued unabated as the college grew and diversified.

The college reorganized in a series of changes prompted by growing pains. Separation from Basic Studies in 1964 was followed in
1967 by formation of departments out of programs. Each division
soon had more faculty and students than a typical professional college, and directors were functioning as deans of small colleges do
anywhere. On Dean Cooper's recommendation, President Allen
retitled these positions as Associate Deans and incorporated them
into the Council of Deans. All five executives of the College of
Liberal Arts now participated directly in formulating and administering the University's whole academic policy, program, and budget.

This development suited Russell Cooper's style of keeping administrative decisions close to the classroom while orchestrating complex programs for the college and the whole University. Almost half of the program and budget planning for the University originated from his office. In effect, he functioned as a coordinate Vice-President for Academic Affairs.

Organization of the Liberal Arts College was effective, but it did not satisfy the expectations of a good many people who looked at the scalar chart of organization instead of the actual administrative network. Some chairmen and departmental faculties perceived their rank to be reduced because they had a box lower on the chart than that of their counterparts in other colleges. They considered their responsibilities and authority to be diminished and their freedom reduced by tight supervision because they worked so closely with the directors and Dean Cooper. Many believed that budget allocations would be augmented if they could present their case directly to the vice-president without this intermediation.

Those who were persuaded that USF worked on the scalar principle and believed that closeness to the top meant more resources overlooked certain pertinent facts. The only way to get a larger budget was for the legislature to increase overall appropriations for USF. Alternatively, the college could capitalize on cost-saving and resource-sharing, as it was in fact doing by diffusing responsibility to small faculty configurations in a close-knit network, bringing program and budget plans to well-finished closure before they went to the vice-president, and taking a major share of the all-University effort in administration.

Actually, the linkages and supervisory functions in the College of Liberal Arts were neither closer nor more remote than those in other colleges and in the Council of Deans' support network for the Vice-President for Academic Affairs. The extra line of boxes on the chart looked as if an extra step were interposed between the departmental faculty and the vice-president. In practice the system branched out from the five principal administrators in the dean's office straight to the departments and saved at least two steps in the planning process.

The arrangement that had evolved by successive stages, keeping pace with growth and diversification, had kept the College of Liberal Arts together as a well-orchestrated network. But the undertones and grumblings over internal strains and external concerns had to come to the surface in order to be resolved clearly. The faculty agreed that these problems called for reassessment of the entire organization of the University. This move came in its fourteenth year—approximately the time for any rapidly growing young person or institution to begin "the awkward age."

REDESIGNING THE UNIVERSITY

Upon John Allen's retirement in 1970, Harris Dean inherited the responsibility for seeing USF through the awkward age. He immediately appointed a 22-member special committee to review concerns of Basic Studies, Liberal Arts, graduate programs, and research institutes, and to prepare a plan for orderly transition to new configurations in the Academic Affairs area.

From September to December this committee held many hearings, discussed numerous proposals, assessed and refined alternative plans. On December 5 it reached its first substantial consensus, on the proposal to reintegrate Basic Studies and Liberal Arts programs and faculties and organize four colleges for the liberal arts out of the existing divisions.

Ordinarily this proposal would have been submitted to the deans and councils of all colleges and administrative areas, then to the University Senate for study, review, and formulation of a finished plan, and to the president for final action. After the Christmas holidays, however, the Board of Regents appointed Dr. Cecil Mackey to assume office as president in February 1971. His involvement in the planning process being both desirable and necessary, Harris Dean and the committee decided to hold all action steps and studies in abeyance until his arrival.

But the proposal did not go through the remaining steps; the planning process stayed in abeyance. President Mackey simply released a three-page memorandum to the University faculty on June 14, 1971, stating his decision and reading in part:[4]

> Almost immediately upon my arrival at the University of South Florida I became aware of a number of proposals and recommendations for academic reorganization. I learned that some of the proposals had had extensive consideration and study by committees within the University, by outside consultants, and by a special study committee of the Southern Association of Colleges and Schools. In order that I could have a complete assessment of the work that had been done on

the subject of academic reorganization, on March 1 I asked Dr. Harris Dean, in his role as special consultant to the president, to review all of the available information on the subject, study the reports that had been compiled, and report to me his findings and recommendations in the three major areas. Especially I asked that he examine the following proposals:

(1) that the College of Basic Studies be dissolved and the responsibility for general education be assumed in the appropriate Liberal Arts departments;

(2) that the College of Liberal Arts be dissolved and its four divisions be constituted as separate colleges;

(3) that the Research and Development Center be terminated and the institutes thereunder be placed in the appropriate academic units of the University.

I received Dr. Dean's report on May 12. He indicated that some of the questions that I had raised had been matters of concern and serious study almost from the founding of the University. He also pointed out that in his role as Vice-President and Dean of Academic Affairs, he had had serious concerns about the adequacy and appropriateness of the existing organizational structure of the University. He questioned whether it was as well suited as it should be to support and facilitate accomplishment of the University's educational objectives.

President Mackey went on to say that he had informally discussed the matter with some members of University councils and with the Chancellor and some Regents who in general commented favorably on the recommendations. Accordingly he announced his approval and his appointment of ten committees to implement the reorganization. He added, "I am sure you will agree with me that every effort should be made to assure personnel affected that their positions will be carefully protected and that moves and changeovers will be planned with the dignity and worth of the individual at a high priority."

Mackey made clear his own belief in the principles of general and liberal education. He felt that the new arrangement would strengthen their purposes. Carl Riggs, who came to USF in September 1971 as Vice-President for Academic Affairs, assumed primary responsibility for seeing the new organization established. He was strongly committed to the value of liberal arts as an integrative center for a university. The faculty generally welcomed the new configurations and the assurance of protection for individuals.

The New Regime

An assessment of the changes made in 1971–73 cannot as yet be definitive but can indicate some of their immediate, traumatic effects. Needs were clear and proposals were proceeding in accordance with the all-University approach and the accent on learning, principles which had facilitated previous transitions. No exceptional dissonance or discontinuity was anticipated in this case. President Mackey, however, took the first rough sketch for reorganization out of this context. He ordered the implementation of a half-finished plan. Many responsible officers and councils were unprepared. Changes came as a sharp, sudden shock. Closing the gaps in the planning process created acute stress and an overload of very difficult, detailed work for many people.

The Liberal Arts College had not prepared the new internal and external configurations necessary to maintain its carefully cultivated linkages across the University and community. These were suddenly disrupted; throughout the whole University lines of authorization, resource-sharing, communication, and feedback were blurred or broken. Systems became erratic in their operation and habits were often thrown out of kilter.

The most disorienting factor appeared to be a shift in the center of organization from the classroom and the teaching-learning process to the president's office and the management team. The consequent changes were often disconcerting and sometimes dysfunctional, painful, and deleterious to morale. Somehow, the new configurations were sorted out but at great cost in time and effort. Many people who had gone through similar transitions before at USF and other colleges considered the procedure excessively costly, even wasteful, because of the sudden departure from well-tested planning systems.

By the end of 1971, the four divisions of the College of Liberal Arts had absorbed Basic Studies faculties and programs and became the new Colleges of Fine Arts, Language-Literature (now called Arts and Letters), Natural Sciences, and Social and Behavioral Sciences. During the transition, Russell Cooper and several other deans and faculty members called President Mackey's attention to a missing link: the important function of integrating general, liberal, and professional studies.

The special committee had studied several suggestions for this function, but these had been left dangling. One proposed to create vice-presidents for Liberal Arts and for Professional Education. A variant proposed only two colleges under these vice-presidents, one for professional education combining Education, Business Administration, Engineering, Medicine, and Nursing, the other combining Basic Studies and the four liberal arts colleges, with deans heading professional or disciplinary divisions. A third was to appoint a high-ranking officer for general and liberal education in the Office of Academic Affairs. And there were other suggestions.

Mackey considered none of these alternatives, and Dean Cooper pointed out that the commitment to integrate general and liberal education now became an all-University responsibility converging on the vice-president. A Committee on Undergraduate Studies was formed, but its broad scope and high volume of transactions precluded careful cultivation of integrative ways of work. It is now difficult for the University as a whole to capitalize on the strong base of experience that had developed in the two original colleges for the liberal arts.

Integrative activities characterizing the College of Liberal Arts, of course, were lost with the college: the faculty meetings, College Council, and Chinsegut retreats. Faculty members still identified with departments, and their division became their college home; but no longer did they have any comprehensive liberal arts organism to bring them together in broad, collaborative undertakings. Many faculty members felt that the new arrangement answered more fully their concern for a home in a special academic territory. Others, especially those committed to interdisciplinary work, lamented their loss of freedom to work beyond a restricted field of study.

FINANCIAL STATUS

Faculty members throughout the University were becoming more and more concerned about well-balanced financing for all the equally important, closely integrated programs of liberal arts and general and professional education. President Mackey corrected the particular inequity affecting Basic Studies faculty in his incisive action of 1972; his directives on the 1973 budget corrected the inequity affecting women faculty members, universitywide. Comparing the total funds per FTE faculty line for 1970 and 1973, independently and as a proportion of the all-University allocation per line, shows how the range of college funding around the all-University level began to diminish as a consequence of these actions and other modifications in program-budget planning.

In 1970 funds per FTE faculty line for the entire University stood at $19,215; the figure increased by 14 percent to $22,028 in 1973. Allocations to the colleges in 1970 ranged from $14,616 in Basic Studies, at 76 percent of the University figure, to $25,637 in Engineering, at 129 percent. In 1973 the range had been reduced by two-fifths (41 percent), from 53 to 31 percentage points overall: the new College of Language and Literature showed an allocation per line of $18,984, 86 percent of the all-University figure, while Engineering showed $25,938 and 117 percent, at the other extreme.

There is little indication that the division of the College of Liberal Arts into four new colleges had much to do with this development. The effort to narrow the range and close some of the most obvious gaps involved the entire University and affected each college in a different way.

Allocations for Education rose by 20 percent and from 90 to 97 percent of the all-University figure in 1973; those for Business Administration rose by 18 percent and from 92 to 98 percent of the overall figure. Funds per FTE line in Fine Arts increased by 4 percent but dropped to 99 percent of the all-University figure, from 105 percent in 1970. Social and Behavioral Sciences showed an increase of 14 percent, equal to the all-University increase, and rose from 95 to 99 percent of the average University line. Language and Literature dropped from 89 to 86 percent of the general allocation while gaining 7 percent in funds per line. Natural Sciences showed a decrement of 6 percent in funds per line and dropped from 121 to 101 percent of the general allocation.

As a set, the four colleges gained 3 percent in funds per FTE faculty member, which rose from $20,487 in 1970 to $21,212 in 1973 and dropped from 103 to 96 percent of the general allocation. The trend toward narrower ranges and more balanced distribution of funds showed in the liberal arts and the whole University. The range of divisional allocations in the College of Liberal Arts in 1970 was 32 percentage points, between Language-Literature and Natural Sciences; in 1973 the range was reduced by more than half (54 percent) to 15 percentage points between these new colleges.

The movement for separate colleges gained support on the unexamined assumption that formal documentation of direct communication with the Vice-President for Academic Affairs would produce a larger slice of the budget pie. This major argument for reorganization received little verification in experience. The results also suggest that some shortcomings were attributable to funding formulae and other factors, rather than to organization. For example, the increment in funds per faculty line of one percent in Engineering coupled with the decrement of six percent in Natural Sciences, 1970–73, seem to reflect changes and pressures on scientific and technical instruction in state and national planning. There was also a leveling off after start-up costs of the new Science Center at USF. And special pressures on costs that tend to escape formulae based on credit hours were also in evidence; as a case in point, the Chemistry department was trying to operate with five cents per student per credit hour for laboratory materials in both graduate and undergraduate instruction.

Such special problems of program development and resource-sharing were little affected by the new approach to organization. Even the regressive effects of the expansion of advanced and graduate studies upon the College of Basic Studies appeared primarily to involve differentials in funding formulae based on level of instruction; these affected adversely its operation as a separate college, but the underlying problems were not resolved by its absorption into the liberal arts colleges.

CHANGES IN DEGREE REQUIREMENT

For students, changes in requirements for the B.A. degree were more important than changes in organization. Both had minimal effect. Most students stayed with the majors in their division as it became a college. The configuration of general-major-elective courses remained the same. Students had the same responsibility for planning, with an added "prefigurative" process for designing the general education block instead of following a standard program.

Fine Arts programs now range from 63 to 91 credits in the major; a student may take all the electives in the college, and this change relieved some pressures that have troubled students in the graphic and performing arts for a long time. Language-Literature faculties now limit majors to 60 credits, with the remainder selected in or outside the college; Natural Sciences follows substantially the same pattern. Majors in Social and Behavioral Sciences must earn at least 90 credits outside the college including those in the general education block.

The new system is more flexible than the old and centers in a common process rather than common subject matter. The faculty has foregone its control over integrative design for general education and now takes a collaborative role with students in the prefigurative design of their whole degree program.

Some critics have charged a few departments with virtually turning themselves into trade schools by pressuring students to take a prescribed set of general and elective courses. There is not much evidence to document this impression. In any event, students would have to go along with the pressure out of agreement with the trade-school idea or out of timidity—since the personalized approach is still the rule and options abound in the catalog descriptions of general, major, and elective requirements. Recalcitrance is a notable feature of student behavior, and the personalized approach would tend to reinforce normal resistance to any informal pressures. Given these countervailing factors, the "trade-school" charge does not seem very likely to have much foundation in actual experience.

INTERDISCIPLINARY THRUST

The Liberal Arts major and Advanced Basic Studies major terminated with their colleges; students irrevocably committed to them were accommodated in one of the four new colleges, most of them in Language and Literature. The development of interdisciplinary courses and majors continued undiminished. Thirteen new programs developed in the colleges of Basic Studies and Liberal Arts between 1960 and 1970 and twelve after the four colleges organized. All twenty-five are interdisciplinary in design. The breakup of the generative center seems to mark the beginning of a period of accelerated program development, with no indication of any loss of fertility in interdisciplinary methods of teaching and learning.

Reorganization centered on administrative concerns for efficiency and followed the scalar principle of organization; it did not seem to be affected by academic concerns for educational effectiveness. In this respect the University was preoccupied with many of the same issues elaborated in studies of the Carnegie Commission on Higher Education and in federal agencies, associations for higher education and the professions, and state and regional authorities concerned with higher education.

This preoccupation seems to have affected minimally the development of academic programs at USF dealing with concerns for quality of life, the natural and human environment, and the culture of cities. Many programs—Rehabilitation, Urban Anthropology, Leisure Studies, Aging Studies, and others—have been designed and conducted in close collaboration with public and private agencies in the community, following much the same pattern set by the fine arts in 1960.

Beyond these observations the long-term effects of the University's reorganization cannot be assessed or predicted. The change was traumatic. Many people felt the loss of an integrative center and a large-minded spirit of concerted study and action with the passing of the College of Liberal Arts. But its successor colleges have manifested much of its fertility in interdisciplinary collaboration. They are, after all, colleges for the liberal arts, and with additional time and opportunity they may prove to cultivate just as fully the sense of coherence and the spirit of reconciliation in the ongoing work of advancing and sharing learning.

THE SPIRIT OF LEARNING

The experience of the University's two colleges for the liberal arts suggests some prefigurative principles that may be generally useful in academic and administrative organization.

First, divisional organization around the humanities and the natural and social sciences clearly has many advantages for a university that desires a well-organized liberal arts college as a generative center. A division for general-experimental-interdisciplinary education may also be desirable as a way to give faculty having these interests a home without undue risk of encapsulation, while still promoting cross-fertilization. Within divisions program configurations provide parsimonious, effective response to changing academic and community concerns, along with close, efficient linkages to the classroom as the primary scene of the action in education.

A broadly representative council will greatly facilitate the development of any college within a large university because of its need for inward configurations compatible with outward responsibilities. This council can promote program development outward around the periphery and the linkages with other colleges that accompany healthy growth; at one and the same time it can facilitate the orchestration of college operations and linkages in the intercollegiate network that holds the university together. Such a council should regularly appraise actual offerings of courses and programs in relation to emerging needs in other colleges and in the community; it should regularly review the actual patterning of degree programs by students and the extent of convergence and diversification, as the indicators of integrative design rather than scattering of interests and efforts. It should cultivate opportunities for faculty development and intercollegiate collaboration in teaching and research.

Resource-sharing is essential. Facilities and budget planning must protect all users against human proclivities to disparagement and rivalries exacerbated by crowded facilities and tight class schedules. Facilities and equipment should provide for multiple use and accommodate the diversified techniques in the instructional repertory. Flexibility in timing will encourage self-directed work by students and guard against disruption of programs by the tendency for interdisciplinary work to expand beyond its original design.

A design for sharing the experience of producing academic work of high quality will probably have more effect on the outcomes of teaching and learning than any factors indicated by statistical data from grades, test scores, inventories, and rating scales. Instrumental approaches to course and program design appear more useful than others in linking the academic experience of students to challenging tasks in the advancement of knowledge and to emergent community needs and opportunities.

The university's planning network must be prepared to capitalize on the inevitable spinoff from general and interdisciplinary education: new courses, new programs, and new techniques for teaching and learning. Strong degree programs in interdisciplinary studies leading to the Ph.D. are particularly needed in order to develop an adequate cadre of teachers and researchers to cultivate these generative resources for higher education.

Just as a liberal arts college must undergird universitywide programs, so an all-University commitment must sustain its organization and program development. The concept of liberal arts is more humanistic and spiritual than institutionalized and practical. Its practitioners are concerned with bringing people together because of their differing cultures, personal experience, and perspectives on the world. Their work relates to the whole struggle of people to sustain themselves as human beings and to affirm generative values in a world of dispiriting change and proliferating technocracy and bureaucracy.

An educationally effective organization for an entire university can draw upon the spirit of the liberal arts in capitalizing upon the shared values at the center of the academic enterprise and sustaining the ongoing quest for knowledge of the whole world of nature and human experience.

7
Professional Education

The Social Setting

The general state of flux in all the professions since World War II may aptly illustrate Margaret Mead's analysis of a trend toward prefigurative rather than postfigurative ways of cultural development.[1] Rising expectations have often diverged, in some cases moving toward prefigurative roles for self-directing action by individuals and groups assisted by professional advice and counsel, in other cases depending on more positive authority, intervention, and direction from professionals in postfigurative fashion. Developing some integrative factors for reconciling these divergent trends in professional roles has perforce involved the universities in challenging tasks.

Indeed, many studies of changing professional roles emphasize the strong infusion of shared values from the universities. In 1955 the U.S. Office of Education conducted the first comprehensive survey of professional education to be made for more than fifty years; its report covered 35 professions and showed how their educational foundations had evolved out of the trade schools of the nineteenth century into strong, influential colleges. Samuel Brownell, Commissioner of Education, considered the narrow "trade-school" outlook to have broadened, with general education becoming the essential foundation for vocational development and the sciences the essential foundation for professional expertise.[2]

Liberal arts faculties, regarding themselves traditionally as masters of all academic territory, resisted the absorption of professional education into universities and often disparaged "trade-school" programs. By the time the University of South Florida came into being, this recalcitrance had generally subsided. It was also becoming quite clear that the professional and liberal arts faculties had to close ranks and share responsibilities for keeping both academic and professional work abreast of the accelerating growth of knowledge. Planning for the University took advantage of this common concern for coherence in the academic enterprise and other social systems. About ten years after USF opened, Paul Dressel observed evidence of such convergence throughout the general system of higher education.

> The sharp distinction between liberal and professional programs is gradually being erased. Faculty members in the basic arts and sciences are often professional in their orientation toward graduate study and thus are more readily accepted by other segments of the faculty. Both liberal and professional faculties are faced with demands to make their programs more relevant to the needs of all segments of society.[3]

In a study for the Carnegie Commission, Edgar Schein found that the expansion of knowledge reinforced trends toward specialization, as exciting new developments emerged around the periphery of traditional strongholds. The older professions were becoming more rigid, bureaucratic, and resistant to innovation at the very time when undergraduate students were seeking avenues for early entry into the most challenging aspects of study and practice. Interdisciplinary innovations would be consistent with both student and community concerns.[4]

The concerns of students and the community also merged in a desire for more different ways of entry to the professions and a shorter period of preparatory studies. The U.S. Office of Education regularly reminds the nation of many rewarding occupations, offering ample opportunity for advancement through lifelong learning, that can be entered directly from high school. A report from the Carnegie Commission estimated that little or no educational quality would be forfeited if the time in undergraduate studies were reduced by about one-fourth.[5]

Vocational counselors typically encourage youth to explore occupational opportunities extensively, to acquire employed experience before and during the college years, and to feel free to change direction in their choice of majors, in order to prepare for mid-career transitions and emerging opportunities in new occupations. The College of St. Benedict (Minnesota) and other colleges have introduced general courses and degree programs in education, counseling, and guidance that deal with the process of career development and the transitions characteristic of adult life and work. Public and private enterprises have developed in-service education, often cooperating with colleges and universities.

All these trends capitalize on the increasing resources for lifelong learning in the general system of higher education and indicate new dimensions for professional education. They open alternative pathways for occupational entry and alternative schedules for career development, moving away from the traditional "career ladder" in a professional bureaucracy. In this social setting the deans at USF developed their program design for professional education.

The College of Business Administration

Professors of liberal arts and sciences have often held business in low esteem; for example, Professor Lowell of Harvard once described business as the oldest of the arts and the youngest of the professions. During the 1950s colleges of business were reassessing their role in the academic world and their linkages to the national and multinational system of corporate enterprise. Both the Carnegie Corporation and the Ford Foundation published studies of business education in 1959.[6] These studies emphasized similar tasks in making the transition from how-to-do-it courses in accounting, salesmanship, and management to systematic studies of the larger issues of policy and planning confronting the management of private and public enterprise. The two studies converged on five principles that Dean Charles Millican considered particularly pertinent to plans for the business administration program at USF.

1. Colleges of Business should raise their academic standards. They should not be a dumping ground for other fields but should have sound admission standards and a challenging curriculum.

2. At least half of the work should be in general and liberal education, to provide an adequate background for managerial decision-making.

3. "The quality of a business school tends to vary in inverse proportion to the number of business courses it offers," declared Gordon and Howell in the Carnegie study. In his study for the Ford Foundation, Pierson recommended a small core of fundamental courses in each of the business fields and control of proliferation in all areas. Students should have breadth in professional education to match a broad foundation in scientific and humanistic studies, giving them greater flexibility to adapt to change and growth in a lifetime career beyond the entry job.

4. Instruction should be realistic and demanding, dealing with practical cases and including first-hand contact with the business community.
5. Colleges must have strong faculties having experience in and commitment to the concerns of business.

The dual focus of USF programs on corporate enterprise and the general economic system, the extensive use of case studies and practicum, and the integration of studies in business and the liberal arts closely paralleled the Ford and Carnegie recommendations.

STANDARDS AND PROGRAM DESIGN

According to the Florida Plan for higher education, standards of admission applied uniformly to each university in the state system. On the all-University principle, standards for continuing study and earning the degree at USF applied uniformly to all colleges and majors. In no way could any college become a dumping ground. University policies did not penalize students for a false start but gave a second chance and supported any change of major within or between colleges.

This approach to academic standards worked out well in practice. Undergraduate programs in Business Administration were fully accredited by the American Assembly of Collegiate Schools of Business in 1968. Data from the Educational Testing Service show that USF graduates have consistently averaged well above national norms in tests for graduate study in business. Levels of performance have been consistent with results from other colleges at USF.

Dean Millican announced at the outset that the college aimed to prepare students "for a succession of jobs rather than their first job or for just top management." Program design followed the combination of general, liberal, and vocational studies established universitywide, with half of the program outside the college. The college has maintained the original design almost intact, but uniform degree requirements have given way to more flexible, personalized patterns since each college assumed more discretionary responsibilities after reorganization in 1972. Business courses now range from 87 to 100 credits maximum in the total 180 credits required for the B.A. degree.

Five basic courses covered accounting, economics, finance, management and marketing. Each major required only three to five additional courses in any field. Advisors emphasized the rapid change and the many emerging opportunities in the world of business and the process of career development with its mid-career transitions, for which students would need both a focal area of competence and a wide range of correlative studies. Each major field opened a cluster of occupations for immediate entry, and the overall degree program gave the scope and flexibility desired for coping with transitions and new opportunities.

Essentially the same philosophy is at work today. Each field has become a department with 27 or more credits in its major. In addition to five core courses all students take a course in business law and one in computer applications; they are urged to include mathematics through Calculus I in most programs.

Over the country, Business Administration faculties have felt countervailing pressures with respect to specialization. In the business world, personnel officers tend to look for recruits with more highly specialized training while other executives are often giving a contrary call for greater breadth in professional study and experience. At USF, interdisciplinary design of courses counteracts the trend toward proliferation of specialized courses to some degree, while independent studies tend to open up new specialties beyond the regular offerings and may evolve into new courses and programs in the course of time. The faculty has not been especially concerned with strengthening the interdisciplinary major—partly because of the multidisciplinary core of courses and partly because of the general use of interdisciplinary methods in teaching, with case studies as the preferred approach.

Since 1970 the college has moved toward joint programs with health, engineering, and newly developing fields of business enterprise. The faculty has developed a program for the M.S. degree, oriented toward administration in public and private nonprofit enterprise, especially in health and other fields of human service. The program design followed social trends toward expansion of services and more systematic planning in nonprofit enterprises and public agencies. But it has run into some difficulties over accreditation, involving questions often raised in public planning bodies, corporate and professional circles, and many universities and community agencies concerning the most effective ways to respond to change and growth in this significant sector of the economic system.

TEACHING AND LEARNING

First-hand experience with the business world has been a lively interest of faculty and students. More than half of the students have outside employment; field studies, internships, and Cooperative Education placements enlarge the scope and variety of practical experience. Most of the courses require some field work; for example, students have helped many small businesses to modernize accounting systems, marketing approaches, or management methods. About 40 percent of the students have supervised field experience of some kind in addition to their own employed experience.

The faculty has developed a diversified repertory of instructional techniques. Independent study is emphasized and is the predominant approach in graduate study. Programed and computer-assisted instruction in business courses augment the lecture-discussion-laboratory format generally employed throughout the University. Heavy enrollments indicate that business programs are well adapted to student experience and expectations, and an increasing number of students in other colleges are choosing electives in Business Administration.

Most of the Business Administration faculty have the doctoral degree and extensive experience in public and private enterprise. Dean Millican's plan for faculty development began with an original cadre sharing as diversified as possible a combination of liberal and professional perspectives; around this group, new positions strengthened each specialty. Because of the shortage of professors, many new positions were filled by specialists having rather narrowly limited experience and perspectives, including adjuncts from the business community on one-term appointments for one or two courses in their specialty. The practice added to the variety in the faculty mix but also reinforced the tendency to proliferate courses and assign teachers to narrower segments of the program.

The faculty has lost some of its cohesiveness through sheer size, specialization, and transient membership. An intellectual breach has grown increasingly evident between teachers oriented toward humanistic, theoretical concerns and those stressing empirical, quantitative methods. Consequent problems of morale have led to short tenure and frequent changes of leadership and to a tendency for faculty to withdraw from collaborative work into a specialized domain. To be sure, similar conditions have spread throughout the University. But a confidential poll by the AAUP chapter in 1974 revealed that the faculty in Business Administration had lost confidence in their own dean as well as in the general University administration. Strong, congenial leadership was needed to restore the spirit of the college and support the faculty's concern for renewal of the diversified and integrative design for teaching and learning.

The College of Education

The history of colleges for teacher education began with the normal schools which many states established in the nineteenth century. In the early twentieth century most of these schools enlarged and enriched their programs; many became state teachers' colleges and some provided the foundations for new state universities. Florida did not follow this typical course of development but depended primarily on the small private colleges and three state universities to educate teachers. But their graduates could not meet the needs of the public schools, and by 1960 over half of Florida's new teachers had to be recruited outside of Florida every year.

A College of Education was therefore included in the planning for USF from the outset. Dean Battle took full advantage of new developments in the teaching profession that were appearing in response to growth and rising expectations in the whole system of education. In 1939 the Cooperative Study of Teacher Education explored new directions for the profession nationwide, financed by a $1 million grant from the Rockefeller Foundation. Cross-sectional and longitudinal studies in a representative sample of 34 colleges and universities produced recommendations to strengthen general education for teachers, to design new content and techniques that would follow more closely the stages and tasks of human development and learning, and to strengthen collaboration between public schools and teacher education programs.

In 1946 the National Education Association's Commission on Teacher Education and Professional Standard (TEPS) recommended action to strengthen teaching as a true profession with thoroughly competent practitioners. The TEPS report emphasized the need for breadth and variety in liberal arts studies, practical classroom experience, and sound knowledge of special subject matter. The NEA generally advocated more flexible, personalized programs of teacher education as a foundation for lifelong professional growth.

A national consensus on directions for teacher education was crystallizing; at the same time, all sorts of new instructional techniques were being tested and proven in research and classroom practice. The knowledge explosion continued to bring new configurations of subject matter into the schools and colleges. Dean Battle and the charter faculty had a wealth of academic and professional experience to use in planning.

ALL-UNIVERSITY RESPONSIBILITY

The typical teachers' college laid down a strong foundation in the liberal arts and sciences—the very stuff of learning in the schools. In the universities, however, schism, vituperation, even open hostility developed all too often between teacher educators and the liberal arts faculties. President Allen and the deans were determined that USF should get along without any such useless cleavages.

Dean Battle proposed an all-University Council on Teacher Education, which was established to plan and monitor development of the program. The Council was an outward and visible sign of the all-University commitment to the "accent on learning" as an accent on the preparation of good teachers. With five members from Education and five from the other colleges it did yeoman service throughout the 1960s in articulating teacher education programs with developments in other colleges and in the public schools.

As intercollegiate linkages became well-consolidated, members outside the College of Education became less active, and President Mackey abolished the Council and similar bodies in all the other colleges in the general reorganization of 1972. The Education faculty now relies almost altogether on in-house planning committees. Because other colleges are necessarily responsible for subject-matter specialties in many of the majors, strong interaction continues between Education and other faculties.

ADMISSION STANDARDS

The College of Education was responsible for administering standards of teacher certification for the state, as well as for securing its own accreditation. Questions about the selection of teachers have exercised educators and communities for generations. The context in which students are selected for teacher education differs from the context in which general standards of admission apply. There are no easy answers to the issues and difficulties growing out of this difference in context and perspective.

General admission depends upon measures of proficiency in past academic work, and there can be no doubt that proficiency in learning is necessary to effective teaching. The difficulty comes from the fact that teachers cannot count on their own effective ways of learning to fit other people—whether they are working with children or adults. Students with brilliant records sometimes fail miserably when facing a roomful of normal, eager, restless youngsters; others of low or average achievement—even people with clearly evident physical handicaps or peculiarities of behavior—sometimes get a class steaming along as if everything in the world was wide open to them and nothing could stop them from learning.

The past record gives little clue to critical differences between effective and ineffective teachers. Neither complete permissiveness nor arbitrary selection seemed workable to Dean Battle and the faculty. At the outset, they asked for a C+ average (GPR=2.5) for entry, but the other colleges protested this departure from all-University standards. It was not fair to students, committed to a diversified general education program and required to study in their areas of weakness as well as strength. For any discomfiture in another field they might be locked out of teacher education, which might be their best choice. The "no dumping" and "second-chance" rules should apply uniformly.

Education, therefore, accepts students through a committee that evaluates academic, physical, and behavioral factors related to professional performance, using a counseling rather than a judicial procedure. The committee looks for candidates who understand their strong and weak points and are prepared to improve in both respects. It keeps students informed of employment trends but does not prevent applicants from pursuing a major in education purely on the basis of market estimates. As a consequence, Education graduates about a third of all B.A. degree candidates at USF. Even though only about half of them found teaching jobs in 1974, the breadth of their programs opened the way to other fields, especially human services and other specialties dependent on knowledge of the learning process and human development.

Selection has thus proceeded through counsel rather than by decree. With swelling enrollment, counseling became more and more perfunctory, except when students pursued the faculty for advice. The system has worked well despite complaints from applicants when some majors have to limit enrollment because of external constraints on internship and practicum placements. The response from accrediting teams and schools employing USF graduates has been generally favorable and frequently enthusiastic.

ACADEMIC PROGRAMS

Six professional courses were designed, common to all majors: Human Development and Learning, Social Foundations of Education, Curriculum and Instruction, Methods, and Internship with its accompanying seminar. In secondary and post-secondary majors, basic requirements represented 36 to 44 credits, leaving 70 to 80 credits available for general education and advanced professional and external electives. In the elementary and comprehensive K–12 majors, students must take content courses along with methods courses, and their work is virtually prescribed for two full years.

For the first four or five years the college was preoccupied with elementary and secondary programs in order to answer increasing needs in the expanding school system. By 1964 it had enlarged its programs and introduced graduate studies to meet expanding needs in counseling, administration, and curriculum leadership. It offered the first graduate program in the University and by 1976 had developed 43 master's programs and a doctoral program focusing on urban education and growing out of the TTT program. In the growth from 64 to 361 courses between 1961 and 1975, the largest increase came at the graduate level.

Part of this growth resulted from an arrangement by the Board of Regents and the State Department of Education to allocate the 67 counties among the nine universities for collaboration between the county school boards and teacher educators on programs for continuing professional development. With 16,000 teachers and 4,000 support personnel in the 12 school systems assigned to USF, many in-service courses, personalized studies, and group projects in institutional research and evaluation were developed. The College of Education and the school boards organized a South Florida Educational Planning Council to give continuity to the work; this arrangement also facilitated collaboration with business and industry, prisons, hospitals, retirement centers, and other non-school settings for teaching and learning.

INTERNSHIP

In 1958 the Florida Teacher Education Advisory Council (a citizens' group advising on certification) surveyed beginning teachers on points of strength and weakness in their preparation. Responses showed that Education students felt the need for more first-hand experience in public schools. Jean Battle was also convinced that public-school internship was decidedly superior to service in the laboratory schools often conducted by teachers' colleges. Local educators were eager to cooperate and worked with the faculty to identify schools and secure master teachers—whose only compensation was a fee waiver on a USF course.

There was no expectation that this choice would be less expensive than the laboratory school; it has proved educationally effective, but it involves distinctive budget problems. Formulae for productivity, based on FTE enrollment in terms of credit hours, do not take into account the investment of real time outside the classroom by Education faculty, time required for observing interns and working with them and the master teachers. As a consequence of this shortcoming in the state's planning system, the college's budget and teaching loads have come under steadily increasing strain since 1967.

Every student observes extensively in the schools, participates actively as a teacher's aide, and then enters internship. Many visitors remark that few if any universities require prospective teachers to spend so much time in the public schools. A year of observation-aide experience and full responsibility for classroom instruction for at least one quarter of the senior year meet the standard internship requirement. Some majors offer an option for continuous internship with half the day in the schools and half the day in University classes through the full four years.

An option to back-track from a B.A. in another field of professional or liberal arts studies has made it possible to enlist many people with special talent and experience who might otherwise be locked out of teaching. Graduates who wish to open up a teaching career may enter the aide-intern program, secure temporary certification, and complete the remaining five core courses while employed.

In actual experience, the internship proved to be the most effective way to find good teachers. Students who found themselves inept in observing or assisting teachers needed encouragement rather than intervention by the faculty in making other choices of major; they discovered their limitations in the school setting very early, and the general design of USF degree programs made it easy for them to shift to another program. Students who took to the school setting and the challenges of the classroom with skill and enjoyment needed little encouragement and capitalized on the advice and criticism of their instructors and master teachers.

ORGANIZATION

Diversified perspectives on content and techniques of learning—developmental, practical, philosophical and methodological—complicate the problems of organizing a college of education. No standard model has proved generally satisfactory. The USF college first organized a department for each of the six core courses and a department for support services, special education, libraries and instructional media. Next the faculty divided into departments according to the three professional areas of instruction, counseling, and administration; each of the six developmental stages (early childhood, elementary, middle school, high school, post-secondary, and special education); the set of core courses in Foundations; and the set of library-media courses and ancillary studies.

In 1973 a new dean, Roger Wilk, worked out a novel arrangement that almost but not quite created a performance contract system. Faculty selected one of four departments (A-B-C-D) as a home base for professional development, faculty assignment, and evaluation. Ten program chairmen presided over courses in the areas of foundations, each developmental sequence, counseling and administration, library-media sequences, and internship. Program heads negotiated with the A-B-C-D groupings for the most effective use of each member's time each term. A professor might have assignments in only one field for one term and assignments in three or four different areas for the next term. Faculty remained flexible and mobile, going where their expertise was most needed as the distribution of students changed across the curricular matrix. The organization moved toward standard departmental forms, however, as the faculty tended to cluster around some professional commonality in each of the A-B-C-D groupings. These now provide the organizational base in departments for Curriculum and Instruction, Communication Arts, Educational Systems, and Human Effectiveness.

The College of Education received full accreditation from the State Department of Education from the outset. The Southern Association praised the program in its initial accreditation of USF in 1965. In 1973 its visiting team reported that the quality of the programs was confirmed by student performance on the Graduate Record Examination and other standardized measures, by the actions and comments of employers, and by the performance record of graduates in their jobs and community service. The college did not seek accreditation from the National Committee for Accreditation of Teacher Education (NCATE), preferring to remain free from any regulations that might tend to restrict growth and future-oriented planning consonant with special concerns in the community. The college seems to have forfeited few benefits by this decision.

The faculty has grown to nearly 200, with attendant trends toward segmented, impersonal organization. Research and publication have steadily increased, especially with the advent of graduate studies. Neither organization nor intellectual interchange has so far satisfied needs for mutual support and solidarity in the faculty—a prime requisite for full and enjoyable professional commitment. Part of this diffuseness, however, comes from the primary commitment of the faculty to personalize the programs for teacher education and to support students in their professional development.

The College of Engineering

Dean Edgar Kopp surveyed engineering colleges over the country and found a pioneering program at UCLA with a focus on the system of technology that proved adaptable to the general design of USF degree programs. Consequently, the College of Engineering was somewhat ahead of its time in its systems approach, interdisciplinary methods, and emphasis on quality of life. In each engineering major, a core of undergraduate studies leads to a four-year baccalaureate degree and provides several convenient transfer points into a five-year program for the first professional degree at the master's level.

Somewhat more slowly than UCLA and USF, other engineering schools were moving toward greater emphasis on the interaction of people, technology, and environment. In 1956 a series of studies on engineering education pointed away from narrowly specialized studies toward broader programs encompassing urban and environmental concerns in keeping with trends in professional practice.[7]

In 1970 the American Society of Engineering Education brought out a comprehensive review of professional development over the past fifteen years. It emphasized interdisciplinary methods and recommended fewer, better-integrated basic courses, theoretical and practical instruction using case studies, and the expansion of graduate study and research.[8] Ten years after the USF College of Engineering opened, the ASEE published a comprehensive Goals Report for 1974 which urged a more diversified education for the beginning engineer, extending if possible to the master's level and emphasizing breadth of learning to include economics, management, and social and humanistic studies. More flexible, individually designed degree programs and continuing education for the practicing engineer were emphasized as strongly as selective admission of candidates with high academic standards and high career goals.[9]

Such new configurations in philosophy and instruction began to crystallize after the USF college was well under way. The principal professional accrediting association, the Engineers' Council for Professional Development (ECPD) denied USF's first application on technical grounds. The ECPD meticulously specified the number of credits required in mathematics and basic science, general engineering science, technical courses, and liberal arts. Its visiting teams, composed mostly of professors from older, conventional programs, insisted upon strict adherence to credit-hour formula and found that the USF programs deviated too far from these standards, despite their general approval of the engineering faculty and the approach to program design.

ECPD accreditation is absolutely essential for placement of engineering graduates. Accordingly, the college rewrote its application and was fully accredited in 1971. The four major sequences held to the original systems design, in keeping with contemporary professional responsibilities; but within this framework the faculty had to add some courses and redistribute other requirements according to ECPD formula: 49 credits in mathematics and science, 56 in basic engineering, 49 in a specialty, and 47 in liberal arts and other studies. The bachelor's degree now requires 201 credits and allows very few electives. Five-year programs for the master's degree provide much greater flexibility but have attracted fewer entering students since 1970; when NASA and other federal programs began to phase down, freshmen became reluctant to commit themselves to five or more years of study in the face of diminishing opportunities in the high technologies.

Nationwide, engineering enrollments have fluctuated with the employment market, but at the University of South Florida they have continued steady growth by small annual increments. About 80 percent of students enroll in the four-year programs; about a fifth of these switch to a five-year program or go on after graduation to advanced studies of the high technologies dealing with urban and industrial development and with economic and ecological concerns for quality of life. The large number of engineers employed in the area look to USF for continuing education and contribute to the steady growth of enrollment for advanced study.

The Board of Regents takes a fairly conservative approach to growth in all areas of advanced study, especially doctoral programs. Demand in the USF constituency for doctoral studies in engineering has steadily grown, and in 1972 the Regents agreed to a proposal that Florida State University close its small engineering college and transfer thirteen doctoral candidates to complete their work at USF. The Regents authorized no further doctoral studies in engineering, but proposals were ready to be presented by USF in 1976, at the end of the moratorium.

The College of Engineering has won high esteem from the profession and from engineering educators. Ninety percent of its faculty hold a doctorate, and all have extensive experience as practicing professionals in a variety of settings. Their contributions in research and publication have been substantial, and much work has been ecologically oriented toward life-sustaining systems.

Another indicator of the quality of the USF College of Engineering is the increasing number of women engineers, actively recruited by faculty and students. And Engineering students and faculty have often challenged other colleges to new ventures. Most recently, a joint task force of liberal arts and engineering faculty and students has undertaken to design an interdisciplinary program addressing the commonalities and differences between science and the humanities that affect the way people approach questions concerning technological development and quality of life.

The College of Medicine

During the 1960s community support of proposals for a medical center at the University of South Florida steadily increased. The two existing medical schools at the University of Florida and the University of Miami met less than half the state's needs for new physicians. Centered in an area holding one-third of the state's population, USF was a logical location for a new program. The Regents and the legislature accordingly authorized the University to establish Colleges of Medicine and Nursing in 1965. As dean from 1966 to 1969,

Dr. Alfred Lawton conducted program and facilities planning until he replaced Harris Dean as Vice-President for Academic Affairs. Dr. Donn Smith carried on the work, and the first students enrolled in the College of Medicine in September 1971.

University people sometimes have mixed feelings about medical colleges. They recognize the necessary linkage of higher education with the system of health care, but they are often irritated by the special prestige attributed to the medical profession and like to entertain each other with heroic tales of battles fought against the all-devouring scourge of academia, the professional dragons with the medical faculty as their chief.

At the University of South Florida many saw in the College of Medicine the conclusive affirmation that this was truly a mature university of the first class; others girded for battle against the new college's voracious appetite for funds. The Board of Regents and the legislature understood the anxiety that the new development aroused, and for the first four years provided separate appropriations for medical education which were heavily reinforced by federal subventions. Both Dean Lawton and Dean Smith further allayed fears by their collaborative approach to their colleagues.

The administrative structure provided a Medical Center with two units, the Colleges of Medicine and Nursing, each headed by a dean. For the time being Dean Smith also headed the Medical Center, reporting to the president in that capacity, otherwise working as a member of the Council of Deans on all-University academic planning. Medical and nursing education were on the same footing as other colleges, an organic part of the University.

The College of Medicine brought a reaffirmation of the University's commitment to teaching and learning. Programs were personalized, and their interdisciplinary design was consistent with the all-University emphasis on a broad, diversified foundation in the arts and sciences. With this approach Dean Smith and the faculty joined a vanguard of medical educators who were calling for more effective community participation by practitioners and for new and varied educational and professional perspectives on health care. Many thoughtful people recognized that medical education had changed little in sixty years and new departures were in order.

The last major change had begun with the classic study by Abraham Flexner in 1910 revealing the sorry state of medical education. Encapsulated in an apprentice system conducted by independent proprietary schools, this "trade-school" or "guild" system had been found lacking in the high standards of learning and practice cultivated by the handful of university-related colleges of medicine and their graduates. Following the Flexner Report, a large number of proprietary schools had closed their doors, and new medical colleges were organized in many universities. A stronger orientation toward scientific studies and research rapidly advanced professional standards of education and practice. The spirit of the Flexner Report dominates medical education to this day.

By the 1960s strong demands for programs having greater flexibility, diversification, and recognition of individual differences in students' abilities and interests expressed this same spirit. More effective professional work should cultivate closer linkages of medical education and practice to community concerns for maintaining health. Beyond the treatment of illness, community and professional concerns should converge on greater attentiveness to environmental deterioration and social malaise as sources of ill health, the expansion of professional opportunities for women and blacks and other minorities, and increasing the number of new physicians to serve the growing population.

A group of 35 practitioners met at Endicott House in 1965 and came to consensus on 80 recommendations for professional improvement. Shortly thereafter, Mount Sinai Hospital in New York published a volume on current issues in medical education as a basis for planning the new medical colleges fostered by federal legislation. The Carnegie Commission on Higher Education published in 1973 an analysis of developments in four professions; the chapter on medicine noted the inordinate length of preparation (as much as 14 years beyond high school) and called for more flexible, personalized program design, eliminating duplicative effort and excessive investment of time. It commended trends toward interdisciplinary approaches, integration of studies around functional competences, and joining preclinical with clinical instruction.[10]

The new USF Medical College was strongly influenced by such trends and studies. The personalized model it selected was further refined and enlarged in keeping with the spirit and the method cultivated at Johns Hopkins.

In selecting students the College of Medicine has simply called for a strong undergraduate record with a broad and varied background and evidence of intellectual vitality and self-initiated, self-directed learning. Applicants who major in any academic field are accepted; two years of chemistry and one each of physics, biology, and mathematics are uniform requirements. Most students present four years of undergraduate study, although they may be admitted after three years.

Faculty members interview candidates having an undergraduate average of B or better and a medical aptitude test score of 500 or more. They conducted over 400 interviews for the 64 places in the class entering in 1974. Twenty-four were admitted in each of the first two years, 36 in 1973, 64 in 1974, and 96 in 1975 (at which number future classes will be held). The medical faculty begin recruiting with the entrance of each freshman class in nearby colleges and universities. They particularly encourage black students and women to enter premedical studies. In 1975 3 black students and 24 women were enrolled, a modest response to affirmative action and well short of the college's goals.

Hospital-centered instruction is the heart of the classic, patient-centered model. After 22 weeks of basic medical instruction, students enter clinical instruction in cooperating hospitals, often working with their own professors, many of whom have an active medical practice. After exposure to many treatment modalities, public health programs, and other health-related activities, each student chooses at least two fields of concentration for the remainder of the degree program. The traditional internship has been virtually bypassed. Three years of study (11 months of instruction with short vacations each year) complete the degree and lead to three or four years of residency, then to private practice. The college also offers the Ph.D. for students interested in medical research and teaching.

The dean and department chairmen select faculty for their demonstrated capability in teaching; many professors also conduct some research (representing about one-fourth of the budget). The college is committed primarily to the preparation of practicing physicians with technical competence, sensitivity, and compassion for the people they serve.

It is still too early to determine how fully the objectives of the college have been realized. But there is no question that the USF College of Medicine has responded to the major concerns of practitioners and educators for developing broader, more flexible and pragmatic approaches to education and professional practice.

The College of Nursing

Nursing has undergone even more rapid and extensive change than has medicine. Collegiate schools of nursing have concentrated on preparing students for the increasing number of new professional specialties related to new treatment modalities, ancillary and support services, administrative, research, and training functions, and health education.

The need for more extensive and diversified programs of nursing education was emphasized in the USOE report, "Education for the Professions" (1955). Consultants noted that the increasing responsibilities of the profession and its humanistic orientation called for a stronger foundation of collegiate education. But 90 percent of all student nurses were then enrolled in diploma (R.N.) programs, predominantly hospital-based and typically physician-dominated. The report recommended a substantial increase in the number of nurses, with the majority of new practitioners having a well-rounded university education. Greater flexibility and scope of leadership from nursing education were needed to meet emerging community concerns and national goals for personal and community health.

The Nursing program requires the same foundation in general education that applies to all undergraduate degrees at USF. Professional prerequisites are minimal: a year of chemistry and biology, two courses in psychology and sociology, one course in microbiology and human anatomy, and one in nutrition or human development. After completing these studies in the University or a community college, students enter the professional sequence at the beginning of the junior year. The field of concentration covers supporting sciences, nursing courses, and some electives, leading to the B.S. degree.

In its program designed under Dr. Alice Keefe, the first dean, the college emphasizes the integration of modes or styles of learning—affective, cognitive, and psychomotor—giving students a behavioral repertory for interaction with people in many different professional activities and services involving different technical and scientific capabilities. Studies in nursing emphasize diversified roles in "prevention of illness, maintenance and restoration of health, crisis intervention, leadership within a health team, and improvement of patient care."

Nursing intervention courses focus on the application of theoretical competence to a variety of health care settings—private home, general hospital, industrial clinic, public health department, and nursing home. Seminars deal with case studies "bringing application of theory to specific patient or family situations into focus." Instructional methods emphasize experience in applying research and investigative techniques to a variety of problems in nursing practice and health services.

Fifty juniors entered advanced studies in September 1973 and graduated in the first class of June 1975. In September 1974, the second class had 63 undergraduate nursing candidates and 14 R.N.'s proceeding to the B.S. degree. The R.N.'s plan individualized programs with advisors in order to capitalize fully on previous study and experience without useless duplication. The first two classes included only one or two blacks and about a dozen males. A faculty committee interviews each candidate and assesses ability, emotional maturity, and professional commitment. The student body has the diversified mixture of interests and the strong commitment and staying power characteristic of nursing colleges in general.

The USF nursing program is broader and stronger in theoretical foundations than the typical collegiate nursing program. It particularly emphasizes linkages between practice and theory. Clinical instruction begins in the third quarter and moves forward with planning and supervision from the faculty in hospitals and other settings.

As part of the Medical Center the College of Nursing has dual connections to the USF administration. Dean Gwendoline MacDonald works with the director of the Medical Center on matters of budget and facilities planning and with the Vice-President for Academic Affairs and the Council of Deans on faculty and curriculum matters. Separation of the Medical and Nursing budgets from general University appropriations apparently pleases most of the people concerned, and no strong disposition to change this arrangement has surfaced so far.

The principal accrediting association, the National League of Nursing, and nursing professionals in general have considerable concern for developing a distinctive role for nurses, independent of the medical profession. They wish to contribute more effectively to improving and developing health-related services out of their special experience. These concerns may develop into a call for some modification of the present arrangements in the Medical Center. Any such change will probably have to be made in the context of current professional emphases on a well-integrated program of general, theoretical, and practical studies, opening up a variety of responsibilities in many settings shared by both medical and nursing educators and practitioners in their common concern for the system of health care.

New Dimensions

The experience of the University of South Florida with professional education underlines some of the factors most strongly affecting higher education and American society in a period of change and development. The organization of the University as a network of colleges has facilitated the sharing of resources and responsibilities. The all-University approach brought the entire academic family together in common concerns for the advancement of knowledge by the universities, for more diversified services and more effective practitioners in the community, and for less stifling, bureaucratic patterns of career development with more challenging, constructive work in the professions.

Like the colleges of liberal arts, the professional colleges have struggled to sustain identity and integrity while capitalizing on new dimensions of interdisciplinary and cross-cultural collaboration, in university and community networks and in major social systems both national and international. The equalitarian spirit of sharing values and responsibilities in university and community may help all professionals to improve their effectiveness in sustaining the quality of life and work in the developing culture of cities.

8
Graduate Programs

Centers of Expansion

Graduate education in the United States expanded more rapidly than any other part of the system of higher education in the twentieth century. All reasonable expectations indicate that growth will continue through the year 2000. From 1900 to 1950, enrollments in M.A. and Ph.D. programs increased fortyfold to 237,000 while undergraduate enrollments increased twentyfold. Graduate enrollments reached 365,000 by 1960, exceeded 565,000 by 1973, and headed for the 2 million mark forecast for 1980.

Growth followed the typical pattern of diversification as new specialties developed around the periphery of traditional strongholds. Regarded as the apex of the educational pyramid by virtue of awarding the highest degrees, graduate faculties became even more preeminent with the phenomenal increase in research that accompanied growth in enrollment and new fields of study.

Many educators began to view graduate education as the foundation, not the apex, of the system. Looking at its actual functions, they saw participation in research as essential to the advancement of knowledge and to the development of new teachers and professional practitioners. While unique discoveries by a few highly gifted persons were impressive, collaborative work by students and teachers at all levels of education prepared the ground and capitalized on the results.

The universities had also discovered rich resources and issues for research in the community. In studies of industry, technology, and the culture of cities, university-community collaboration opened new frontiers for high-level study and research. The tradition of the community of scholars as a worldwide network, advancing and sharing knowledge in campus and community, reinforced trends toward expansion, diversification, and diffusion of graduate study and research into the community.

A trend toward "domestication" of graduate education in urban centers thus became a positive factor in planning for higher education after World War II. The nation needed thousands of educated adults who would complete advanced degrees and move into teaching and other expanding professions. In the traditional way, they left their work, family, and civic responsibilities and went to some remote, prestigious graduate center, the more remote the better. The medieval tradition of the wandering scholar persisted in the common persuasion that the purest quality of high scholarship depended on this ritual detachment of students from their native heath.

In twentieth-century America the practical and educational advantages of domestication outweighed this tradition of detachment and disengagement from community affairs. State and national plans could be designed to save money and gain added value for the community by establishing new graduate programs where people were living and often already at work in the very enterprises that most needed new M.A.'s and Ph.D.'s.

Graduate students discovered how to capitalize on employment, not only as a way to defray some costs out of current income but as an added resource for study and research. They learned that helpful, competent teachers who are available daily can facilitate completion of research projects and degree programs, often at a faster pace and more effectively than some of the distinguished professors so often involved in external affairs.

Modern technologies facilitated resource-sharing between older and younger universities. For instance, a well-designed university library of moderate size became adequate for high-level study and research when backed up by interlibrary networks and computer-assisted information retrieval; new universities could share older collections both rich and rare. Resource-sharing meant that new graduate centers could rapidly develop the high quality that older ones had taken years to build up step by step. Domestication could thus be managed without loss of quality; and it clearly reduced some critical problems of cost, access, geographic distribution and diversification of programs, and pertinence to community needs and expectations. Developments in higher education after 1950 capitalized heavily upon these advantages.

The Florida Plan

In 1954 graduate education at the University of Florida and Florida State University was expanding, but at a rather slow pace by comparison with other universities and state systems. By 1960 graduate enrollment totalled just over 1,300 in each center. Limited resources were strained by their special commitments, such as programs in agriculture and home economics that contributed to a significant segment of the state's economy.

The Brumbaugh Report proposed further expansion in the two graduate centers and recognized the practical necessity to keep many options open for diversifying M.A. and Ph.D. programs and distributing them over the state to meet growing needs in regional constituencies. As soon as their undergraduate programs matured, USF and the other new universities would have to take a major share of responsibility for graduate education.

The domestication of graduate education answered both academic and community concerns. This mutual interest was particularly evident in the USF service area. In 1956 its seven counties included more than a million people and in 1976 probably 2.5 million or more, one-third of the state's population. No other graduate center was available in the area, a community rich in opportunities for advanced study and research. New forms of theory and practice were needed and research could be tested and applied readily in this burgeoning urban-industrial complex, impinging on an agricultural hinterland, located on a narrow peninsula whose fragile terrestrial and marine ecosystems might or might not sustain the life of cities.

Its location in a major center of commerce, transportation, and communication gave the University of South Florida some advantages in access to the wider world of scholarship. The entire university network stood to profit as USF capitalized on its location, communications, and community resources. Accordingly, the Comprehensive Development Plan of the State University System (CODE) in 1969 specified that "The University of South Florida at Tampa is a general purpose university which will place increasing emphasis upon advanced graduate and professional studies during the next ten years."[1]

Community service strongly influenced the plans of universities and state systems for graduate education, considered to be a major national asset. Lewis B. Mayhew learned from a national survey that new and developing universities tend to emphasize graduate study and research closely related to community concerns, cultivating diversified expertise in research; older ones tend to emphasize expansion in traditional disciplines. These trends are expected to continue through the 1980s.[2] The University of South Florida, like other new centers, emphasized linkages to the community in graduate education as it did in undergraduate study.

Plans for the Florida system capitalized on such diversified roles and shared resources for graduate education. USF had a comparatively young faculty, a new plant and modern equipment, rich community resources, and a constituency eager to participate. The faculty included a strong cadre with experience in interdisciplinary method, particularly useful for studying many of the complex problems presented in the community.

On equalitarian principles the University had to provide studies to the most advanced degrees in order to facilitate the students' "advancement to the extent of their capabilities." The faculty was eager to bring in graduate students whose energies and maturing powers provided essential resources for scholarly inquiry, as well as to give them the experience as teaching and research assistants needed for their professional development. But the primary concern was for the contribution of graduate programs to the generative capacities of the entire academic program, infusing the most advanced studies throughout its organization and making USF truly a university.

Universities generally share this concern for graduate education as a generative system, as shown in a 1974 report on graduate study and research.

> Graduate education and research are not a mere appendage to the university, but are instead its defining element, infusing a spirit of inquiry and concern for scholarship throughout the institution. . . .
> The vitality of most academic disciplines requires the continuous renewal that new Ph.D.'s bring to the university, and yet many universities are now staffed by a high proportion of tenured faculty, with relatively few retirements expected in the next decade. The nation can ill afford to lose the intellectual excitement and vigor that the brightest young professors provide on every campus.[3]

USF had a continuing infusion of new, young professors. Its need was for graduate students to contribute to the faculty's research undertakings, which began even before classes opened. In solving this problem the University turned to collaborative work with people in the community on study and action projects that often involved undergraduates also. Older universities were similarly discovering that community participation in lifelong learning supplements the time-honored way of maintaining vitality by turnover in the faculty.

Research Programs

At USF, each department and college administered those research projects within its particular domain. Interdisciplinary approaches were frequently necessary in dealing with emerging theoretical and practical issues. By 1962 so many projects of both types were underway that a center of coordination became necessary, and Leslie F. Malpass, chairman of the Human Behavior program in Basic Studies, assumed the responsibility. His office provided a place for faculty to join together for interdisciplinary inquiry and facilitated planning, evaluation, and funding of research within the colleges.

In 1966 President Allen approved a plan for a larger Center for Research and Development with the added function of providing a home for special research institutes funded primarily by federal programs and private contributions. Within a short time six institutes were underway: Marine Science, Gerontology, Exceptional Children and Adults, Clinical Speech Pathology and Audiology, Leisure, and Rehabilitation.

These institutes differed from those in other universities that tended to be loosely connected to the general academic organization. At USF they developed dual-purpose programs for research and graduate study with feedback into undergraduate programs. Each one offered a few core courses and involved students concurrently in related research, field studies, practicum, and action projects. Related colleges and departments established the courses in their offerings as the base for a major in the field and seconded additional faculty to the institutes.

The deans of the USF colleges viewed with approbation the function of the center in facilitating their research and graduate programs within the disciplines and the linkage of the research institutes and interdisciplinary projects to their departments. The additional grants coming through the center and the number of distinguished research professors in the institutes added ballast and balance to University resources. On the other hand, the deans were apprehensive lest USF experience the "brain drain" that other universities had suffered when particularly inquisitive, provocative teachers and students moved into peripheral units. Apprehension increased as the center and the institutes began to move ahead of some research and graduate programs within formal disciplines, an equally important element in balanced growth.

In 1970 the mixture of apprehension and approbation came to a head when William Taft, director of the center and professor of geology, proposed in the reorganization of the University to include a new College of Special Studies, consolidating the institutes into a separate faculty. This proposal seemed to depart distinctly from the all-University approach and the effective practice of sharing responsibility in each college for both undergraduate and graduate education. In the 1972 reorganization each research institute was placed in an appropriate college, usually as a department in its own right. The Center for Research and Development was dismantled and its function of coordinating projects and grants passed to the Office of Sponsored Research, with Dr. Taft as its director.

Systemwide Development

At the same time, the Board of Regents was strengthening planning and support for research and graduate study in the whole SUS. Proposals for concentrating on one or two centers continued to surface; many people were still persuaded that "the higher, the fewer" was a basic principle that guaranteed quality in Ph.D. programs. This approach was not consistent with either experience or expectations in American higher education, which continued to diffuse rather than concentrate responsibility for graduate study and research. The SUS councils and the Board of Regents continued to move in this same direction.

The Board of Regents wished to develop criteria of adequacy in planning that would assure sufficient quality and clientele in new programs to represent real gains for the whole state. Its guidelines asked each department proposing a new Ph.D. program to outline the resources required, to weigh present resources against future needs, and to design a plan to bring them up to strength. A timetable for monitoring progress would indicate the point at which the department would have a strong base for the startup investment in graduate study. As major criteria the board emphasized research experience and capability in the faculty and a record of experience in directing graduate studies.

With respect to clientele the regents argued that a department which did not attract many undergraduates probably would not attract many graduate students either. The sus councils and chancellor's staff worked out formulae on this principle: a department proposing a master's program should have graduated 15 undergraduate majors in the past year or 30 in the past three years; one proposing a Ph.D. program should have graduated 8 with the M.A. degree in the past year or 15 in the past three years. Variances were expected in such fields as astronomy or classics, essential to the whole scholarly enterprise but not very popular as fields of concentration; even in these cases, consistency between enrollment and completion of the degree program would still be a useful indicator.

The approach was effective. Graduate enrollment expanded and new programs were added in all the universities over the first five years of operation under the Board of Regents. But in 1971 the Regents declared a five-year moratorium on all new Ph.D. programs while they considered other urgent matters that affected the role and scope of each university in the system and its responsibility for graduate education.

One urgent matter was a class action in the federal courts that mandated all states having any predominantly black universities to integrate their state system and offer equal access to educational opportunities throughout the state. Under this mandate, Florida Agricultural and Mechanical University, highly prestigious in the state and among the old-line black colleges of the South, located near Florida State University in Tallahassee, would have to assume a new role and scope. This change would affect the rest of the universities.

Then the national economy began sliding into recession, and the usual anxieties surfaced over an "oversupply" of people with advanced degrees. Some analysts predicted and others hoped that the period of exponential growth in Florida was nearing its close and the rate of development leveling off.

The planning system for the state government was now based on steady-state assumptions. While this approach can be consistent with the future-oriented planning necessary for universities, the implications were not well-clarified at the outset, and it was sometimes hard for legislators and others to understand how universities keep a steady state. Their faculties have to plan for developmental changes in knowledge and professional practice, which quantitative changes in population and economic productivity will not necessarily indicate.

Linking university and state planning systems, dealing with estimates of manpower needs, and developing a unitary university system, fully occupied the Board of Regents and the chancellor's staff. The moratorium gave them the time they needed for this work; since it applied only to doctoral programs, new master's programs at USF and other universities continued to develop. Plans to carry Ph.D. candidates into new programs were being designed and refined in readiness for the end of the moratorium in 1976.

The University of South Florida Graduate Program

Planning teams for graduate studies began work even before USF opened classes in 1960. Administrators and faculty wanted these programs to differ from conventional forms, often criticized by students and educators as too narrow, theoretical, and impractical, excessively prolonged and encumbered by archaic requirements unrelated to the present state of the art or to future opportunities, and monopolizing entry to college teaching while developing no mastery of instructional techniques. USF planners resolved to design graduate studies that would be distinctive for their contemporary design, pertinent to future concerns of universities and society.

One distinctive contribution could capitalize on interdisciplinary methods of research and teaching, emphasized in the academic program and in the selection of charter faculty. Considering the nationwide shortage of teachers with strong interdisciplinary experience, the University had a special interest in the preparation of college teachers. The growing number of community colleges sought faculty of demonstrated effectiveness in the classroom as well as in research and publication. Working closely with these institutions and the four-year liberal arts colleges, Sidney French was convinced that USF could make a distinctive contribution in the teaching of college teachers, who would be outstanding for their spirit of inquiry and enjoyment of learning, skilled in a variety of instructional techniques, and strong in a broad intellectual foundation.

Dean French outlined a comprehensive graduate program for this purpose: a broad undergraduate foundation and a strong concentration in a single discipline enriched by studies in ancillary disciplines (or an interdisciplinary field of concentration); at least one course in techniques of college teaching and one in curriculum and administration of higher education; a culminating internship in a two- or four-year college near Tampa. The plan had good support from faculty and administrators in the service area. French obtained a grant from the U.S. Office of Education for a cooperative in-service study of college teaching in introductory courses, involving USF and several neighboring colleges.

The College of Education developed some advanced programs along these lines. First, the faculty introduced a course on the community college and one on college teaching for master's candidates seeking certification in community colleges. Then it developed an Educational Specialist degree (Ed.S.), virtually a Ph.D. without the dissertation. Requiring 60 credits beyond the M.A. degree and qualifying a graduate for the state's Rank I-A certification, the Ed.S. opened opportunities for administration, supervision, and counseling as well as teaching in schools and community colleges. For active teachers, in-service observation and critique substitute for the internship. By completing additional seminar, research, and dissertation requirements, a student can proceed from the Ed.S. to the Ph.D.; nothing precludes graduate students in other colleges from completing the internship and seminar components in the College of Education and securing state certification along with a Ph.D. degree.

A third distinctive contribution lay in the determination to design graduate programs of high quality, free of obsolete requirements, adaptable to contemporary conditions of adult life and work. Requirements should contribute to scholarly competence, not simply set up roadblocks and locksteps for administrative convenience. The faculty could capitalize on personalized design, traditionally emphasized in graduate education and cultivated in undergraduate studies at USF.

In 1964 President Allen appointed an Interim Committee on Graduate Study to prepare a long-range plan. It set a conservative rather than innovative course. The members argued that USF must first establish a reputation for conventional respectability in the traditional liberal arts specialties before it branched out into innovations of interdisciplinary design that might be interpreted as lowering standards. The first Ph.D. programs, in natural sciences, emphasized research and set the pattern for subsequent developments. The approach was conventional, even pedestrian. Replicating a traditional, specialized, research-centered program, as a basis for later development of innovative, creative elements, seems in retrospect to be a very strange choice for a new university which had to overcome little or no resistance from established conventions and traditions when it first embarked on any academic enterprise.

Standards for admission to graduate study followed customary practice: at least a B average in the undergraduate major and a score of 1000 or better on the Graduate Record Examination. Customary standards for earning a graduate degree were adopted: a cumulative B average or better, a comprehensive examination, and writing and defending a dissertation for the Ph.D. (many M.A. programs also included a thesis and oral examination). According to research methods in the discipline, each program should require one or two foreign languages or an alternative such as statistics or computer science. Standard procedures for waiving requirements for promising students failing on one criterion applied as they do in undergraduate admission. The USF Graduate Council, which took over responsibility for program development in 1965, and ultimately the Board of Regents' systemwide standards held to these requirements. Departments handled their own recruiting and admission for the most part, and actual records of applicants who were accepted often surpassed the minimum requirements.

The organization for graduate education was decentralized, and this rather unconventional approach proved effective. President Allen and the first college deans agreed that graduate studies would lodge in each college and develop out of the same resources as undergraduate programs.[4] As the planners hoped, the diffusion of responsibility to the colleges proved to avoid some of the fragmentation and divisiveness that troubled other universities. Coordination and planning for graduate programs proceeds through the Graduate Council of representatives from each college. In 1971 its chairman was designated director of graduate studies, responsible for such administrative procedures as admissions and records, monitoring progress toward the degree and certifying completion of requirements, and certification for financial aid, fellowships, and out-of-state tuition waivers.

The arrangement provided a network of graduate programs closely linked to undergraduate study and faculty research. Its primary strength appears in the economy of operation realized by resource-sharing. In any event, a university library, facilities and equipment, and support services must be used by graduate and undergraduate students alike. In addition, the University's approach left the allocation of faculty time and expertise to the departments and colleges. Overall enrollment rather than level of courses would be the principal planning factor, and faculty time would be applied where expertise was most needed, rather than being locked into a single discipline or level of studies. Administrative costs would be held down by avoiding duplicative functions at undergraduate and graduate levels.

While the argument to confine advanced studies to a few graduate centers at the apex has some attraction, the experience of the University of South Florida and the sus suggests that domestication and resource-sharing may represent realistically the trends that realize major gains in graduate education as a national asset.

Groundbreaking Ceremony, 1958. Photo courtesy of Special Collections, USF Library.

Billboard on Fowler Avenue announces site of coming University. Photo courtesy of Special Collections, USF Library.

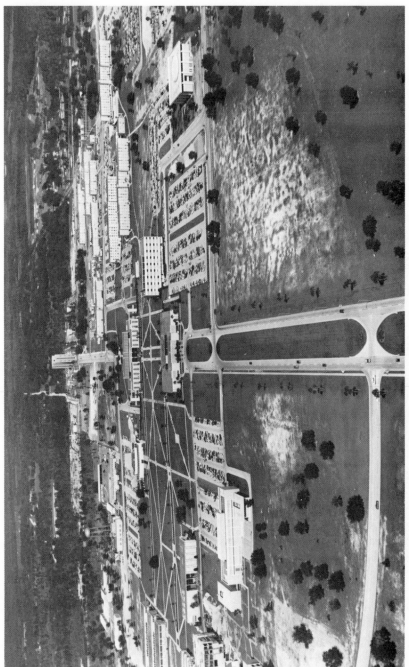

USF campus, early 1960s. Photo courtesy of Special Collections, USF Library.

USF students protest the Vietnam War. Photo courtesy of the *Oracle*.

A Question of Access

The Double Door

Florida's plan for higher education succeeded in making some type of postsecondary institution accessible to the entire population, by capitalizing on the distinctive features of open-admission community colleges and selective-admission universities. A separate network for each type of institution functions in a branching rather than a two-track system. Several different pathways open beyond the "double door" for transition from high school to college. In recognition of its merit, universities also award the A.A. degree to generic students who qualify. A statewide council of institutional representatives monitors the branchings and linkages that facilitate resource-sharing, the paralleling of A.A. with B.A. degree programs, the interchange of credits among degree, certificate, and continuing education programs, and transfer and dual enrollment between community colleges and universities.

In the 1950s and 1960s statewide planning centered primarily on expansion and access to higher education, leaving each college and university to deal with other factors affecting equality of opportunity and quality of education "beyond the open door." In general, President Allen and the planning team relied on the all-University approach as a criterion for inclusiveness and cohesiveness and on the personalized approach as a criterion for equality of opportunity. They were primarily concerned with serving as many people as facilities and finances would permit; they tried to make studies pertinent to individual expectations and experience and to interfere as little as possible with personal responsibilities. Sometimes the planners had firm constitutional principles to follow; in other instances, common sense and the accent on learning had to guide policy and practice.

Racial Integration

John Allen was determined that the costly, unjust caste system should not take hold in the University. One of his first presidential announcements stated simply that admission was open to any person qualifying under guidelines of the Board of Control. He did not even take counsel on this declaration, knowing full well that Florida's educational policy must eventually follow constitutional principles.

Allen immediately started to work very closely with Dr. George Gore, President of Florida A. & M. University, on their common task of recruiting an integrated faculty. By 1958, Jean Battle, Dean of the College of Education, who had long been assisting public school boards with integration, was working with teachers and counselors in black high schools on their concerns; and the registrar, Frank Spain, gave special attention to them in recruiting students. The Tampa Urban League appointed a special committee to recruit black applicants and raise funds for grants-in-aid.

The University of Florida admitted a few blacks to advanced study in 1958, and President Allen heard rumors in Gainesville that USF would be "inundated by hordes of black applicants." However, in September 1960, not one black student enrolled and no black faculty member or administrator was employed at USF.

Perhaps a dozen or so blacks filed applications in 1959 but none qualified for admission. During the second term and summer session of 1960–61, perhaps 20 or 30 black students enrolled as transfers. Ernest Boger enrolled in September 1961, with a scholarship from the Tampa Urban League; he is believed to be the first black who ever enrolled full-time as a first-time freshman in any Florida university other than FAMU.

Faculty recruiting was difficult for all the Florida universities. Their salary scales were not competitive in the academic marketplace. FAMU was at a disadvantage among the foremost black universities. Half their "peer group" of 58 public universities enrolling 10,000 or more students could outbid USF and FAMU, whose salary scales were close to the mean for this comparison group over the entire period 1960–65.

The unsettled social climate tended to raise doubts in prospective candidates about any offer from Southern colleges and universities.

Many felt that they could enjoy more comfortable social conditions elsewhere as well as higher salaries, and the teacher shortage gave them a wide range of choices. Those wishing to work for civil rights and integration could do so almost anywhere else without taking the extra risks, costs, and constraints of the Southern caste system.

Before a president could confirm a contract, many prospects tired of waiting and took another position. In every state institution or agency, all salaries above $10,000 (raised to $12,000 in 1962) required line-item approval by the Cabinet; the procedure might require six or seven stages over a period of six months or more. USF was under particularly heavy time pressure from this procedure in recruiting and hiring more than a hundred new faculty members and administrators in less than two years.

COMMUNITY CONCERNS

By all reasonable predictions, more than a handful of blacks should have enrolled at USF. The staff knew they were recruiting in competition with the nationwide talent search that creamed off the top 10 percent of graduates from Southern high schools for the larger, more prestigious institutions of the Northeast and North Central regions. They asked all the schools to refer applicants from the next 20 to 30 percent of the rankings. They promoted advanced study by black teachers to prepare for many opportunities emerging in the transition to a unitary system.

The approach did not achieve the expected results. In the schools and the community, the meritocratic persuasion that top-ranking students make a top-quality university prevailed. USF itself was seeking graduates in the top tenth of high school classes to set the academic pace and prove its quality. Black schools and communities were preoccupied with the talent search; they were also committed to the strategy of selecting the very best students to challenge segregation laws. These "pathfinder" and "test case" approaches had become almost habitual over many years of legal action.

Enrolling at USF did not appear to answer the concerns of the black community for participation in the mainstream of higher education. It was accredited only as a "new institution," and black students were as dubious as whites about taking a chance on its prospects of earning full accreditation before they graduated. Unproved in community relations and higher education, USF was not yet in the mainstream.

However earnestly they tried, the planning staff simply could not dispel the immediate impression that USF recruiting was just one more instance of tokenism, paternalism, and white self-gratification from "doing good for the less fortunate as far as the law allows." Like all the other white universities, USF appeared only to seek a few students who could be "whitified" and to disregard the heartfelt concerns of black people to participate fully in society in their own right and identity.

Many black educators thought that Florida officials were playing at integration while actually perpetuating the caste system. Meritocratic access models based on grades and test scores looked like an academic caste system reinforcing the color line. Professional people in several fields had often protested to the State Department of Education against the two separate normative scales for the Twelfth Grade Test Battery, used for evaluating schools and for setting standards of university admission. The use of a separate scale for blacks seemed to be a transparent subterfuge, attempting to make black schools look better than they actually were and maintain the illusion of a "separate but equal" educational system.

In 1961 the department finally adopted a uniform scale, and the Board of Control raised the FTGT score required for university admission from 200 at the 40th percentile to 300 at the 50th. Under the articulation agreements, the score was changed periodically in order to maintain balance between university and community college enrollments. Blacks objected that the practice tended to steer them away from universities and threatened to weaken FAMU and change its historic role as an open-admission university.

THE UNIVERSITY'S RESPONSE

Vigorous, widespread protest greeted the new FTGT requirement. At USF Lew Mayhew investigated the probable effect on students from the five counties of the service area that had no community college. He found 284 charter students (over 14 percent) who would have been excluded had the new rule applied in 1959–60. All were in good standing at the end of their freshman year with a GPR above 1.5; 90 had 2.0 or better, and 5 had 3.5 or better. These and other results showed predictive errors of a size that rendered unreliable the use of any FTGT score as an automatic cutoff point. The practice did not allow for the fact that students can improve their academic performance, which makes predictions inaccurate in many individual cases.

Mayhew advised the president that any criterion would be not only unreliable but extremely unfair and counterproductive if it excluded 14–15 percent of a cohort—applicants whose records were similar to those of students who had actually earned good standing. Other educators observed that the arbitrary use of test scores as a single, independent criterion penalizes many students who tend to perform better in academic work than on standardized tests. This seemed absurd: not test scores but students in their academic work contribute to the advancement of knowledge.

President Allen therefore proposed to the Board of Control that the present policy of considering admission on the basis of the total academic record should continue, with the universities retaining the discretionary authority to qualify students who fell short on any single criterion, given other evidence of capacity to do creditable work.[1] The board continued the policy, which was recommended also by other universities and agencies, although it still raised the required score to 300. Several board members and other officials urged universities to hold closely to the standards, in order to avoid excessive risk to students and maintain the high quality of the universities.

Mayhew's study underlined the arbitrary nature of fixed cutoff points—in many respects just as arbitrary and inequitable as the color line, which they often reinforced. Black educators, aware that the University had taken particularly strong exception to such arbitrary policies, began to entertain the possibility that the *Accent on Learning* meant what it said, in practice as in principle.

This inclination was reinforced by the matter-of-fact way in which Ernest Boger entered USF, with no public fuss and fanfare, as one of 3,500 other good students. One night, however, the Concert Band went to a nearby restaurant to celebrate after a performance, and the whole membership walked out when the manager refused to serve Boger, the principal tuba player. At once President Allen appointed Elliott Hardaway as chairman of a special committee to confer with the proprietor, who explained his dilemma: he did not want to violate state segregation laws at the very moment when a new Civil Rights Act, nearing adoption by Congress, would enable him to serve all comers without jeopardy. Students and faculty picketed the restaurant until the day the act passed and the proprietor, serving all comers, proved as good as his word.

Such no-nonsense, straightforward actions led a few more people to believe that the University might practice as well as advocate equality.

The Company Store

Deeply rooted in the American experience is a strong persuasion that any wise and prudent person will mistrust any offer of gains and benefits to be purchased by forfeiting independence. "I owe my soul to the company store" means a lot more than just a line in a folk song. It rings true to the history of a long struggle to realize shared values and shared visions of genuinely human lives sustained in the face of mindless, depersonalizing systems, arbitrary actions, and disregard for the facts of life.

Folklore teaches, "Them as has, gits." Educators discovered in the early 1950s that this also applied to financial aid practices; independent colleges and universities began to consider the implications of studies that showed a direct relation between the level of family income and the ranking of students on grades and test scores. The correlations indicated that the customary practice of awarding scholarship money solely on the basis of high competitive rankings often had the effect of giving much of their limited funds to those who least needed aid. Accordingly, institutional members of the College Entrance Examination Board changed their financial aid policies; other colleges and universities quickly followed suit. They still recognized competitive achievement by awarding scholarships, but they gave financial assistance in proportion to the student's need.

Federal programs of financial aid followed the same principle of basing the award of funds on need, designed into the National Defense Education Act of 1960. Congress also included a forgiveness feature as an incentive for students to fill the need for teachers in the expanding educational system. Loans at nominal interest were repayable over a ten-year period. Up to 50 percent of the outstanding principal could be forgiven at the rate of 10 percent for each year a graduate spent in teaching.

The University participated in the NDEA program, and federal programs are still its principal source of funds for financial aid. The USF Foundation raised NDEA matching money; it also secured funds for a small number of scholarship grants, and established service awards for talented students. Twenty-seven awards were given in the first year, fifteen of them in athletics, most of the others in the arts. In 1964 the legislative budget sharply reduced the allocation for part-time personnel and student assistants. The University partly compensated for the cutback by converting all service awards and scholarship grants to work scholarships requiring 100 hours of service per term on a selected assignment.[2]

Advisors found that students and their parents often objected to loans. Many students wanted to be as independent from the University and the government as from their parents. They objected to giving anybody "a lien on the diploma" and wanted to "earn a degree free and clear." Parents often advised against "mortgaging your future." Beneath the expressed aversion lay inexpressible memories of the Great Depression, the company store, and the sharecropping system.

Some people considered the incentive in the NDEA program to be coercive and unfair. Just as the sharecropping system and company store locked people onto the land or into a job, students choosing the forgiveness option might be locked into teaching and closed out of other opportunities. To some the policy looked like a penalty for choosing any other profession. Some critics considered the incentive to have counterproductive effects: no policy should even appear to lure or inveigle people into any important commitment; and if you wanted trifling, ineffective professionals, forgiving a debt would be a good way to get them.

Black people felt themselves at a loss both ways. It looked as if they could expect more competition and fewer opportunities in teaching—historically the most prestigious profession and the most readily accessible in the black community. On the other hand, strategies for integration and equality of opportunity called for blacks to compete for entry to other fields where they were not so well represented—but in these fields students would have no forgiveness option to ease the financial burden.

These objections highlighted some pertinent questions about the general approach to financial aid. Reserving grants for top students and giving others only a choice to work their way or take out a loan seemed to produce inequities in very much the same way that a caste system does. People on one side of an arbitrary line gain most; people on the other side take most of the costs and risks. And the line will not change no matter how much the people in lower ranks may accomplish. Whether the system used the color line or rankings in grades and scores, the principle of low risks and high gains at the top, high risks and low gains below the line, did not seem to alter. Even the language used in admissions and financial aid sometimes described the situation almost literally; for example, "high-risk students" meant those from poor families who stood below whatever cutoff point a college was using and were deemed to have little chance to move up in the rankings.

Colleges and universities seemed to have translated a rather dubious meritocratic assumption that "top-ranking students make a top-quality college" into a self-serving principle of investment. The institution made the low-risk investment in top-ranking students. The choices left for other students involved more cost and risk: to draw a loan and put their future career at risk or work their way through college and put their academic record at risk. Some people found the whole approach puzzling, particularly in light of the fact that most of the costs of a college education come from the general revenue and private contributions. Plain common sense, and certainly "card sense," suggested more productive investment strategies with more favorable odds for success, reducing risks for both the college and the student at any level of achievement.

For instance, top students should be able to work their way from the beginning with comparatively little risk or to handle loans with good prospects of repayment from a profitable career. Grants could buy time for lower-ranking students to concentrate on study for the first year or two in order to consolidate their academic standing; then they could obtain loans or work their way in later years, with lower risk and better prospects for repayment. The Tampa Urban League took this commonsense approach in raising funds for grants to students in the top 20–30 percent of classes; USF took this approach in turning grants and service awards for top students into work scholarships.[3]

Developing Public Policy

USF was not the only institution encountering resistance, by virtue of tradition, location, social climate, and financial resources, in trying to reduce barriers to higher education. Many other schools, colleges, and universities encountered similar difficulties and made similar recommendations for more effective, commonsense approaches, converging on several points.

First, federal financial aid programs should offer more options, including work-study, and grants-in-aid for students "below the scholarship line." Second, advisors and students should have more flexibility in designing personalized packages. A mixture of work, grants, and loans should be changed from term to term to match changes in academic standing and other commitments and to allow ample time for academic work. Third, part-time students should be eligible for aid in proportion to the segment of the degree program taken each term. Fourth, special services should be added to facilitate the transition from high school or employment to college study.

Amendments to the Education Acts in 1967 followed these recommendations. They also strengthened services for handicapped students and other programs that helped institutions to diversify and expand developmental instruction and academic and career counseling for students from many different cultural and economic backgrounds.

The Education Acts and their amendments may represent a significant turning point in public policy. New programs went beyond the matter of equal access and dealt with the quality of the student experience, with ways to equalize the costs and risks for students at all creditable levels of achievement, and with changes in the system to facilitate progress toward a degree.

But even in the acts and guidelines, such pejoratives as "marginal" and "high-risk" students and "remedial" and "compensatory" instruction, thinly disguised the deeply ingrained habit of viewing individual differences in style and rate of learning as differences in the quality of students. K. Patricia Cross in her study of students new to higher education, 1950–70, remarked:

> We are in the grip of a "deficiency" conception of New Students. From nursery school to college, we give more attention to correcting the weaknesses of New Students than to developing their strengths. . . . Those who over-assist the New Student show the same basic lack of confidence in his learning capacity as those who have quit trying to teach him. "Over-assisters" may be more dangerous in the long run because they deny the student the opportunity to take the real risks that learning involves. The reorientation to learning comes from the student's knowledge that, through his own effort, he has accomplished a difficult task.[4]

New Students predominated at USF; 70 percent or more of its freshman classes were the first of their family to attend college. Most of the experience of USF faculty and administrators stood in the meritocratic tradition, and they tended to mingle meritocratic and equalitarian principles in planning and program design. But they tried to avoid the tendency to key on the presumed weaknesses of New Students. The best strategy seemed to be a personalized approach, capitalizing on strengths in the whole student body and on changes in the system that would help more students succeed.

SPECIAL PROGRAMS

Meritocratic and equalitarian approaches mingled in the Special Senate Program adopted in 1965. It made no change except to permit an advisor to waive the required GPR as long as a student stood a chance to earn a degree and wanted to continue. The approach was frankly experimental, genuinely "high-risk" for the University, in admitting students who could not qualify in the ordinary way and testing the hypothesis that their chances to continue were little better than zero. Ten faculty volunteers admitted two candidates each on evidence of good performance observed by a teacher, counselor, or supervisor. Student and advisor worked one-on-one, making the best plan possible out of standard courses, resources, and services. As soon as they became eligible, students shifted to standard financial aid packages. The rather hair-raising experiment ended in 1968 when federal programs provided for students in similar circumstances. Reports cannot be located, but at least half the participants are known to have continued into the second year and at least six to have graduated; one was attending USF in 1975. This two-year experiment at least disproved the "no chance" hypothesis; the learning experience also indicated that USF had to add group interaction to "one-on-one" arrangements.

The "marginal students" program in the Developmental Center was introduced at the same time and included group orientation and counseling components. A hundred students, not quite admissible, took an option to enroll conditionally in the summer. They took English or mathematics for credit according to their major strength, developmental instruction in the other subject, and a non-credit orientation course in program planning, study skills, and social interaction. They qualified for fall enrollment with a grade of C or better in both credit and non-credit courses. Followup studies showed the group performing at about the same level as their freshman cohort; and its retention rate of 70 percent was similar to the rate for all students. The program changed the system, adding a standard "breaking-in" routine that capitalized on group interaction. Those who enrolled recommended enthusiastically that all freshmen start with this type of program.[5]

HEP, an outreach program for migrant and poverty-level youth with qualifications similar to Special Senate students, and Upward Bound, oriented toward urban high school students and unemployed youth, followed the marginal students model. Each federally funded program operated like a "cluster college" centered in a residence hall and employed team teaching and group counseling techniques. Directed by Richard Pride, Upward Bound has been especially successful, with 83 percent of all participants from 1967 to 1975 having enrolled and continued in college studies.

FACULTY AND STAFF

Deans and program chairmen continued to recruit black instructors with disappointing results. In 1965 Ed Martin, Dean of the College of Basic Studies, suggested an incentive which the University Senate adopted. Any department ready to hire a minority candidate could fill the position without regard to productivity formula from a pool of 10 new faculty lines reserved off the top of budget allocations. Fine Arts, Education, Engineering, and Natural and Social Sciences promptly claimed new positions, and others were soon filled. The number of black teachers still stood at ten (1.6 percent), according to the first Affirmative Action report in 1969, and rose to 21.5 FTE positions (2 percent) in 1975.

In Career Service, blacks were at first concentrated in food service and physical plant; they held 307.5 FTE positions (21 percent) in 1975 representing all ranks and areas. In 1975 black administrators held 6.75 positions (5 percent), the first being appointed in 1971. In total employed personnel, the proportion of blacks has remained at about 13 percent from 1960 to 1975, approximately the proportion in the community.

ENROLLMENT

The best guess about the proportion of black students at USF is 5 to 6 percent for 1975. The proportion of students of Hispanic and Mediterranean extraction has usually been about equal to figures for the "Other" category on ethnic checklists. Given the cosmopolitan population of the area, minority classification has had little practical significance, aside from special concerns for blacks. New immigrants from Cuban and other Caribbean, Korean, and Southeast Asian origins, and students from bilingual and trilingual families, have special needs that USF has particularly addressed. Personalized services, rather than programs designed for special minority categories, have predominated because of the considerable differences among students within particular ethnic groups.

Accurate figures on ethnic background are not to be expected in any event. On equalitarian principles USF kept no ethnic data until 1967 or 1968; since then, the responses to items on ethnic identification have steadily diminished in frequency. In 1976 fewer than 15 percent of all students gave this information. If one equalitarian concern is to dissociate public records and transactions from color and ethnic background, the trend in student response goes decidedly in the desired direction. It also follows the University's inclination to organize student participation according to role and setting rather than personal appearance and background—following typical patterns in the modern culture of cities.

Removing Architectural Barriers

Just as President Allen decided to deal with racial discrimination by not establishing the practice in the first place, so he decided to build no architectural barriers into the campus. Providing access for the handicapped seemed a simple matter of following recommendations from the Easter Seal Society and the American Institute of Architects.

Governor LeRoy Collins envisioned a beautiful waterfront campus along the Hillsborough River, but this location had to be rejected in the face of periodic flooding and the need for protection of a fragile riparian-wetland environment. The high sandy ground actually chosen was more accessible and more suitable but had to be protected for future expansion. Since "buildings in place protect space," Allen, Clyde Hill, and Bill Breidenbach, the architect assigned by the Board of Control, decided to construct an initial ring of buildings as far apart as utilities costs would permit. Even though he could not center the whole campus plan on a compact, readily accessible library-media center, Breidenbach designed into the plan a network for closed-circuit TV and other instructional media, using many suggestions enthusiastically advanced by his friend Dr. Frank Stanton, President of the Columbia Broadcasting System.

The able-bodied as well as the handicapped, however, found the distances between buildings too great to cover in ten-minute intervals between classes. The *Oracle* sponsored an annual Bunion Derby, politely but firmly insisting that one John S. Allen compete in a walk with ten pounds of books and papers over the longest stretch— almost half a mile. Allen never won but always came on strong in the backstretch. In 1964–65 a revised class schedule (requiring the most complicated, detailed, and difficult planning process conceivable) provided a twelve-minute interval—giving the able-bodied less vigorous exercise, helping handicapped students not at all.

Arrangements were more successful within buildings, and handicapped students regularly advised Clyde Hill and the physical plant staff on other modifications. Sections of Beta and Gamma halls were equipped for handicapped residents.

Beginning in 1963 the U.S. Office of Education held annual workshops to keep planners, architects, and engineers abreast of new designs and technologies for improving access and the federal standards applied to facilities grants. The Handicapped Students Association provided advice and representation on USF committees writing new building programs. In 1973 the association surveyed all facilities and recommended improvements that were quickly carried out. Its president, Louise Friderici, prepared and the Office of Student Affairs published the University's *Handbook for Handicapped* in print and Braille.

"LOOPS" AND SPECIAL ARRANGEMENTS

President Allen decided in 1960 that handicapped students should function as self-directing participants and provide their own special equipment, materials, and services according to their regimen. When the Student Affairs deans considered this way of "mainstreaming" students, they realized that hidden costs and unforeseen barriers could produce a "revolving-door" effect unless a workable plan was prepared in advance. They offered to the handicapped the advice they gave anyone choosing a college: visit and see how well it fits you. Dean Fisher arranged with the Admissions Office for handicapped students to follow the standard "loop" for any personalized decisions, petitions, and discretionary action. Admissions staff identified handicapped applicants; the University physician identified those who should follow the loop; the dean invited them to visit before they decided to enroll.

This informal "dry run" evolved into a systematic procedure

documented in Policy Statement No. 34 of 1964 (revised 1968). Each visit followed an individual schedule of conferences that always included the Health Center, Admissions, and faculty advisors and might also include residence, counseling, developmental instruction, and financial aid staff. Usually a visitor would test-run the schedule of classes and could confer with instructors on course work, special equipment and other arrangements, or special interests in academic work.

After each conference the staff member gave a rough estimate to the dean of men or dean of women; occasionally, a staff conference had to assemble to order to make an adequate assessment. Typically, the visitor and dean went over the plan with the staff recommendations and came to a decision by consensus, having much the same information to go on. The dean then sent a recommendation to Admissions for consideration as part of the total record in making the final decision. In only a few cases did the dean and staff recommend denial of admission because of special needs that the student and the university could not meet. Those going through the loop left with a class schedule in hand, completed enrollment by mail upon receiving notice of admission, and avoided the ordeal of mass registration.

CELEBRATION

In September of 1969, Assistant Dean Linda Erickson suddenly realized that registration was approaching, but she had cleared very few handicapped applicants. She called Robert Egolf, the University physician, who was the first to realize that this was the first high school graduating class ever to escape a polio epidemic, thanks to the Salk and Sabine vaccines. Two University offices had a small celebration that day.

There was a dramatic dropoff in the number of applications going through the loop after that date. Subsequent developments in the University reflect other gains in the national effort to bring handicapped people into the mainstream. The expansion of public and private services has made participation easier and resources more readily available, staff and students more knowledgeable, and students more independent in their plans and activities. The loop no longer functions in the admission process. The state Vocational Rehabilitation Service has seconded a counselor to lodge in and work closely with the Personal Resource Center. Housing and other physical facilities have improved on campus and in the community. Handicapped students work with an advisor in the Activities Office to initiate activities and improve services, facilities, and program planning. In 1976 the physical plant director reported that USF facilities had passed inspection under new federal guidelines with minor exceptions.

Academic Standards

The majority of USF enrollment would be New Students about whom planners could safely assume only one thing: interests of the University and the students would converge in the concern for effectiveness in teaching and learning. The approach to academic standards should accordingly avoid the dubious meritocratic assumption "the higher, the fewer" and aim to increase the chances for most students to succeed. In the first *Accent on Learning* (pp. 110–11), Sidney French emphasized the flexibility provided for students in planning their studies and the arrangements provided for "late bloomers," "slow learners," and mature students returning to studies interrupted in the past, so that their plans could capitalize on their greatest strengths and most comfortable ways of work.

Frank Spain, Registrar, and the Committee on Academic Standards set up policies and procedures designed to ease constraints and reduce risks inherent in the system itself. These followed the "Accent on Lagniappe," a principle having several implications. One was "sudden service" in making decisions on admission, waivers, and petitions and in delivering records. Fast response was self-serving, given the stiff competition for topnotch applicants. It also helped to allay students' anxieties over being admitted and making a final choice of college, or securing records for job applications.

Another implication was the consideration of a student's shortcomings as the basis for a joint exercise in risk-taking, rather than an arbitrary cutoff indicator. The deans and Dr. Spain were inclined to take any reasonable risk to the University that students would accept for themselves, for several reasons. Five of the counties in the service area had no other college when USF opened, and most students could afford no other available choice; statistical predictors were known to be unreliable when applied to individuals; and the academic program was designed for personalized teaching and learning, so that administrative procedures should be equally flexible.

A third implication applied to both students and staff, equally deserving of a little lagniappe. Removing administrative artifacts, redundant functions, bottlenecks, and roadblocks would give students a better chance and also reduce work load for the staff. Clarifying staff and student roles would avoid duplicative functions and would tend to reduce errors; in turn, these improvements would reduce the number of appeals for discretionary judgments while preserving guarantees of due process in dealing with grievances, waivers, and petitions.

In assuring due process the principle of shared responsibility applied; if a reasonable plan could be worked out, a student assumed responsibility with as much assistance as the University could provide under standard programs. Applicants below admission standards and students not in good standing consulted an advisor or counselor to prepare a plan and present a petition for waiver of standards or administrative decisions to the Committee on Academic Standards. The committee made a recommendation to the registrar, whose action was subject to appeal to the Vice-President for Academic Affairs and the president.

Academic standards at USF generally conform to customary practice in universities. USF provides a "breaking-in" period before establishing the C average required for the degree, so that the cumulative GPR required for good standing increases with the number of credits (in quarter hours): 1–45 credits, 1.5 GPR; 46–89 credits, 1.7 GPR; 90–180 credits, 2.0 GPR.

Below these levels, the Records Office placed a notice of warning on the term's grade report; a second consecutive notice gave final warning to improve over the next term, in order to avoid disqualification. Students who were improving could continue on warning, especially when the next term's GPR was 2.0 or better. Students could appeal a disqualification, and advisors often encouraged them to do so when their grades were showing improvement and were above a C average for the term.

Both students and University needed a little lagniappe. Each was an unknown quantity to the other; some benefit of the doubt, some mutal accommodation in planning and risk-taking were necessary at least to get USF started. The Registrar's staff and the Committee on Academic Standards carefully monitored academic standards and procedures and shared results with the faculty and staff, for general use in planning and administration.

MONITORING AND FINE-TUNING

The committee carried a heavy load in designing a personalized system of academic standards. For the first three or four years, Frank Spain typically brought to its meetings not only petitions but also selected admissions applications and academic records that illustrated some special problem or some opportunity to improve policies, reinforce student achievement, or reduce work load. End-of-term review of the overall enrollment and grade record provided additional information.

Petitioners were uniformly required to present their proposals in writing, but some were encouraged also to appear in person when they seemed to have special experience or understanding that might help the committee. A few would return to report on the results of previous action—usually to crow a little—and they were always welcome. But as a rule, students were urged to confer with an advisor on their plan, rather than to use the committee for a group counseling session.

Because each recommendation was specific to a unique case, the committee found only a few patterns that applied to general types of situations or categories of students. Members sometimes teased each other about personal predilections, but they knew very well that few generalizations could be drawn about students in any category. Institutional studies confirmed the general well-being and effectiveness of students and University, but quantitative factors could not provide accurate estimates of future performance.

The committee had to look for commonalities that tend to escape statistical treatment. Little by little they began to identify some indicators likely to have some bearing on academic performance. None of these could serve as cutoff points for administrative policy, but it was convenient and time-saving for Admissions and Registrar's staff to use them in rough screening in order to identify records that called for more careful study and perhaps for additional information.

    • Unusual disparity in quality of work or scope of previous studies, related to one field of study and another or one cognitive skill and another.
    • Accidental interference (e.g., frequent changes of school; illness or injury; changes in family life or working conditions).
    • Breadth of interests, variety of work experience or volunteer service.

• Interaction with the family, especially in relation to educational and career expectations and experience.
• Financial resources and money management (in relation to overall work load and other responsibilities).
• Indicators suggesting "failure anxiety" or the "nonachievement syndrome."[6]
• Fallacious folklore (e.g., "If you once drop out, you'll never go back").

The staff and committee began to find some relations between grades and scores that could be used for reasonably equitable decisions in the ordinary procedure. They developed a sliding scale combining grades and test scores, which the Admissions staff could use in considering conditional admission on warning or final warning. Based on regression tables correlating high school and USF grades and FTGT scores, the sliding scale worked according to ranges indicating convergence and divergence between grades and scores. For example, an applicant showing a cumulative GPR between 1.6 and 1.7 with a FTGT score above 350—suggesting the nonachievement syndrome—might be considered for admission on final warning, if he agreed to confer with a counselor to assess more fully the factors affecting his performance and develop a plan for coping more effectively with academic work. A student with a FTGT score between 200 and 275 and a GPR from 1.8 to 2.0 might be considered on warning or might be given unconditional admission if the GPR were higher than 2.0. "Other things being equal" always applied; the total record had to be taken into account.

The staff and committee tried hard to avoid "the fallacy of uniform equality"—the tendency to treat everyone exactly the same. Procedural guidelines would assure fairness, but uniform rules of thumb usually worked more for administrative convenience than for fairness to students. Designing equitable safeguards for due process and an effective approach to each unique applicant required a great deal of patient, careful work.

In 1962–63 the committee reviewed 794 petitions representing 21 percent of the student body and approved 40 percent of them. In 1964–65 it reviewed 1,334 (20 percent of enrollment) and approved 42.5 percent. In 1964 the system of advising was changed, and a small corps of advisors was organized within each college. Given more extensive training and interchange with a smaller group, faculty advisors could make an increasing number of recommendations to the Admissions and Registrar's staff on which action could be taken without committee review. The committee's load then leveled off at approximately 10 percent of enrollment. In 1970 it reviewed 1,444 petitions representing 9 percent of enrollment and approved 55.9 percent of them. After the 1972 reorganization, each college became responsible for monitoring students' progress toward the degree, and very few petitions concerning all-University policies had to go to the Academic Regulations Committee, which succeeded the original body. The 1975 figures show 1,588 petitions, one percent of enrollment, with 81 percent approved.

This leveling off reflected the growing confidence in student performance and in the general standards of academic work at USF. Institutional research and evaluation indicated the effectiveness of the system overall and the general reliability of discretionary judgments. Students and faculty shared more reliable information and guidelines as a basis for planning. Developmental instruction and counseling were being used earlier and more often.

The committee found other ways to reduce work load based on feedback from experience. For example, in 1962 it recommended the elimination of the original practice of warning for any F and the practice of duplicating a copy of the warning to the advisor. About 10 percent of USF grades turned out to be F, and students knew very well what the grade signified. The warning was a work of supererogation, and the Senate agreed to eliminate it. The committee reviewed the registration procedure and the processing of records each term; some redundant functions and data had to be retained as safeguards, but a good many others could be combined or eliminated.

The committee had the responsibility to develop policy on honors and awards. In 1960 it recommended a minimum cumulative GPR of 3.5 for each term in order to qualify for a special certificate at the Honors Convocation. In July 1962, as graduation of the first full class approached, it recommended a minimum cumulative GPR of 3.5 in the major as a basis for departmental faculty to award Honors at Graduation; and it adopted Grace Allen's suggestion to award each honor graduate a green-and-gold fourchette to be worn at Commencement.

The committee supervised early admission after the junior year of high school, and in May 1964, it also adopted guidelines for dual enrollment of high school juniors and seniors in one University course. This variant of early admission provided opportunities for students who were prepared in one particular field but were not ready for a full freshman program.

SCALAR PRINCIPLES AND RISK-TAKING

It was important for the University of South Florida to earn a reputation as a university of high quality, and critically important for it to earn accreditation immediately. Consequently, anxieties repeatedly surfaced over the lack of highly talented students and the abundance of New Students who were considered not to be "up to college quality."

In March 1964, Dr. Spain replied to an inquiry from Sidney French concerning the 302 students conditionally admitted in 1962–63. Ninety-nine percent of them had enrolled; only 6 percent had withdrawn during the first term; at the end of the year 76 percent were eligible to continue and 32 percent had earned a cumulative GPR of 2.0 or better. More conditionally admitted students enrolled than did those admitted in the ordinary way; they also seemed to stay with their academic work more consistently. The proportion continuing through the full year, 76 percent, was greater than the figure for all students, 64–65 percent from 1960 to 1963.

Entering freshmen were generally encouraged to enroll first in a summer session taking a light load, for a "breaking-in" period to consolidate their academic standing. Continuing students on warning also went this route as often as possible. The president and Executive Committee then became apprehensive over the mix of such "marginal" students and public-school teachers; they desired genuine year-round operation, not a conglomeration of "summer people."

Accordingly, in 1966 E. L. Flemming, Director of the Developmental Center, reported on students attending the summer term while on final warning. He found 258 new and continuing students in this category, 6.6 percent of total enrollment for the term, and concluded that "the University of South Florida did not have a disproportionately high number of serious academic risks." He particularly noted the wide range in FTGT scores among them—from 37 to 485 out of a possible 500. Like Lewis Mayhew in 1961, Flemming could not accept the validity of these test scores "as a predictor of academic success in any of the colleges in the University."[7]

Actual experience at USF proved to be somewhat out of line with the "double door" access model used in planning the state system of higher education. It indicated that students could often break out of low levels of performance and succeed in academic work if the system were modified even minimally. They gave back some lagniappe to the University in the process of risk-sharing.

Grades and test scores became even less reliable predictors when students were given a chance in their planning to identify and accommodate conditions of life and work more directly affecting their performance. The registrar and committee received many recommendations from other committees, students, faculty, and staff on ways to remove roadblocks and make the system more flexible, and they adopted some proposals that could be applied in general policy.

For example, two modifications in the grading system removed administrative artifacts based on dubious applications of scalar principles. In 1969 the Committee on Instruction proposed to give students the option of taking a limited number of additional courses to be designated by the departments, on a pass-fail basis with an S/U grade. The Committee on Academic Standards had to postpone action until the changeover to a new computer configuration was completed, but in 1970 the proposal was adopted by the University Senate for one-year trial and has continued in standard practice. S/U grading, of course, is the most practicable approach to many types of work which do not lend themselves to scalar measurement for evaluation; internship, Senior Seminar and other special seminars, independent and directed reading and research, field studies, and a number of graduate courses were already using pass-fail grading. But the "experimental" approach to the new policy appeared to reflect a persuasion that the quality of work has to be quantifiable on a graduated scale in order to be evaluated; and some faculty members were apprehensive about diluting the quality of students' work by changing to a two-point grading code or downgrading the level of instruction in courses designated for S/U grading.

In 1973 the Senate approved a policy on "forgiveness" which Joe Howell, the Vice-President for Student Affairs, had proposed. The practice, followed in many community colleges, allows students to repeat as many as three courses in order to raise a grade and discards the previous grade and credits in calculating the cumulative GPR. With dual enrollment between the University and neighboring community colleges, the change removed some inequity between generic and transfer students.

Dr. Howell was more concerned about removing an administrative artifact that perpetuated every failure in calculating a student's ranking and gave a lower reading than the actual level of accomplishment after repeating a course. For instance, if a student earned one F and one A and earned a C on repeating the failed course, his cumulative GPR would remain at C. Under the forgiveness policy, the B average would be much more in keeping with his actual level of overall performance.

These modifications in the system of academic standards counteracted tendencies to apply scalar principles that work for administrative convenience at the expense of students' progress. They removed some administrative artifacts conducive to frustration and failure. In general the faculty and administration were disposed to accept some risks and costs to the University rather than put most of the burden on students; they were willing to exercise discretionary authority to keep students moving toward the degree rather than follow a strict "up or out" formula. These departures from meritocratic tradition alarmed some people, but they were consistent with the personalized approach that the first president and deans had established.

The "Accent on Lagniappe" rang true to the *Accent on Learning*. It seemed reasonable to expect these principles to work equally well in dealing with other questions of equal opportunity, fairness, and shared responsibilities of the University and the students.

EQUALITARIAN STRATEGIES

President Allen and the deans departed with equanimity from the traditional view of college as the domain of young men making the turbulent passage to adult life and work. The volume of applications from mature men and women, eager to resume advanced studies, led the deans in 1959 to recast the class schedule and add advanced liberal arts and professional courses for the charter class. Mature students enrolled in large numbers and quickly earned a reputation as academic pace-setters, more than adequately replacing youthful "stars."

Large numbers of women of all ages and walks of life enrolled, more or less in accordance with the expectations of the planners. The proportion of women in the total enrollment exceeded national figures from the outset, ranging around 45 percent annually through the 1960s, approaching 50 percent in the 1970s, and appearing likely to follow national trends and exceed that figure early in the 1980s. By all indications USF seems to have attracted women students primarily "because it was there" and affordable, rather than through particular efforts to concentrate on women as a special target group or as a minority—which they did not represent in any statistical sense. By coincidence, the first graduates of the University, in December 1962, were mature women, Lucas King and Evelyn O'Neill, who promptly established the first alumni endowment for an annual award to the top-ranking graduate.

Programs in the Student Affairs area did not often develop through parallel same-sex activities such as Dean French's suggestion of men's and women's self-government. All Student Association committees and activity councils had coeducational membership. Most voluntary associations were coeducational; separate sports clubs and intramural leagues organized where separate rules of the game applied; men's and women's fraternal societies organized according to practices of national fraternities with which they hoped to affiliate. As long as a single-sex group had no other discriminatory provisions, and as long as both men and women had ample opportunity to participate in activity areas where any same-sex groups were organized, the Vice-President and Committee on Student Affairs were not disposed to invoke a nondiscrimination rule with respect to sex, as they did with respect to color, religious, and ethnic barriers.

President Allen and Howard Johnshoy set up the table of organization for Student Affairs on a functional basis and tried to recruit professional men and women in approximately equal numbers. Johnshoy preferred functional titles and did not use the titles of Directors of Men's and Women's Activities originally designated for the central office. Herbert Wunderlich, his successor in 1962, adopted the traditional titles of Dean of Men and Dean of Women, partly to give prominence to their functions in serving the special interests of men and women and partly as a convenient way to divide equitably the unpredictable load of referrals, individual conferences, and problem-solving and disciplinary proceedings, while still giving students the choice of a same-sex or opposite-sex mentor.

The architectural design for residence halls enabled the University to change the assignment of men or women to each self-contained living unit for 40 to 50 students as the mixture of applications changed. In developing the system of standards and discipline for residence halls, the traditional double standard—strict parietal rules for women, less regulation and more independence for men—fell into place in 1960.

When the 47 women living in the University Center were formulating regulations with Phyllis Marshall, Howard Johnshoy, and Margaret Fisher, the three administrators were in general accord on certain matters. First, locking people up was a last resort, the worst possible way to protect them against harm to their own persons or property. Second, a curfew would be counterproductive to the University's academic purposes, curtailing participation essential to develop high-performance capabilities in studio, theatre, and concert work, typically involving late hours, and laboratory work often requiring around-the-clock monitoring or other operations. Third, a curfew put men and women equally at a disadvantage in developing supportive peer relationships essential to academic and professional development—not to mention dating, courtship, marriage, and family life.

Knowing that 1960 plans would set patterns for the future, they tried every way they could think of to avoid a curfew. But they ran into the hard realities of an isolated campus with its attendant security problems and lack of money for more than a small complement of campus police. In order to provide even minimum security, the small force had to rely upon closing all buildings at the earliest convenient hour of 10 P.M. The rest of the double-standard system then fell into place. Most ways to provide open access after closing hours cost more than the residents or the University were willing and able to pay. Students and staff settled for access by prior arrangement, setting the pattern for a complicated, irritating signout system that entailed followup by residence hall officers and staff on frequent abuses and violations of security arrangements.

Jim Decker, who assumed responsibility for residence hall staffing and programing in 1961, described the policy as "open hours, closed halls." This simply put a good face on an equivocal situation. He went through many trials in developing the residence hall program, beginning with an uproar over a feature article in the local press. The reporter commented accurately and favorably on the residence hall plan, but the headline hailed the opening of Alpha Hall as a bold new "coeducational dormitory" and provoked public outcry, shock, and criticism of "immoral behavior" lasting for several weeks. Undergraduate resident assistants even offered to strike in protest against the equivocating policy that thinly disguised the double standard and put them into conflicting roles as "helpers" and "enforcers" with their peers (although these issues were eventually resolved in the course of in-service training).

In 1962 Herbert Wunderlich separated the duties of residence hall programing from the responsibility for standards and discipline, incorporating the latter into the University's general system. The Deans of Men and Women, Charles Wildy and Margaret Fisher, worked with separate councils of standards chairmen, resident instructors, and resident assistants on adopting standards and following due process in handling complaints and violations. But the load on the entire women's staff in the system of standards and discipline was far out of line with the convenient and equitable division of labor in other respects. Only the stresses, strains, and role conflicts engendered by the curfew and double standard were equally divided among all concerned. Besides, anyone could readily see how the residence hall policy was at cross purposes with the University's personalized approach to student responsibilities in other respects. And in all the halls, both the security system and the standards system leaked like a sieve.

During the 1960s periodic open houses and visiting days evolved into a systematic plan for daily visiting hours to be set by each hall. In 1971 a regent vigorously denounced the visitation policy in public and at board meetings. The Council of Vice-Presidents for Student Affairs took up the matter and recommended uniform visitation guidelines which the Board adopted systemwide. This action, and increased numbers in the campus security force, made it possible for USF to terminate the curfew and the signout system in women's halls.

More than any other single factor, acceptance of a traditional double standard seemed to put the Student Affairs deans in a highly equivocal position in carrying out their responsibility for open, equal access to participation in University life and work. When they tried to develop new agenda and plans to counteract inequities, racism, and sexism, they often came up against countervailing pressures, sometimes of their own making. For the University often tried to mingle meritocratic and equalitarian approaches to policy and practice. And in a political and social climate that was often unfavorable to academic freedom and equalitarian gains, its low-key, low-profile initiatives and actions were often equivocal, confusing, and easily misunderstood.

Equalitarian strategies became more positive and prominent as the social climate became more favorable, especially as federal programs and guidelines consolidated into a firm base for affirmative action. Women students and faculty had worked together since the University opened on many mutual interests; their effort gained momentum as more positive guidelines emerged. In 1969 Dr. Maxine MacKay, a humanities professor who also had a law degree, conducted a study for the AAUP chapter on the status of women faculty in rank, salary, and tenure. Around this study a group of women faculty and staff came together to develop agenda and to encourage participation in joint initiatives by women students. In the fall of 1971 the president appointed a special Committee on the Status of Women in addition to the Affirmative Action Committee. From this point forward the University as a whole began to develop more active programs for women and their special concerns.

The University, indeed the entire system of higher education, stood in need of nationwide advances in understanding and support of equality of opportunities for effective teaching and learning. Long before 1956 the high costs of a caste system, race and sex discrimination, and the double standard had been demonstrated over generations of institutional and community experience. The experience in higher education over the 1950–75 period simply underlines these exorbitant costs and indicates how inequities compound themselves when questions of equal opportunity and equal protection under law for all persons are left unsettled from generation to generation.

10
Breaking the Lockstep

Things New and Old

The University of South Florida stood to gain administrative convenience and educational and economic advantages by more prefigurative approaches to the passage through college, sharing responsibility with students for more personalized ways of learning. The system of higher education generally was turning away from postfigurative methods towards prefigurative, collaborative ways of work, aiming to help more students succeed.

In private colleges and universities, budget, admissions, and student affairs officers perennially worried about drop-outs. Enrollment attrition meant budget attrition. Public institutions confronted similar anxieties in terms of the return on the taxpayer's investment. Nationwide, the majority of any freshmen cohort were more likely to disqualify or drop out than to complete a degree over the standard four-year period.

In 1970 K. Patricia Cross observed that education from kindergarten through graduate school seemed to have fallen into a rigid lockstep, operating on the meritocratic principle that students must earn the right to advance their education by competing for high rankings, and they dare not fall out of step for fear of forfeiting all future opportunities. Many educators had discovered more effective ways to facilitate learning, but the only way that was open for most youths involved a "counting-out game" along the line of musical chairs, with fewer and fewer places available at each level of education. Many students grasped early in their schooling the implicit assumption that few would make the grade, and they stopped competing. Even gifted students often tended to play for low risks of failure rather than for the enjoyment of learning and the challenge of exploring new worlds. Many studies showed how "failure anxiety" and "the nonachievement syndrome" impaired the effectiveness of many competent students at all levels.[1]

Christopher Jencks conducted a particularly thorough survey of sources of inequality and considered this competitive approach to be a major contributing factor. It tended to reinforce a dubious and dispiriting assumption that rankings will change little from kindergarten forward, regardless of the students' experience and effort. For teachers and students alike, the actual educational experience seemed to discount important values in the human encounter across generations and cultures that enhance the quality of life and work in a school, college, or university.[2]

Studies of this sort were scarcely needed to persuade many youths and adults that education—and other social systems—were lacking in the "spirit of things that *work*." Many were asking how any sensible person could tolerate, let alone enjoy, the standardized, regimented turnover of interchangeable people in the typical "rat race": make that grade, make that score, be first on the list, win promotion, win a diploma, and earn—the right to start all over again in college, and again in certification for professional practice, and again in occupational entry and promotion on the career ladder, in order to earn—retirement. Did this scenario really mean equality, life, liberty, the pursuit of happiness?

The founders and the faculty of the University of South Florida looked for ways to break the academic lockstep, ways of work more in keeping with the process of human development, the enjoyment of learning, and the actual conditions of life and work in an urban university. In many instances a more effective approach included flexible timing to accommodate individual differences in rate of learning or changes in conditions of work. Usually new departures were experimental primarily in terms of some application of a special technique to an unusual field of study or stage in the passage through college. At first the faculty, in postfigurative style, reserved innovative methods for top-ranking students, but the results often indicated the potential value of these methods as an option for all students. Many things, new and old, were shared with colleges and universities throughout the country in mutual concern for gaining greater quality and effectiveness in higher education.

The Educational Contract and Modular Design

The University follows the customary practice of confirming the catalog under which a student first registers, or any subsequent catalog from which the student may choose, as an implicit educational contract. The faculty undertakes to provide the courses and services described; the student undertakes to produce the academic work specified for the degree.

From the outset the deans adopted the rule of contracting in writing for individually designed ways of completing standard courses and for independent and directed studies or personalized degree programs. The practice had proved helpful in guarding against the tendency of students and teachers in independent study to become excited about early results and expand the work beyond all reasonable limits. In 1971 the Committee on Instruction recommended and the University Senate adopted the present policy of contracting for every course. The syllabus presented in the first session must state the timetable and minimum requirements for student work and the evaluation procedure and criteria for grading. The syllabus represents the educational contract, and it involves a commitment for students to contribute out of their own work and their personal experience to the resources for learning available to the whole class.

Students were eager to have the syllabus–contract generally adopted in order to help them plan their work around multiple academic and community commitments. The shift to the quarter system in 1967 (and a fee-per-credit schedule introduced in 1973) called for more than ordinary prudence in managing their investment of time and money. The syllabus–contract gave more settled, reliable information for planning. The practice actually facilitates creative, innovative teaching and learning by identifying the principal conditions of work in advance of the student's choice of alternatives for personal study, so that neither accidents nor faculty whims nor student enthusiasms may unduly increase costs and risks of any departure from routine.

MODULAR DESIGN OF DEGREE PROGRAMS

As it now stands, the general design for USF degree programs represents a matrix filled in course by course in any convenient sequence.

Other institutions have applied the educational contract to modular programs with a degree completed in blocks of extensive, long-term studies. Each module represents a personalized contract by a student and instructor that typically allows variable deadlines, according to the scope of studies and the student's most comfortable rate of learning. The Basic Studies program failed to realize fully its original modular design, but two effective examples of modular contracting have developed at USF.

The University introduced in 1969 the first program for an external degree to be offered in the Southeast. Three modules (in Humanities, Natural Sciences, and Social Sciences) are required under personalized contracts for independent study, reading, and research. On completing each module, students attend a three-week resident seminar in the discipline, in which intensive integrative studies with a faculty team culminate in a comprehensive examination. A fourth thesis-oriented contract integrates the entire program through an interdisciplinary investigative study. An oral and written comprehensive examination completes the program for the Bachelor of Independent Studies degree.

Credit is not interchangeable with other programs for the B.A. degree, but participants may waive one or two modules by examination, on the basis of previous study or life experience. The B.I.S. program requires no more than nine weeks of on-campus study and offers opportunities for higher education to people whose commitments preclude regular enrollment.

The second case was serendipitous. In 1974 the state purchased New College for USF's regional campus in Sarasota. This twelve-year-old liberal arts college organized its degree program around the modular contract in three fields identical with the B.I.S. program. Contracts specify goals, activities, timetable, end product, and criteria for evaluation; they may run from a term to a year, and long vacations give plenty of time to tie up any loose ends. The B.A. degree is awarded upon satisfactory evaluation on nine contracts, four independent study projects, a comprehensive, integrative senior project, and a final comprehensive exam.

New College continued this modular program and became a unit within the University of South Florida, adding a small liberal arts college with a demanding, self-directed program and the strong student-faculty interaction that the USF founders valued so highly. Its actual cost of instruction is somewhat higher than standard appropriations and fees will provide, so arrangements were made for a special advisory board to raise supplementary funds.

While it is too early to see how New College will fare within the University, initial experience indicates that its program will flourish. The B.I.S. program is well-consolidated, and its comparatively small enrollment primarily reflects the limited number of available staff.

Personalized Learning

For USF the emphasis on personalized learning was sound theory and almost a necessity in practice. The University had no chance to prove itself on meritocratic principles. Most of its students would be new to higher education; therefore, its only alternative was to prove that New Students produced good academic work.

The 1959 Conference on Intellectual Tone emphasized the real value of academic work, which is not to be measured by the past experience of participants but by their breadth and depth of learning in the course of study. Realizing this value depends on diversifying the experience open to students and faculty. Many educators believe that state universities, enrolling a large, diversified student mix, should also provide more diversified ways of learning that will ultimately enrich both higher education and the community.

Personalized studies would serve another important purpose in providing the feedback from independent work beyond standard courses, typically coming from graduate study, that USF needed to sustain development of its academic programs before it was fully accredited and ready to develop graduate programs. Many small colleges have conducted much of the advanced work in some majors by using personalized, independent studies typical of graduate programs. Small faculties often provide full coverage of a field in this way, without committing themselves to a plethora of courses that few students will take. Coming from a small liberal arts college, Dean French was convinced of the educational advantages as well as the economy of this approach for USF.

INDEPENDENT STUDY

Independent study for credit by examination in nonlaboratory courses was at first reserved for top-ranking students, especially those taking advanced or honors classes in high school. If the application was accepted, a student took the uniform course examination and earned credit with a grade of A or B; otherwise he took the course in the ordinary way.

Independent or directed study, reading or research went beyond material in standard courses; an instructor certified the educational contract planned with the student and the grades and credits earned upon its completion.

These special arrangements were at first considered experimental and accordingly were coordinated by Lew Mayhew in the Institutional Research Office. The deans approached independent study with great caution and some ambivalence. USF needed to exploit the technique; but on traditional principles, any special opportunity should be rare if it were to reward outstanding students—and few students, especially freshmen, should even be allowed to expose themselves to its unusual demands and risks.

The Faculty, Staff, and Advisor Handbook, 1961–63 (pp.44–45) took a postfigurative approach, assuming that faculty must take responsibility for managing these challenges and risks. Lew Mayhew urged full exploitation of independent study but with great caution. Perhaps 10 or 15 students might merit the fullest use of the technique and "might be freed from academic regulations some time after the first semester." Even for a single independent study contract, a student should have strong motivation, strong high school preparation, high grades and test scores, and high scores on the Inventory of Beliefs—indicating their tendencies toward flexibility and adaptability rather than rigidity of habits and beliefs. "In general a person who is authoritarian, who is rigid in his outlook finds himself uncomfortable away from the guidance of day-to-day classroom work. These authoritarian students though academically apt should be discouraged from attempting independent study the first year."

Students could arrange informally for short-run study, free from any required class attendance, to meet contingencies such as illness or change in working hours without stringent tests. Some "goofed off" and some abused the privilege, but the practice saved considerable numbers of students from forfeiting their whole investment and enabled them to complete their courses successfully. In general, performance under these informal arrangements did not often seem to be adversely affected by factors measured in tests and inventories. Evidence from experience with both formal and informal arrangements suggested that independent study was generally effective and could be subject only to the safeguards of the educational contract.

Postfigurative styles of administrative intervention gradually dissolved, leaving only the standard procedure for registration under an independent study contract. The number of contracts settled at a steady 5 or 6 percent of enrollment per term; the 1973 Self-Study showed approximately 150 per term in regular offerings, 750 in personalized studies, fairly evenly divided between undergraduate and graduate students (pp. 60–61).

As anticipated, feedback from independent study aided in the development of new courses and programs, and much of the content related to community concerns. The Women's Studies program provides a good illustration: students designed special projects and term papers on women's concerns in related courses, and contracts for independent study and research appeared in increasing numbers. Next, students and faculty organized special topics courses and seminars which enrolled sufficient numbers to merit formal program design and supported the divisional majors that some students began to center in women's studies. Finally, in 1970 a block of Women's Studies courses in the Department of Interdisciplinary Social Sciences became a field of concentration.

This developmental process has helped faculties to make the case for new and modified academic programs. Students already studying in related areas can be identified as a basis for enrollment projections; they can help the faculty confirm points of convergence on community, national or international concerns as a basis for program design. The process yields hard evidence, anchored in actual experience, to support probabilistic projections.

GROUPING BY ABILITY

A time-honored, well-intentioned meritocratic practice separates highly talented from less gifted students. Theoretically, grouping by ability allows the talented "eagles" to gain more in scope and depth when they are not held back to the humdrum pace of the "turtles"— who will not become so anxious or discouraged when competing with their peers rather than with "eagles."

At USF each Basic Studies course offered some honors sections, indicated by an asterisk in the class schedule and reserved for students having a GPR above 3.0 with FTGT scores of 400 or better. A "starred section" might be organized as a seminar reviewing independent study and research or as a team conducting a laboratory or field project; it might simply include more laboratory or studio work or more extensive reading of professional treatises and journals.

The purity of experimental design was impaired from the outset. Severe pressure on scheduling classes in multipurpose facilities made it necessary to admit some "turtles" to starred sections, and some "eagles" chose standard sections, in order to provide a full-time schedule for the term. Followup studies found little significant difference in results from the uniform examination for starred and standard sections or in comparisons of ability groupings within and between them. The evidence suggested some infiltration of special techniques from honors into standard sections.

This was indeed the case. The faculty was collecting and sharing innovative techniques for general use, and there was no way to prevent special techniques from being used anywhere. Students learned about different methods from their friends or in Education courses and either used them or asked instructors to introduce them in other courses. The instructor of a standard section once remarked that the students simply ate everything up and asked for more; they did not seem to understand that certain types of content and techniques—even things reserved for graduate study—were supposed to be beyond their capacity!

So the honors sections faded away, like the Cheshire Cat, leaving only the "grin" of the stars in the catalog indicating that the class would do something special.

TEAM TEACHING

The College of Basic Studies set up a team teaching project introduced in 1961 by James Parrish of Functional English and continued through 1965 under Gerald Robinson of Biological Sciences. Any student could elect to register for a block of sections combining two, three, or four Basic Studies courses in which they worked with the same group of faculty and students. Participants took the uniform final examination for each course included in the block. These teams developed into strong support groups capitalizing on special strength and experience in every member to enrich the whole class.

In an English–Biological Sciences–Mathematics–Human Behavior combination, teams concurrently worked on mathematical methods, principles of logic and strong inference, and laboratory studies of animal and human behavior, from which they extrapolated concepts of behavior and social organization and biological and ecological theory. A single integrative project or term paper satisfied requirements in all four courses, or any combination within them, as well as a special study for each one. Instruction in Functional English centered on reading and writing in social and natural sciences. Another option combined Functional English and The American Idea taught by a two-member team. The present American Studies program germinated out of this experience.

Team teaching ended when the trimester calendar made block scheduling difficult and the faculty eliminated the uniform final examination yielding the principal evaluative evidence. No significant differences appeared in team and standard sections, high- and low-scoring students within them, matched pairs of resident and commuting students, or other groupings. Integrative effect was hard to assess although students responded positively in nonquantifiable ways. The drop-out rate was very low; students stayed with the team unless illness or other unavoidable circumstances intervened. They developed high spirit and morale; one team even held a reunion six or seven years later, and members came from all over the country.

The principal outcome may have been this ineffable effect on morale, especially in the face of recurring concern over school spirit at USF, where people could usually think of nothing but football as a way to generate spirit and identity. Results of team teaching added strength to many other observations that academic work could and did generate university spirit and cohesiveness.

PROGRAMED INSTRUCTION

In the late 1950s programed instruction came into extensive use, applying social learning theory[3] in its step-by-step, cue-response-reinforcement schedules for developing concepts and techniques in developmental or logical sequences. The USF faculty used programed instruction in many fields. Laboratory programs in Functional Foreign Languages enabled students to move at their own pace in mastering skills of speaking and listening. Functional Physical Education developed self-instructional programs, some with videotape playback for comparison with high-performance examples. Education, Business Administration, Engineering, and many fields of liberal arts used the technique extensively. The Computer Center reserved 55 percent of its time for teaching and research including computer-assisted instruction, and the allowance was more than fully used.

The Human Behavior course, organized around social learning theory, was a natural field for the technique, and a group of instructors wrote programed texts for it.[4] Some of its faculty conducted research on the theory and its applications. One study found computer-assisted programing effective with retarded children; some learned basic reading and arithmetic beyond predicted capabilities.[5] Another compared standard and programed textbooks, concluding that they were equally effective and the choice could rest on preferences of students and teachers.[6]

In computer-assisted instruction, USF may have fallen a generation or more behind institutions leading in this field, such as Dartmouth, because of strict limits on new computer configurations, especially for interactive and self-directed applications. A comprehensive plan for an integrated computer network in the universities and state agencies matured more slowly than anticipated in 1960, when the Cabinet brought design and procurement of computer systems under uniform guidelines. The network was still not fully designed and implemented in 1976. Consequently, USF computer services were useful for processing information but often lacked the capacity for extensive use as an alternative form of programed instruction. This situation may change with completion of the master plan and with advances in microcomputer technology.

STYLES OF LEARNING

Developments in learning theory have also distinguished cognitive, affective, and psychomotor modes of learning and styles of coping with developmental tasks. These can be loosely defined as thinking, feeling, and doing. Thinking not only involves abstract concepts and ideas, "book-learning," and the use of language, symbols, facts, and theories, but also the understanding of how knowledge meets the test of experience both logically and pragmatically. Feeling, or affective learning, involves aesthetic experience and sensitivity to positive reactions that bring people together and aversions that impair "affection" for oneself or others—or for learning itself. Psychomotor modes involve "all-over" learning that includes skills of hands, mind, and body in movement, doing and making things.

In any case, people seem to learn with their whole selves, so that each mode can facilitate or interfere with the others. (Even cognitive modes involve psychomotor skills in reading and writing.) Effective instructional techniques can integrate different modes of learning and capitalize on strengths of particular students and teachers. For example, the College of Nursing designs teaching techniques in both ways. Each course combines learning by each mode to the fullest extent practicable; and instructors also capitalize on strength in one mode to help students with other ways of learning—for instance, to work back from affective and psychomotor learning in clinical instruction into cognitive learning in related sciences.

The 1959 Conference on Intellectual Tone specifically emphasized the importance of affective and psychomotor learning in relation to the aesthetic values in the intellectual encounter. The report urges students and teachers to learn "to use reason and feeling as tests for their respective validity" in integrating learning and in confirming mastery of content and technique (p. 3). In keeping with this emphasis the first Faculty, Staff, and Advisor Handbook (pp. 60–61) described 49 different instructional techniques compiled from a survey of the faculty. Nine applied affective modes, 14 accented psychomotor learning, and the remainder described cognitive ways of learning integrated with one or both of these modes.

From 1966 to 1971, during the period of greatest pressure on faculty resources from expanding graduate studies, the Committee on Instruction organized the exchange of techniques and distributed a set of "fifty nifty" special approaches recommended by teachers and students. The SACS team commended its strong focus on active student involvement in such "whole person" forms as team-building, role-playing, and exercises in creativity. The committee also conducted workshops in 1970 and 1971 to introduce new faculty and graduate assistants to the variety of techniques and styles of learning at their disposal.

New technologies augmented resources and techniques in the instructional repertory, especially in the use of nonprint media and closed-circuit and broadcast instruction. The Instructional Materials Center included in the Education building has equipment for students and faculty to use in preparing all sorts of print, graphic, and nonprint material; next door the Learning Laboratory has more than a hundred audio stations, half also video-equipped, with materials also accessible by telephone. In 1972 YOU (Your Open University) introduced broadcast instruction in courses specially designed for the medium. All these resources enable people to vary the setting and medium as well as the process, mode, and content of learning.

194

Learning in the Community

International exchange of faculty and students was particularly emphasized in public policy during the 1950s. In the 1960s student activity in the community opened another avenue of international and intercultural learning at USF where many worlds are open on the doorstep. From the first day, the College of Education coordinated activity with public schools in order to keep local systems from being overwhelmed by faculty and student projects. Off-campus learning became so extensive that administrative coordination had to be provided; centers developed for study abroad, national and international student exchange, and field studies that pooled resources of all the colleges.

COOPERATIVE EDUCATION

President Allen had long been active in Cooperative Education and included this type of work-study program in the initial plan. Under George Miller in Personnel Services, the program began in the spring of 1961 with the barest possible lead time to recruit and place students. Through good and bad times it has maintained a steady enrollment of 150 to 200 per year, considered optimum for its setting and resources. Initially there was much anxiety that students might flock to it in such numbers as to exceed all expectation for placement. But this tendency to use Cooperative Education as another form of financial aid did not materialize; the results of counsel and orientation went the other way, encouraging students on their own initiative to apply the Co-op principle in opening opportunities on the job to relate employed experience to academic work.

THE OFF-CAMPUS TERM (OCT)

In 1969 Keith Lupton came from Cooperative Education to coordinate field studies, applying the Co-op model to the Off-Campus Term program. A small staff helps faculty and students arrange field studies and manages linkages to collaborating agencies over the country and abroad. Its formal program centers in group projects, including two-week field studies in Jamaica scheduled several times a year, an Urban Survival package offering up to 16 credits for a term in studies of urban interaction in New York or another metropolitan area, and a number of prepared projects giving 3 to 5 credits in studies of environmental interaction, government and international relations, and cultural, community, and economic development. These can accommodate about 250 students per year, are regularly filled and overflowing, and have to be scheduled far in advance. The small staff cannot keep track of all the people they assist in designing other off-campus studies, whose numbers may approach four or five times the enrollment in prepared projects.

DEPARTMENTAL AND VOLUNTARY PROJECTS

An excellent example of student initiative is the American Studies Cooperative organized in 1972 to produce special seminars and lectures. During 1973–74 the Cooperative also organized field studies, some teams securing grants from the National Endowment for the Humanities. One team conducted an oral history project on Southern folk arts and crafts, traveling through Florida and parts of Georgia and Alabama. They documented the study with artifacts and written, filmed, and taped records that remain at USF as a general resource. They were the first undergraduates to appear on the program of the American Studies Association and also conducted lecture-demonstrations in many Southeastern schools, colleges, and universities.

Faculty and students in Fine Arts Education organized a center in Ybor City—a historic Latin neighborhood that now includes a substantial black population—for children to produce their own art and crafts and to work in music, theatre, dance, film, and other media. "The New Place" now operates as an independent agency with MDA funding from the city and continues to use USF volunteers.

An Intensive Tutorial Program (ITT) has put as many as 1,500 volunteers per year into individual tutoring for school children of all ages, in cooperation with the Hillsborough County Public Schools and with some federal funding. Faculty members and public school teachers provided intensive training for tutors during their assignments and helped them bring as much breadth and variety of experience as possible to children, using campus and community resources.

In 1970 the Office of Information Services answered a request to help Alpha Phi Omega, the Student Association, and other groups to organize a general clearing-house for volunteer service, now entitled CAUSE (Community and University Service Encounter). Some of its leaders also initiated a loosely coordinated statewide network of volunteer services in colleges and universities that mounted several workshops and planning and training conferences annually during three or four years of activity. CAUSE has remained firmly established at USF, serving as many as 4,000 students per year. Both ITT and CAUSE promote volunteer service for its own sake, but students can independently link volunteer experience of any sort with academic work and arrange with instructors for appropriate credit.

When Sargent Shriver visited in 1963 to find out how this new university provided the highest proportion of Peace Corps volunteers, in relation to enrollment, of any institution in the country, few ready answers were forthcoming. Only a few guesses can be made today about the wellsprings of voluntarism. The University simply seems to have capitalized on a community spirit that matched the frontier spirit cultivated by its founders. Certainly the participation of community people in planning, the emphasis on personalized learning, the flexibility for modifying the mode, setting, and technique of learning, and the emphasis on student initiative and contributions inside and outside the classroom have capitalized on the volunteer spirit and may also have cultivated its growth in the University's membership.

But where it comes from is as hard to understand as where it will go next. Formal and visible ways of volunteer service at USF seem to represent only the top of a tree that puts out myriad feeder roots that go deep and wide. In a very real, historical sense, a university is a special kind of voluntary association and USF may simply be drawing on a deep, vital "spirit of things that *work*" in the American experience with its shared values of freedom for voluntary association.

HONORS PROGRAMS

Plans for an Honors Program began in 1960; the 1965 Self-Study reported that a proposal was expected momentarily from the Committee on Instruction. From 1967 to 1971 a loosely coordinated Honors Program functioned in the Liberal Arts College, modeled on the Advanced Basic Studies program and requiring four honors courses to be added to any major sequence: the Honors Program Reading Seminar, Special Topics Seminar, Individual Research Program, and its own Senior Seminar (in addition to the all-University one). The 1973 Self-Study reported that about 100 students had participated and that a special committee was considering this design and other alternatives for an all-University program. But no further action has been reported, and no honors courses have been listed in the *Accent on Learning* since 1974.

The Philosophy faculty developed its own program for the award of Honors at graduation; it requires additional independent work in three courses of the major sequence, an independent research project, and a cumulative GPR of 3.5 or better in this block of four courses and 3.2 or better overall. The department has recommended extension of this program throughout the University.

The off-again on-again history of honors programs has raised occasional doubts about the commitment of USF faculty and students to the enjoyment of learning and the pursuit of scholarly excellence. The planners considered such questions and decided that this commitment had to apply to the entire experience of academic life and work at USF. Honors created for students and faculty should enlarge the choices, challenges, and opportunities open to everyone, rather than create an artificial scarcity of rewards. President Allen felt strongly that the all-University approach involved such generous commitments to open opportunities for earning honors and to recognize excellence in every form.[7]

From the student perspective, honors programs requiring a prescribed set of courses and grades approaching an A average may look more like an added cachet than an added opportunity, among all the other possibilities for challenging, self-directed academic work. In fact, some Honors List students say quite frankly that they prefer to keep all their options for selecting courses and to settle for Honors at graduation as an ample reward.

In the 1961 and 1962 policies, the faculty did not withhold any opportunity to earn Honors at graduation in the ordinary course of study; a cumulative GPR of 3.5 or better would qualify a student for consideration by the departmental faculty. On this basis, a number of different honors programs could probably be created by departments, colleges, and the whole University, to enlarge rather than limit opportunities to seek new challenges and rewards in the enjoyment of learning.

The Developmental Approach

Committed to the pursuit of excellence, the president and deans could do nothing much about the quality of students' academic work except to follow the process of human development and learning, as far as it was understood. The theory did not describe a smooth, well-oiled process, but one that seems almost literally to go by fits and starts.

Learning seems to begin with a period of steady progress, as new skills and habits progressively fit into a well-integrated repertory equal to each new task. This leads to a "plateau" where the process seems to stall and may even fall apart. Then a stage of reintegration proceeds by the use of strong skills and habits to backtrack and practice up in areas of shortcoming, so that the whole repertory once again comes back into balance. Then a new stage of steady, integrative growth and development proceeds to a new plateau, reintegration, and so on.

Basic cognitive skills (reading and writing, speaking and listening, thinking and figuring) are likely to develop at different rates, and one or another may come out of balance from time to time in anybody's repertory. Students appear to become frustrated over imbalance in skills more frequently than they do over the level or rate of learning—even when performance is consistently above average. And people will often find some skills out of balance with the volume of required work, especially in a field new to their experience; for instance, many a good, fast reader has had considerable trouble keeping up with work in an unfamiliar field of science, humanities, or professional study.

Teachers and investigators working with people of all ages and all levels from kindergarten to graduate school have developed an array of techniques that facilitate the process of learning and often help students break out of successive plateaus. Some of these have proved useful in easing the transition from high school to college and keeping the repertory of skills in balance over the passage to a degree. Involving changes in role and responsibility, a new environment and schedule for learning as well as new tasks, new fields of study, and usually a heavier burden of studies, college work is neither the ordeal nor the triumph of tradition and folklore; but it is hard enough to test anyone's capacities, and developmental services can often smooth the way.

Accordingly, plans for USF included an array of developmental instruction and special services available for any student. The 1959 Conference on Intellectual Tone set the developmental approach in the context of higher education as a process of planning and risk-taking, capitalizing on gains as a resource for further ventures. Early intervention at the first sign of difficulty would reduce risks and costs and, at the first sign of opportunity, would facilitate gains in skill and performance.

ASSESSING SKILLS, ADVISING, AND PLANNING

Lew Mayhew, with the chairmen of English and Mathematics and the staff in developmental services, compiled a test battery administered prior to freshman orientation for use in advising and program planning.

The College Qualification Test, an arithmetic proficiency test and a reading test, and the Cooperative English Test on Mechanics and Effectiveness, were chosen in order to give advisors some indication of students' general knowledge, their understanding of material covered in general education courses, strengths and weaknesses in writing, and understanding of business transactions and simple statistical interpretations.

The Inventory of Beliefs, Form 1, covered beliefs about matters of general education and a scale indicating degrees of rigidity (authoritarianism vs. flexibility) that was used as one indicator of readiness for independent study. (This test drew heavy fire from the Johns Committee in 1962.) A simple, ten-minute screening for speech and hearing by interview and audiometer gave many students such a test for the first time in their lives.

The Faculty, Staff, and Advisor Handbook and the training sessions for advisors emphasized the use of the whole academic record and personal information about experience and expectations from the student as the context for interpreting results on this test battery. The Handbook advised, "Test scores . . . simply reflect a central tendency of a student in a particular area. . . . Any given individual can perform in direct variance to expectations established through a test."

The process of planning, assessing risks and costs, and selecting courses, special services, and special opportunities was outlined as a joint responsibility of student and advisor. Test results could not be used as independent indicators; the whole body of information had to be considered, especially the student's expectations. For instance, a student considering a waiver of Functional Mathematics and also expecting to do some advanced study in math, statistics, or computer sciences should not only have a high math score but a good, solid high school course in trigonometry.

Conditions of personal life and work would affect academic performance. Advisors should listen to a student's account of any personal concerns and give practical advice and information ad lib.

When in doubt they should refer the student to a counselor but should not shy away from all personal matters just because they were not trained in counseling or therapy.

Students would need to learn a great deal about the University, partly because it was new, partly because they were typically the first of their family to attend college. Advisors could often clear up blind spots and points of resistance with clear explanations, positive reinforcement, and encouragement of effective choices and plans. For instance, financial aid advisors had encountered blind spots in the system itself; managing time and money might present new tasks for some students; and some students might be offended, assuming that anybody must be considered stupid or mentally ill, to have counseling and developmental instruction even suggested to them. In order to keep the total investment of time somewhere within compassable limits of 60 to 70 hours a week, the Handbook suggested that advisors should help students taking Developmental Reading to avoid "excessive reading courses" and choose those relying more on discussion, studio or laboratory work. Many students scoffed at the very idea of finding any other sort of course; a beleaguered freshman in 1960 probably expressed the general reaction: "I've already bought sixteen books and now they are handing out stacks of reprints in every class! What do they think we are!"

Some faculty members thought they were, on the whole, pretty poor students. Usf has had its fair share of people with a mind above the facts of life and learning, who view students in general with condescension, students in distress as incompetent, and developmental services with undisguised loathing. And it has a typical student mix, varying from the very brightest and most productive to the least gifted and most recalcitrant. The University challenged them all to enjoy learning and gave as much support as its limited resources would allow.

THE DEVELOPMENTAL CENTER

The Developmental Center in Student Affairs supported classroom instruction with personalized programs for individual and group services. Dr. Rose Spicola, the first Director of Developmental Reading, also taught a section of Functional English on writing skills and worked with the faculty in planning general instruction in communication skills, as did Dr. Harris Pomerantz in the Speech and Hearing services. Both worked with the Mathematics faculty on ways to help students having difficulty that involved more than the mastery of quantitative methods.

Screening in speech and hearing being the first such test for many students, the service was almost swamped with participants, including some wishing primarily to improve in polish and style of speech. The staff simply had to leave stylishness alone, as long as students could speak and hear clearly enough to understand and be understood. No one even thought of "stamping out Black English" or any of the profusion of regional American, Oriental, Spanish, Italian, Hungarian, and other distinctive idioms heard on campus.

The same heavy load appeared in developmental reading; as anticipated, a substantial number of slow readers had to be given priority, but some students in all levels of proficiency wanted a chance to improve—as the planners had hoped they would. In 1961 Robert Zetler of Functional English introduced the Evelyn Wood method of speed reading, and fairly proficient students had a choice of this classroom method or the personalized programs in Developmental Reading. This did little to reduce the load on the Developmental Center.

Clinical and counseling psychologists and psychiatric social workers helped students with the assessment and management of other skills and habits pertaining to the developmental tasks of adults. Diagnostic testing and psychometric services supported all the developmental programs, especially in counseling and psychiatric assessment. The counselors provided short-term, intensive modes of service, often emphasizing affective learning and using both individual and group techniques. They referred students to community agencies for long-term, extensive treatment modalities. Consulting psychiatrists served both the Developmental Center and the Health Center, assisting in diagnosis, medication, and referral for hospitalization or other treatment, and sharing in training and program planning for counseling and guidance.

As new staff and new services were added, the Developmental Center also strengthened the links with Cooperative Education, Placement, and career development services in Administrative Affairs, and with faculty in many academic areas. Dr. Tom Rich became director in 1961 and began to strengthen linkages with residence halls, faculty advising, and the Health Center. As collaboration became more extensive and the emphasis on counseling became more pronounced, the title was changed to the Counseling Center for Human Development; and in 1972–73 the unit was joined with Cooperative Education and Placement in the Personal Resource Center.

EARLY INTERVENTION

Dr. Rich was concerned about suicide and crisis intervention and brought consultants to USF for workshops to train staff and many faculty members in these techniques. He also applied some of the techniques of early intervention to failure anxiety and the non-achievement syndrome, seeing an analogy between academic intervention and suicide intervention: both had to deal with a self-fulfilling prophecy of alienation, failure, frustration, hostility, and despair. Support from friends and advisors and peer reinforcement would be important factors in early intervention, facilitating referral to professional services and sustaining gains in personal devlopment and learning.

A great deal of the success of New Students at USF may be attributed to the effectiveness of the services and the training provided in the Developmental Center, facilitating the work of professional specialists through understanding and support by students, advisors, and teachers.

Linkage of the center with residence halls was particularly emphasized. Their staffing plan included joint training for professional resident instructors and undergraduate resident assistants with the Developmental Center staff and paraprofessional student aides. In 1964 E. L. Flemming, the new director, set up "satellite services" in Argos; each counselor visited one night a week for drop-in conferences or group sessions. In 1966 the center moved into the Andros classroom building, and Fleming's successor, Ed Allen, added a schedule of counselors on call 24 hours a day.

Peer managers in the reading and study skills services were trained to assist the professional staff. They also helped with the academic improvement network set up by volunteers in each living unit to provide information, tutoring, and referral for special services. Peer management was extended to services for other areas of interpersonal relations, special concerns of women and blacks, career development, drug and crisis intervention, and smoking and weight control.

For the year 1970–71, more than 25,000 contacts were reported by the center, exclusive of career development services, out of a University enrollment of about 15,000. This volume of service was handled by a professional staff of 12 (FTE) in 10 distinctive types of service. Coordinated programs, extensive use of group techniques, self-directed programing, peer management, and cross-training among specialized staff made this work possible with a very modest staff and budget.

Testing and psychometric services supported the whole program, especially *counseling* and *psychiatric consultation. Reading and study skills, speech and hearing services,* and *tutoring* were closely linked to counseling and career services and to academic departments. *Cooperative Education and Placement* included the *Career Information Center,* a library and laboratory with print and videotaped materials. The *Vocational Rehabilitation Service* seconded a professional counselor from the state office, housed in the center and collaborating with all staff. *Research* related to the student experience, program evaluation, and special problems of theory and practice (e.g., studies on stuttering and test anxiety).

This developmental approach to counseling as a way of teaching and learning, with diversified services diffused to all three administrative areas, had disadvantages as well as advantages. Duplication of community services was a recurrent concern, but evidence indicated that planning should move toward enlarging community resources rather than limiting student services. For instance, even as the Personal Resource Center was being formed, the Speech and Hearing Service was scheduled shortly to move into new facilities providing a clinic for general use in the Department of Communicology, formed out of the Research Institute in Speech Pathology and Audiology.

The lines between credit courses and noncredit developmental instruction were sometimes hard for students and advisors to understand. Dual appointments of staff confused some faculty and many students. The linkages of developmental services with Student Affairs and Administrative Affairs officers created confusion and misunderstanding.

The distinction between traditional treatment modalities and the developmental approach at USF was never quite clear and hard to clarify in any event for students, staff, faculty, and the professional community. The concept of counseling as a form of teaching seemed to forfeit traditional roles, values, and professional standards in treating mental and behavioral disorders. Professionals in the universities had much the same problem with systems in flux that practitioners had throughout society.

In 1971 C. M. Warnath analyzed some intricacies of policy and practice and some role conflicts that counselors and therapists confronted in a campus setting, over the whole period of change and expansion.[8] Most of these surfaced at USF. For instance, concerns over confidentiality and privacy, legal guidelines and institutional policy, and linkages between counseling and administrative functions in disciplinary action often evoked complaints and protests, created role conflicts, and disrupted congenial professional relationships.

Disadvantages seemed to be outweighed by the effective developmental gains made by many students. Interdisciplinary approaches and personalized, self-directing program design proved to be as effective in developmental services as in other academic programs.

A Question of Effectiveness

Planning and Polity

Presenting the temporary organization during the 1960 orientation, President Allen emphasized the responsibility to be shared by the entire membership in the all-University approach; in the State University System the Board of Control followed much the same principle of locating authority and responsibility at the scene of the action. Since a university centers in teaching and learning, feedback from student and faculty experience would be essential to the development of an effective organization. Temporary planning and administrative systems had been tested over two or three years of work. Immediate responsibilities involved the implementation of academic programs and concurrent design of systems for general evaluation and feedback to planning; this work had to be done quickly in order to prepare for accreditation and the subsequent growth of advanced and graduate studies.

Allen anticipated a period of increasing strain on facilities, personnel, and finances. Beginning about 1963–64, as USF approached accreditation, the second round of new universities and community colleges would start their initial period of exponential growth. Despite internal and external pressures the University could realize important values through ingenuity in planning and parsimony in sharing resources—given strong capabilities for evaluation and feedback to planning. The temporary organization was designed for the membership to develop these essential components around systems already in place.

The first question was "When do we vote on it?" Allen explained that there was no occasion to vote; the University was already operating on a temporary organization which the faculty must rapidly consolidate as the evidence accumulated from experience.

"How do we get a constitution?" was the next question. The University already operates under the Florida Constitution, Allen explained. He did not think that he should even consider a constitution for USF at all. The very concept seemed out of keeping with its actual position as part of the network of universities under the Board of Control rather than as a private corporation.

The faculty generally recognized the need for some falsework to hold the University together, and they worked agreeably within the fairly standard pattern of administrative and collegiate responsibilities embodied in the temporary organization. There were the usual criticisms and complaints, and some things went against the grain of tradition. Faculty members were in the majority in all committees and councils and the University Senate, but some were outraged at having students and nonteaching staff ("freshmen, librarians, secretaries, and janitors") participate in governance. Some considered dual appointment to administrative and faculty positions and the involvement of faculty in administrative and student affairs to "dishonor the tradition of a university as a community of scholars."

Clyde Hill was troubled over an apparent oversight that left physical plant workers out of elections for the Senate. This looked like an invidious distinction, perhaps related to "menial work" or to the large number of blacks on the staff. The distressing impression was not relieved when some people defended the omission "because physical plant has nothing to do with higher education."

The principle of diffusing responsibility according to function rather than rank or status puzzled some people who had little experience with anything other than the scalar principle of organization. The temporary organization was laid out in a standard bureaucratic chart, but the principal organs and systems had connections in every direction, disregarding rank and level of instruction and crossing over traditional areas of student, faculty, and administrative jurisdiction. The degrees of freedom, authority, and responsibility that everyone had to exercise in multiple roles were hard to understand. Instead of trying to understand how they could initiate plans and carry them out, some people concentrated on figuring out why the temporary organization could not possibly work. Others considered the whole complicated arrangement to make a feeble pretense of democracy, designed so that the president would make all the decisions anyway.

Of course, there was nothing to do except to proceed as planned, and the organization turned out to "embody the spirit of things that *work*." Formative principles stood up even in the process of adding new colleges and reorganizing others; and the systems continued to function even when decisions by the new management team of 1971 sometimes threw the process into reverse.

Positive results predominated over grumblings and grouchings. For instance, the efficient communications systems and accessible decision-making locations were a pleasant surprise. The lines on the chart did not put up barriers; persons could often get closure on a matter by telephone. People soon became accustomed to the "Accent on Lagniappe" and "one-stop service"; complaints about a few "ping-pong matches" that still bounced them back and forth between offices helped to improve administrative systems. Feedback to the president and Executive Committee actually did result in improved policy based on the test of experience; only 3 of 82 policy statements promulgated by President Allen from 1957 to 1970 remained unchanged (those on smoking, gifts, and boats).

In practice, the plan of governance made little change in traditional roles, and it capitalized on much of the traditional vision of the community of scholars. Puzzlement seemed to come from the necessity to clarify themes and action in traditional roles where people were accustomed to rely on habit but now had to think everything through from the beginning. The planners may have clarified too little and left too much for charter members to work through—out of a desire to share the camaraderie and frontier spirit they enjoyed. But most of the members responded in that same spirit to the challenge of developing a university of the first class.

New Configurations

The deans had chosen most of the faculty for their interdisciplinary experience and had designed the organization to capitalize on their sharing of resources and responsibilities. Very few novel practices were involved. Universities typically own facilities, libraries, equipment, and land to be used for the benefit of all members; they typically give each member a home in some collegiate form of organization with some responsibilities for work with people in other disciplines and other colleges. Plans for USF simply capitalized more fully and more visibly on effective principles and practices to be found almost everywhere in higher education.

Still some faculty members had trouble understanding just where anybody stood in the organization, with all the dual memberships, intercollegiate councils, and multiple work assignments. Some had trouble with Jean Battle's account of teacher education as an all-University responsibility, and found it hard to grasp the fact that students would simultaneously belong to Education and another college. The concept of a degree program as a plan that students administer eluded some and alarmed others who did grasp its implication. Some people felt uneasy about taking on unfamiliar tasks—teaching in more than one college, advising students in non-academic matters, and serving on committees out of personal interest and expertise without necessarily representing any department or college.

Sidney French tried particularly to reassure those who were perturbed over "teaching outside their field" in interdisciplinary courses. Explaining that teachers probably know more than they think they do, even outside their specialty, he added, "Besides, it's really easy to teach what you don't know. Say you don't know—just as you have always done. Then go look it up—better still, have the students look it up. That will be good for them; they're supposed to contribute to academic work."

The idea of students as contributors also made some students and faculty uneasy; it opened up unfamiliar roles on both sides. In fact the whole faculty had a heavy burden in helping New Students learn to manage their roles in the University, on top of dealing with some new ways of work and a more diversified repertory in the teaching role. Personalized studies may appear "independent" of supervision, but in practice students and faculty have found them to require much the same shared responsibility that uniform assignments involve; sooner or later, the work comes back for evaluation. Some students find self-directed studies to require added responsibility and effort; teachers find the responsibility and the effort in planning and evaluation of personalized work to differ distinctly from ways of assigning and grading uniform exercises and examinations. While such principles and practices were not shockingly innovative, taking on a new role in a new setting called for both faculty and students to form some new habits.

In general, "transfer shock"—the usual stress of adapting to a new setting—undoubtedly accentuated feelings of disorientation and disaffection. Certainly, more than ordinary planning, patience, discretion, and hard work are required to start a new university. Even today as in 1960, there are complaints that "this University does everything for students and neglects the faculty." Frontier life seemed hard, confusing, unrelenting in the pressure to do more and do it more effectively.

Faculty Status

The 1959 Conference on Intellectual Tone took particular note of adverse effects of rank on the genuine intellectual encounter. Floyd Reeves, and other founders and consultants viewed distinctions of class among students and rank among faculty as counterproductive, especially where rich resources could be cultivated in a new university free from some traditional barriers, privileges, and "artificial scarcities."[1]

During the orientation workshops Russell Cooper presented a modest proposal for a system of faculty assignment and evaluation linked to salary schedules, as an alternative to the traditional rank-salary-tenure model. He considered tenure to be misplaced as a reward or an earned right linked to rank. Tenure belonged to the system of mutual support for standards of scholarly integrity and freedom of inquiry. In Cooper's estimation, an instructor needs tenure the moment he walks into a classroom to confront resistant students and recalcitrant subject matter in a social climate that is sometimes forbidding. The traditional linkage of tenure to rank seemed to deny those who most need its protection: young people trying their wings, older people bringing worldly experience into the novel setting of a campus, and those on part-time or short-term appointment. He proposed to extend protections for academic freedom to all the faculty from the first day of classes under traditional guarantees of free speech and due process.

Cooper was convinced that an effective system for faculty assignment, evaluation, and salary schedule would disregard rank and would provide some effective reward—such as cash. He suggested that the faculty propose to the president the adoption of a single, ungraded, "topless" salary scale that would provide two types of reward: small annual increments for effective performance and substantial sums for outstanding and creative contributions to University planning and development, community and professional service, teaching, and research. An ungraded salary scale would make it easier for chairmen and deans to project general appropriations and distribute salaries more equitably to new and continuing positions. Linking reward to performance would offset the tendency for trustees and legislative committees simply to increase salary scales by a fixed percentage across the board—a practice that in effect gave a greater net increment to faculty in the higher salary levels, regardless of their actual share of the work load and the actual quality of their performance.

In the face of rapid expansion such modifications might be essential, in order to avoid foreseeable dysfunctions in traditional systems and adverse conditions of stress from unpredictable enrollments and predictable financial constraints. Some adverse conditions did come to pass at USF as Cooper expected. Instructional funds were in fact strained by rapid growth, imposing urgent requirements for new positions and leaving meagre increments for continuing faculty; accelerated growth in advanced and graduate studies put additional stress on all funds for lower-level and general education courses and their instructors. New faculty often came in at a higher salary than some counterparts on continuing appointment; the disparity generated resentment and disaffection. Administrators were tempted to substitute rank for money as a reward, and "dry promotion" was conducive to cynicism and deleterious to morale at USF as elsewhere.

An effective system for evaluating faculty performance, with feedback to planning faculty assignments, work load, and salary budgets, would be the principal factor in making any type of incentive and reward for scholarly effort serve the mutual interest of both faculty and university. Cooper suggested a multivariate design covering the entire spectrum of teaching, research, governance, and community service. Criteria specific to each area with measures pertinent to evidence on each criterion would have to be designed and linked to the salary scale. "Publish or perish" makes good sense; without publishing knowledge, the whole culture of cities may perish. Other criteria and measures would have to be designed especially for University and community service, areas rarely included in faculty evaluation systems in other institutions.

Cooper considered rank to be dysfunctional in evaluative design; it tends to predispose toward useless, even fallacious, rank-order comparisons. Performance measures should relate to operational criteria describing the unique assignment of each faculty member and instructional unit, which vary from term to term for people of all ranks.

Less than two years later the Johns Committee and AAUP censure caught the University off balance on two factors that Cooper particularly emphasized: tenure as a general safeguard for academic freedom, and performance evaluation of unique responsibilities. Twenty years later, his modest proposal seems more elegant than ever in its simplicity and fairness.

Many critics have found rank and tenure counterproductive in developing a support system for scholarly work. Some recent studies find in the traditional rank-salary-tenure system the source of some general inequities that tend to affect academic women even more strongly than men. These raise some questions about the effectiveness of rank and tenure as rewards for scholarly productivity and about the effectiveness of universities in providing both opportunities and resources for scholarly work.

Studies by Bayer and Astin[2] have shown significant, direct correlations of rank, tenure, and salary with years of teaching experience, and less significant correlations of these rewards with factors presumed to measure quality or productivity. For example, volume of publication increases as the years of service increase. This relationship is to be expected, in view of the time required to develop scholarly work and get it published. Total years of service, however, correlate much more closely with rank, salary, and tenure than does volume of publication.

A good many women take some years' leave from academic employment; and the status of academic women as a group is lower on all counts than that of their male counterparts. The differences relate directly to the aggregate number of years in teaching, which is lower for women as a group than for men. If the traditional system actually rewarded high performance, the gap between men and women faculty would not be as great—or else it would relate to some specific performance criteria that women do not meet while they are teaching. But this does not seem to be the case; no other factors appear to have as considerable an effect on the status of men or women faculty as the length of service alone appears to produce.

Men as a group simply show more years of service than women as a group; and rank, salary level, and tenure vary with total years of service more than any other factor.

Findings of the Bayer and Astin studies on the size of salary increments also suggest that time in service is the most significant variable. Experience at USF also indicated little connection between evaluation of faculty performance and provision of salary increments. The USF Self-Study of 1965 included a comparison of its faculty salaries with those in a set of 58 public universities enrolling 10,000 or more students. For the period 1960–65, increments in total funds allocated to faculty salaries averaged 3.3 percent per annum at USF, 5 percent in the comparison group. In the 58 universities, annual increments began to approach the rate of inflation toward the end of the period but consistently lagged behind the rate of enrollment growth. Annual increments at USF consistently lagged behind both inflation and enrollment growth over the entire period. Findings suggest that all 59 universities received just enough appropriations to keep going, with none even beginning to approach the level of funding required for modest rewards for scholarly work.

These studies suggest few significant effects of an incentive-reward system on actual funding for teaching and research. The evidence bears out other observations on the lack of incentive for governing bodies of colleges and universities to secure funds that will provide rewards for excellence. As alternative rewards, rank and tenure may actually function as *disincentives* for funding salary increments of any considerable size—beyond just keeping up with rising costs of things in general.

Difficulties in setting up an effective incentive-reward system have led some educators to suggest a different approach to scholarly productivity. Some consider productive teaching and research to be functions primarily of personal curiosity and energy, modified principally by opportunity. In this context, an effective support system might be designed to create opportunities for innovative teaching and research and to provide resources in libraries, laboratories, communications, and publishing—giving particular attention to the protections for academic freedom that Russell Cooper emphasized.

THE COUNTERWEIGHT OF EXPERIENCE

Cooper's modest proposal did not get much of a hearing. President Allen, the faculty, and other deans showed no particular interest. This may be one of the more useful proposals advanced and one of the more important opportunities missed during the University's formative years. In retrospect it is easy to see how the suggestion fell on deaf ears. Aside from general disorientation and "transfer shock," both faculty and students were almost too full of novel ideas and eager to latch onto anything traditional to higher education that was in sight. Moreover, many faculty members had strong commitments to AAUP standards based on the traditional rank-salary-tenure system. Roughly 43 percent of the charter faculty were assistant professors, many of them having become eligible to earn tenure very recently.

It was hard to imagine how USF could design and adopt any support system for standards of academic freedom and integrity, replacing tenure as an earned right. In consequence, many people understood Cooper to propose eliminating tenure—an alarming idea—when he actually proposed to extend tenure immediately on appointment to any position, and to deal with salary directly without intermediation of rank. The actual proposal was still alarming to many of the faculty who generally valued rank as a reward contributing to self-esteem and recognition among peers. Anticipating meagre salary increases was even more reason to preserve rank as a reward—even as a "dry promotion." And rank at USF was considered requisite to any negotiations with other universities operating on traditional systems.

The faculty may also have been indifferent because they were fairly content. Most people found the working arrangements, unrelated to any reward system, to be rewarding by comparison with past experience and conducive to effective work. Telephone and clerical service, student assistants, a private office, allowance for outside consulting and travel for professional development, a temporary procedure for evaluative decisions on promotion, tenure, and salary fairly consistent with AAUP principles—these conditions, added to the self-esteem that came from contributing to an exciting venture, gave many comfortable reasons for taking a leisurely approach to the development of institutional systems that must grow with experience in any event.

Faculty Employment and Evaluation

The planning team followed the traditional process of peer review in hiring charter faculty, as Floyd Reeves suggested, and proposed it as the base for faculty assignment and evaluative systems.[3] Well tested over generations of experience, the practice had become almost a habit in assessing plans, progress in the work, and values from results and their applications in universities, accrediting associations, publishing houses, and other agencies. A formal system had to be designed for feedback to planning, budgeting, and policy development in the University and the Board of Control; and it must incorporate information needed for accreditation studies by the Southern Association. The faculty accordingly adopted a standard form for the annual report, covering research and publication, teaching, other University and community services, and honors and awards; this report was the primary source of information for peer review.

TEACHING

For evaluating courses and instructors Lew Mayhew recommended a questionnaire from the Center for the Study of Higher Education at Michigan State University. Standard items covered course design, instructor effectiveness, student experience and expectations, and sources of satisfaction. The faculty adopted the instrument and administered it in each section at the end of each term. Individual instructors and program faculties often added special sets of items related to experimental variables or to special projects and individual contributions to classes.

Results were highly gratifying. Mean ratings were satisfactory or better in section, course, program, and college dimensions. They indicated a good fit between student experience and expectations, and effective connections between classroom experience, the community, and the scholarly world. Few unsatisfactory ratings appeared, most of these indicating improvements immediately feasible. The most effective use of evidence was in term-to-term fine-tuning of course and program design, the reliability of the instrument for other applications being open to considerable doubt.

APPOINTMENT AND ADVANCEMENT

Allen and French outlined a temporary procedure for new appointments and for awarding promotion, tenure, and salary increases. Peer review by the program faculty began the process; each faculty quickly had to work out an evaluative design including self-evaluation. On the basis of peer review the chairman would interview each faculty member or applicant and forward a recommendation and supporting evidence for review by the dean of the college and the Vice-President for Academic Affairs.

These stages laid the foundation for the Executive Committee to fit recommended faculty appointments into the overall enrollment, program, and budget projections. A comprehensive plan would go to the president for final review. He would confirm salaries for continuing appointments and recommend to the Board of Control all new appointments, grants of tenure and promotion, and salaries above the level requiring Cabinet approval. The board followed much the same procedure in the systemwide policy completed and adopted in 1963.

ASSIGNMENTS AND WORK LOAD

Two conventional ways to match faculty assignments and work load to enrollment have developed in the American system of higher education. These grew primarily out of experience in residential colleges and universities, typically having few members enrolled or employed less than full-time and showing fairly small variations in enrollment from one term to the next.

First, a standard credit hour was taken as a basic unit of time for generating faculty positions from enrollment figures. As a rule of thumb, the credit hour was considered to represent a block of 3 clock hours, each hour in the classroom requiring approximately 2 additional hours of work per week by each student and instructor over the standard term.

Second, a standard number of credit hours set by policy to represent a full-time load was divided into aggregate credit hours of student enrollment, actual or projected, to produce a proportionate number of full-time equivalent (FTE) faculty positions.

In 1963 the policy adopted by the Board of Control set 15 credit hours as the standard full-time load per FTE teaching and research line. On the "two-for-one" rule each FTE line provided approximately 45 clock hours per week, with 12 hours in the classroom, 24 in class-related work, and 9 in all other activities combined. The annual report on faculty effort called for the percentage of time spent in instruction, research, and University and community service, but no base in actual or estimated clock hours was given or requested.

The board also established the standard full-time faculty contract to cover 9 months' employment with a 10-month pay period. Under the Florida Plan, universities were committed to year-round operation, and the board introduced the trimester calendar for this purpose. For each university the 1963 budget added a small number of 12-month positions, estimated on the basis of recent summer enrollment, each carrying a salary increase of 20 percent based on 2 months added to the pay period.

Experience at the University of South Florida began to indicate shortcomings in these conventional formulae from the first day of planning. In many fields of study and administration, variables pertaining to special configurations of people, techniques, setting, and materials had direct bearing on the actual work load in real time for students and teachers; but their effects almost entirely escaped the FTE formulae based on credit hours. The new dimensions of community service and the actual work load in developing research and educational programs in the nine expanding universities appeared likely to call for an investment of real time somewhat in excess of the 9 hours per week allowed by formula. And many people considered the expansion of a 9-month work period to 12 months to indicate a salary increase of 33 percent, not 20 percent, under the trimester plan.

Studies of actual experience dealing in real time were clearly needed. The 1965 USF Self-Study reported that the Committee on Institutional Research was designing but had not mounted a study of work load—one of the urgent tasks outlined in the 1960 orientation, particularly in Dean Cooper's modest proposal. In general the faculty seemed disinclined to put much effort into evaluative studies. Many were persuaded that the results would make little difference to the people who actually made the ultimate decision—and if they did mean something, then the president, chancellor, and Board of Control should design the system.

Political interference, questions about accreditation, and AAUP censure seem to have contributed to this apparent lack of interest by eroding much of the original enthusiasm for creative planning and program development.

Counteracting Folklore

Russell Cooper liked to elaborate on an ancient metaphor used by Phi Beta Kappa, likening the process of learning to a lifelong voyage into new worlds. Charting a course for a degree required cross-bearings on experience and expectations and the University's mission—both for midcourse corrections in teaching and learning and for the work of mapping the widening world of knowledge. Academic folklore tended to regard faculty as preoccupied in research; while they were opening worlds of knowledge, students merely followed well-charted courses and career channels. But even on this assumption, the design for teaching and learning should provide the same checkpoints and cross-bearings for both faculty and students, in both individual and institutional plans and mid-course corrections.

From a postfigurative perspective, meritocratic traditions primarily emphasized the administrative process of selecting students according to competitive rankings. Accordingly, the common academic folklore tended to emphasize concentration, hard work, high motivation, and perseverance in competition for top rankings at transitional points on educational and career ladders: it had little to say about what occurred between the checkpoints. From a prefigurative perspective, in relation to the responsibility shared by faculty and students in launching the University and launching their personal careers, competition had little meaning, and folklore gave little guidance. For students, faculty, and the University as a whole, skill in navigation counted most.

Many colleges and universities were swinging away from postfigurative approaches. Many educators were trying to counteract misleading folklore, especially such common fallacies as "If you just concentrate on studying hard, you will succeed," or "You only have one chance—if you once drop out, you'll never go back."[4] Neither teachers nor students could expect to continue in the traditional way. The knowledge explosion alone gave good and sufficient indication that they could not expect to work in the same kind of university their professors attended, but had to find new ways of learning in collaborative effort.

Plans for the University of South Florida often took a prefigurative approach. Assuming that the interests of faculty and students converged on the art of navigation, all members would have to learn to chart a course for themselves in a university new to everyone's experience. Until they were tested in experience, no rules of thumb, no traditional readings and checkpoints, could be expected to give reliable bearings for a new university serving a constituency new to higher education during a period of expansion in higher education and tremendous growth in knowledge.

Prefigurative ways of work had to be evaluated for their educational effectiveness. Simple rank-order comparisons with other universities would give little guidance, especially if the rankings depended on progress in the postfigurative "academic lockstep" and the meritocratic practice of selecting fewer and fewer students for advancement to higher levels and degrees. New Students and new universities together had to prefigure an uncertain future. Their effectiveness would depend on the outcomes of planning, and on the convergence between the educational experience and the expectations for performance in future responsibilities and new roles coming over the horizon. In focusing on educational effectiveness in relation to expectations, USF was working against a tradition of evaluation by competitive rankings that strongly influenced the public understanding of the quality of higher education and the student experience.

The Double Bind

In the face of meritocratic tradition, almost any evaluative approach would put the University in a double bind, a "no-win" situation. If students did well, the conclusion would follow that faculty were lowering academic standards and practicing "grade inflation." If they did poorly, the University would clearly have the wrong kind of students, "poor college material." Any evidence, favorable or unfavorable, on the actual student experience was not going to prevail against the self-fulfilling prophecy that a university improves its quality by enrolling more students from the talented top tenth and flunking out more students from the bottom of the GPR rankings each year.

The evaluative design for USF implicitly tested the folklore against the actual student experience. At best the results indicated that the hypothesis about top-ranking students making a top-quality university was not proven.

Lew Mayhew devised an evaluative plan taking evidence from grades, GRE scores, course and instructor evaluation, and the College and University Environment Scale. For the first three years the evaluation of Basic Studies courses provided two additional measures that could be compared. The uniform final examination was considered to be comparatively free of interaction with the instructor's estimate of performance in class and to deal with the general mastery of elements common to all scholars in the field. Instructor grades could be taken as a measure affected by social interaction, students' special interests, and personal conditions of work.

The design assumed that students produce work which the instructor grades and helps them improve. Doing work of good quality is the student's ultimate concern; mastering content and technique is simply a means to that end, and an exam simply indicates directions for improvement.

The evaluative design measured congruence between instructor and examination indices as an indicator of the tendency either to teach students or to "teach toward the exam." Correlations should *not* indicate congruence between the indices if instructors were in fact emphasizing the students' exploration of the field of study rather than routine performance of standard assignments; the results should indicate considerable *incongruence* and discrepancy as evidence of effectiveness in personalized teaching and learning.

The initial study produced correlation coefficients too strong to be favorable.

Mayhew concluded that instructors were measuring the same variables that the uniform examination measured. Either they were not diversifying instruction as much as they could and should, or else they were not evaluating individual work in calculating grades but relying on tests and exercises standard for all students. He added, "This is too strong an agreement. It may be that one would want to assume that whatever the examination measures should be virtually the same as what is judged in the classes. I would be distressed if we made such a assumption."[5]

The faculty were generally making this assumption. Much concerned about fairness to students in competitive grading, they took pains to remove topics and items that were not covered in every section when they reviewed the preliminary draft with the examiner. They were not designing the examination to cover the range of scholarly interest, and they were not teaching toward the examination. But they were indeed assuming that the exam should cover only what every class covered. And in the process, part of the test of effectiveness in relation to the broad fields of scholarship was lost in the overall evaluative design.

Followup studies cannot be located but corrective measures are known to have been taken. The program faculties in the second term avoided the checking of exam items against the content of classroom instruction. They generated a greater variety of materials and techniques and were even bolder in challenging students to do independent work. For instance, files of material shared in the Human Behavior faculty in Term II are more than double the volume for Term I (1960–61). And results on the course and instructor evaluation for Term II showed a decided shift away from preoccupation with the instructor and the exam toward reading, independent investigation, and the possibilities open in the broad field of study. For instance, on one item students in Term II rated textbooks and other readings above all other techniques in terms of their value in learning, a decided shift away from results in Term I. They also indicated that they were improving in critical thinking and rated it much higher as a significant factor in learning during Term II.[6]

So the problem of excessive congruence seems to have been cured to some degree, if only by broadening the outlook of the faculty and the students on the field of study. And the higher ratings for course and instructor in the second term indicated that this change was in keeping with the interests of students.

Perceptions of the Student Experience

In general students saw themselves as performing well under exacting conditions of "high academic press." They indicated in conferences, class discussions, and evaluative reports that they were exerting genuine effort to meet challenges and contribute to the University. They knew they were doing better than expected, and they were very proud of themselves.

As most of the charter class approached graduation in 1963, these perceptions were assessed systematically by administering the College and University Environment Scale (cues) to a stratified sample of the student body each term.[7] In this study and in the analysis of scores on the Graduate Record Examination which all seniors had to take, usf results were compared with those from a group of 50 colleges and universities selected to represent a cross-section of high-quality institutions. A set of profiles compared data from usf, Antioch, Purdue, and the University of California at Los Angeles. The following five scales are utilized by cues:

> Practicality: indicative of an emphasis on procedures, personal status, practical benefits, order, supervision, school spirit, and student leadership in campus activities.

Community: describing a friendly, cohesive campus, congenial, with feelings of group welfare and group loyalty, the all-university sense of support and community.

Awareness: reflecting an emphasis on personal, dramatic, poetic, and political meaning, a search for self-understanding, opportunities for creative, esthetic experience and the expression of ideals in commitment to human welfare.

Propriety: suggesting an environment that is polite, cordial, prudent, considerate in decorum and personal relationships, with an absence of inconsiderate, demonstrative, assertive, and unconventional behavior.

Scholarship: indicative of an environment of competitively high academic achievement, commitment to scholarly work and the advancement of learning.

On all five scales, student ratings of the University of South Florida environment were consistently high. Only Antioch students rated theirs higher, on Awareness and Scholarship, than did USF students; in all other cases, USF ratings were higher than any others. The report states, "We are atypical in this regard, since the usual pattern is for a single school to be low on some scales and high on others."

The response pattern was consistent within and between different groups with a few variations. Seniors perceived "the USF climate as being less scholarly and conducive to less 'awareness' than any of the other classes." All classes rated USF lower on Practicality than any other scale. Ratings on Propriety suggested that "those living on campus perceive the environment as being less conventional (or more demonstrative and assertive) than those living off campus."

The developmental approach to services, activities, standards, and discipline in Student Affairs had been accompanied by criticism and predictions of disaster and disruption. While some people were surprised, the Student Affairs staff were pleased to find that students perceived the environment as characterized by high academic press, orderliness and mutual consideration, and a strong sense of community—in spite of the much-criticized "radicalism" of students, "looseness" of standards and discipline, and lack of school spirit due to the "ban on football."

The Graduates and the Grading System

In the words of the Scottish dominie's prayer, USF students had "a guid conceit o' theirsel's." Their self-esteem extended to the Graduate Record Examination. Some seniors went so far as to say they looked forward to the GRE and actually enjoyed it. Knowing that their qualifications would be assessed in light of the University's reputation, many of the charter class were as eager for the general results as for their own scores.

Results on general and area tests consistently showed USF seniors to have mean scores higher than those for the comparison group of 50 colleges. Indications that students had gained both depth and breadth of learning were in keeping with expectations of the founders and the charter faculty in designing programs with the accent on learning.

Vis-à-vis postfigurative, meritocratic models, evaluative results did little to get USF out of the double bind. There remained the persuasion that its obviously low-ranking New Students could not make the grade, unless the faculty practiced "grade inflation"— another self-fulfilling prophecy.

Evaluation Services accordingly constructed a performance model using high school grades and test scores to predict probable distribution of course grades at USF, verifying the model against actual grades at institutions having a similar student mix.[8] Since correlations of USF grades with high school grades and test scores were not reliable predictors, the performance model was designed to check the consistency in direction, as USF grades followed the general trend in high school grades and scores for each successive freshman cohort.

The actual distribution varies from the model by no more than 2–3 percentage points in any given year. The percentage of F's was lower by 2–5 points than the model indicated and the tendency for this proportion to decrease over the years was consistent with the trend to be expected as each cohort progressed through the degree program. Changes in general were too small to indicate any grade inflation. Proposals for strict cutoff points at the low end of the GPR rankings seemed to introduce an administrative artifact likely to have little or no effect on the overall quality of academic work.

Results were compared with data from the University of Florida and Florida State University; both enrolled a higher percentage of students scoring above 400 on the FTGT and a larger number of those having grades in the top tenth than did USF. The percentage of A's was higher at each institution than at USF by two or three points. The University of Florida showed the highest proportion of F's with USF next and FSU lowest, all within a range of two or three percentage points. Differences between grades earned at USF and the older universities did not even begin to approach the magnitude predicted on the basis of standings at admission.

But there was yet another place to look for grade inflation—in the "pabulum" dished out in Basic Studies and the "Mickey-Mouse" courses in Education. Evaluation Services compared grades against the predictive model and found no significant variances within or between colleges.[9]

Another study[10] tested a proposition that grades must become inflated as each faculty tends to treat its majors more generously than students taking electives. This hypothesis was not proven: in no college did majors consistently earn better grades than they did outside of the college.

As anticipated, majors in all colleges had their lowest combined averages in Basic Studies courses, which involved all students in academic work related to both weakest and strongest areas in their repertory of skills. Basic Studies majors did not fare as well as others; but this result was largely an administrative artifact: their numbers included those who had not yet declared a major or could not do so until they attained good standing, along with students committed to the very demanding Advanced Basic Studies major.

Combined GPR's for Education majors were higher than others in almost every case. Students from other colleges earned combined GPR's in elective Education courses below the level earned by the majors. But if this meant that Education instructors were grading majors generously, then instructors throughout the University must also be grading Education majors more generously than their own majors and other students taking electives: an absurd notion contrary to the original hypothesis.

In general the results of the evaluative design for assessing educational effectiveness showed the University doing a good job, and the students performing well in a strong academic program. No grade inflation appeared; the meritocratic assumption was not proven; no pabulum was being dished out in thin, undemanding courses; and the teachers were trying to make the exams fair to students but were not "teaching toward the exam."

Against the folklore all this evidence simply tended to reinforce the impression that something was wrong with the students, the academic program, the faculty, the grading system, or everything about the University of South Florida. It was just so *different* that it could not possibly attain high quality.

All of this bothered the charter class not at all. Enjoying all the benefits of coming new to higher education, they paid little heed to detractors. They were opening a new world of expectation and experience for themselves. They were doing good work and they enjoyed it. They were full of self-esteem and pride in the University.

Actual experience evaluated on a prefigurative model showed that USF was effective, not because it selected the best and brightest, but by virtue of the overall performance of the students and the faculty in their shared responsibilities. As students saw it, the quality of the University came primarily from their effective academic work, their initiative, and their contributions to others in their courses and voluntary activities. And that was the way the people who planned the University wanted to go. They wanted to work with students not as "college material" but as contributors to the advancement and sharing of learning, as navigators and explorers in their own right and responsibility.

12

Diversifying Administration

Transition to the Board of Regents

As its name indicated, so had the Board of Control functioned since 1905—primarily as an instrument of formal control by the state Cabinet over a small family of universities. With six new universities on the horizon, the board would clearly have to assume a broader scope of responsibility, in order to keep the growing administrative burden from overwhelming the Cabinet. Accordingly, their role as trustees needed clarification; educational concerns for orderly growth, service to regional constituencies and fields of scholarly study, and protection from arbitrary political interference called for greater autonomy in the universities and their governing board. And the board shared with the Cabinet the responsibility to serve the general public interest and to make government more fully accountable to the people for fair, honest, effective political dealings.

In 1963 the legislature passed a constitutional amendment designed to replace the Board of Control with a Board of Regents having 9 members. Appointment of one member each year for a 9-year term would guard against political domination by any governor or legislature. The Board of Regents would take greater responsibility to develop and manage academic, fiscal, personnel, and administrative policy. The Cabinet would no longer control transfer of funds and line-item expenditures but would rely primarily on its responsibility for quarterly release of funds under block appropriations in proportion to actual revenues, under the time-honored "pay-as-you-go" principle. Although regional representation was not contemplated—and impracticable—the selection of 9 members could be informally designed to insure some familiarity with each major constituency

225

and field of study related to the mission of the university system as a whole.

The legislature adjourned with much important business unfinished, and the governor immediately called a special session. The budget director and other advocates of centralized control persuaded the legislature to recall and reconsider the higher education amendment and to delete sections concerning the broader scope of responsibility and authority given to the Board of Regents in fiscal and personnel matters. The legislature finally passed an amendment that left the Board of Regents under Cabinet authority in almost the same position as the Board of Control.

The voters approved this amendment in November 1964. In January 1965 the Board of Regents came into being after much haggling over rival claims of the outgoing and the incoming governor to the prerogative of appointing its first members. Accountable for action within a rapidly growing, increasingly diversified university system, while lacking the necessary autonomy and capability for effective response to changes affecting higher education, the Board of Regents represented a classic example of "Latham's principle of administrative absurdity": it could only relay decisions even farther from their educational context to an even more remote political process.

Accreditation Standards

Into this situation came the visiting team from the Southern Association of Colleges and Schools, to make the final study and recommendations that advanced the University of South Florida to fully accredited membership in December 1965. The team found the University to be in violation of standards for administrative and fiscal autonomy, authority, and responsibility:[1]

> There can be no doubt that the University, through no fault of its own, is in violation of Standards Two and Four. It, and other units of the University System, *is* subject to outside influence, and other officers of the state, specifically the State Board of Education and the Budget Commission, *do* have authority to alter budgeted figures approved by the Board of Control. . . .
>
> It should be noted, however, that the University of Florida and Florida State University also are in violation of these Standards. If the Committee on Admissions considers the University of South Florida meets all Standards except these, then this Committee does not believe

membership should be withheld because of this situation which is beyond its control.

The Committee is unanimous in its belief that the situation in Florida is so grave that it merits careful consideration by the Council of the Commission.

The Southern Association followed through on the recommendation and sent representatives from its Council to confer with university administrators, regents, and members of the Cabinet and legislature. Impending changes in federal law reinforced proposals from sacs and the universities to reduce Cabinet controls over expenditures and to increase the autonomy and scope of responsibility for the Board of Regents in personnel matters and other administrative affairs. Effective July 1, 1967, new statutes gave the Board of Regents a broader, more diversified role and scope commensurate with the accreditation standards of the Southern Association.

In formulating the original amendment of 1963 to create the Board of Regents, the legislature had addressed problems of coordinating a complex university system and reducing arbitrary political intervention such as the Johns Committee exemplified. It also had anticipated the extension of federal acts on fair labor practices to include colleges and universities. In 1965 it began to prepare for compliance, directing the Cabinet to bring all state employees into the Merit System except faculty and other categories exempt from the wage and hour acts. The Cabinet authorized the budget director to employ Cresap, McCormick, and Paget to design an expanded Merit System taking in 33,000 additional positions.

The consultants apparently carried out the survey as specified. The plan presented in April 1966 followed the *scalar principle of organization,* assuming that a single employment category and the job classifications, serial rankings, and salary scales within it would fit every type of agency, mission, and program, and that rank would determine the degree of responsibility in each position. In conducting the survey, the consultants found a Merit System category whose specifications seemed to match each position in the universities and then established job description, qualifications, rank, and salary scale according to the Merit System listings. For instance, positions for psychologists had the same specifications whether in a university, prison, employment service, or health and welfare agency.

The consultants also graded the salary scale in each category according to age and size of the university, with the top grade III for the University of Florida, grade II for Florida State University, and grade I for all other universities. For example, heads of colleges at USF, classed as Dean I, had a lower salary scale than counterparts at Gainesville classed as Dean III. The Cresap, McCormick, and Paget report downgraded the salary scale for 46 percent of the 650 positions classified at the University of South Florida.

OUTRAGEOUS LACK OF MERIT

Every single university registered outrage. One respondent stated simply, "This study fails on every count." John Allen wrote that the proposed system was unworkable and much more effective systems were already in operation. Based on actual functions rather than dubious comparisons with jobs unrelated to higher education, the USF personnel system required less than half as many categories and ranks. The report listed whole sets of job descriptions that had not been used in the general system of higher education for 25 years or more—if ever. It disregarded many categories in current use, especially in student personnel administration. Grading universities defied all logic: each was growing so rapidly that neither its age nor the size of its enrollment would affect its overall responsibilities or the tasks assigned to any particular job.[2] The University of Florida also objected that grading universities and introducing competition for advancement on a career ladder within the state system would be counterproductive, especially with its general disadvantage in a highly competitive national market.

The personnel committee at the University of Florida probably expressed the general reaction. It observed feelings of "frustration . . . a sense of near helplessness" pervading the faculty and staff; its members considered that "mere presentation for review has done severe damage to employee morale." The proposal would disrupt effective systems already consistent with most of the necessary standards. Job descriptions were regularly validated against annual reports for updating to fit the actual, unique combination of functions in each position. The specifications for the survey and the consultant's report required no such validation; they identified no commonalities, applied no standards of professional practice, and recognized no interaction among functions in each position and unit in the universities. For example, the uniform qualification of counselors based on a high school diploma and six years of experience was at best an anachronism; it disregarded completely many current standards requiring advanced degrees, professional certification, and special experience, in many types of positions related to counseling and guidance.

In short, the design was devoid of theoretical principles and applied unexamined assumptions without essential tests against actual experience. The original specifications rendered the entire merit system plan invalid on its face.[3]

AUTONOMY FOR THE UNIVERSITIES

The principal conclusion to be drawn from the Cresap, McCormick, and Paget report was that general principles and procedures could be established in compliance with federal acts and Merit System regulations. Beyond that point, responsibility had to go to universities and state agencies for designing and validating job classifications and descriptions compatible with actual requirements on the scene of the action.

Under a legislative act of 1967, the Board of Regents assumed responsibility for personnel policy and practices concerning Teaching and Research, Administrative and Professional, and Career Service employees. The sus councils and Board of Regents restored the personnel systems in the universities and brought systemwide policy and procedure into line with federal acts and Merit System principles for classifying jobs and setting salary scales. At usf 90 percent of the downgraded positions resumed their previous classification and salary, and a few Career Service salaries were brought up to par with Merit System scales. The Board of Regents simply ignored the grading of universities I–II–III.

Out of the whole experience came considerable clarification of roles, principles and procedures, some stronger guarantees for fair practices and equal employment opportunity, and the right of university employees to organize and bargain collectively. The administrators and personnel staff at usf had incorporated most of these principles and safeguards in the original personnel system. Procedures and documentation had sometimes been less formal than the law now required, and more options had been left to supervisory judgment than the new guidelines sometimes permitted. Adjustments were tedious but usually involved little modification in the general approach to personnel services.

Delegation of responsibility to the Board of Regents, and removal of the cumbersome procedure for Cabinet approval of promotions and high-level appointments, facilitated recruiting and compensated somewhat for disadvantages in the academic marketplace. Above all, legislation and systemwide policy had once again followed the principle of diffusing responsibility through an institutional network, instead of establishing a monolithic organization for centralized control.

Gains came at some cost. The scalar principle of organization was firmly embedded in government, and the scalar concept of a "career ladder" was embodied in federal guidelines for equal opportunity and fair employment practices.[4] The universities had developed an orderly process for validating job descriptions against annual reports as a basis for updating them, modifying classification and salary scales according to the changes in programs and conditions of work. But documenting this action also to the state Merit System and the U.S. Department of Labor more than doubled the burden on the personnel staff in the universities and the Chancellor's staff. Moreover, in justifying some modifications, documentation to government agencies had to go beyond the evidence from experience and show that the changes conformed to a career ladder within the employment category and its specifications for advancement with training and experience.

Given the unique configuration of responsibility required for almost every position in relation to the process of planning and administration for the whole university, it was hard to document the career ladder. Steps on the ladder were assumed to correspond to serial ranks within bureaucratic levels determined partly by the distance from the center of control and partly by the number and rankings of positions under supervision. As a consequence, some positions could not be assigned a rank or salary scale commensurate with actual requirements of competence, experience, and volume of work, because they involved no supervision. For instance, secretaries to deans and directors and receptionists for Admissions and Registrar's offices carried a heavy burden requiring expertise in facilitating participation in all sorts of academic and administrative affairs by members of the University and the general public; but this significant responsibility for participation did not count because they supervised few if any other employees.

Still, the career ladder had to be documented somehow in order to meet tests for equality of opportunity in employment entry and career advancement, salary equalization, and other criteria of adequacy in affirmative action. The "Peter Principle"—the tendency for competitive systems embodying a career ladder to advance people to "the level of maximum incompetence"[5]—consequently began to operate. Through provisions for dual appointment, lateral mobility, advancement in salary with increasing responsibility, and flexibility in assigning tasks according to function in administrative systems, the University had capitalized on special personal experience and competence throughout the ranks of faculty and staff. Without disrupting orderly systems, departmental faculties and the staff of administrative units could often share opportunities to enlarge experience and cultivate shared resources for career development, without changing their table of organization or job classifications. These advantages began to diminish as the Peter Principle began to take greater effect.

Irrationals surfaced frequently enough to strengthen an impression that the universities were in the grip of depersonalized bureaucracy. People began to grumble about becoming mere cogs in the machinery and to complain about dysfunctions in the apparatus. The personnel system had to draw lines distinguishing employment categories in administration, faculty, and general staff. These began to form barriers interfering with carefully cultivated linkages in planning and communication systems. Complaints over many consequent dysfunctions tended to center on dissatisfaction with the all-University approach. Proposals for solving problems began to crystallize around a governmental model as an alternative, having a separate senate for each employment category with legislative functions in planning and policy development. A growing concern for equal representation in governance came along with concerns for equal opportunity and fair employment practices.

Autonomy and Accountability

In 1967 under the administration of Governor Claude Kirk—an entrepreneur strongly inclined toward centralized management—the state appeared to settle on a problem-solving approach to planning with maintenance of equilibrium the prime objective. At the same time, public outrage over shady deals in the state administration and legislature called for statutory remedies. Based on the principle of government's accountability to the people, legislation typically proceeded on the assumption that strong controls must be imposed by centralized authorities operating "in the sunshine," with proceedings and records open to press and public. The general approach to planning and accountability, favored by press, public, and legislature, seemed to follow Mark Twain's maxim: "Put all your eggs in one basket—and *watch that basket.*"

Organization and administration in the universities were developing along other lines. The general approach followed the principle of diffusing responsibility to those points where people collaborating in study and action are first of all accountable to each other for the results and then to the whole organization for the effects of their action on its mission.

Various proposals were consequently advanced to bring the State University System into line with the principle of accountability under centralized control. The most retrograde would have restored Cabinet control over personnel and budget matters or created a monolithic State University with undergraduate branches serving regional constituencies.

In the matter of accountability, the scalar principle of organization once more had to give way. The universities had developed beyond the point where the system could be brought under centralized control; programs were too diversified, and the burden of planning and administration was too great for any monolithic organization to carry. Accountability had to go with the responsibility that had to be diffused throughout the university system and within each institution. In the face of increasing needs in all the regional constituencies for postbaccalaureate studies, constraints on program development could not be justified: the principle of accountability for action in the public interest stood in the way. The network of universities developed in 1956 stood the test of experience and the test of accountability.

Many urgent tasks still remained in linking the universities with the state's planning stystem. In 1967 Broward Culpepper, the chancellor who saw the State University System through its first phase of exponential growth under the Board of Control, went to Texas Women's University. The appointment of his successor, Robert Mautz, in 1968 marked the beginning of a second phase involving the development of more formal policies and an augmented staff to manage the network of universities, their interaction with community agencies and social systems, and the linkages of the State University System with the state government under the new Board of Regents. Dr. Mautz came from the University of Florida, where he had been a professor of law and Vice-President for Academic Affairs. Having a strong sense of order in administrative proceedings and their documentation, he was also knowledgeable about communication and planning systems and the complex statutes, guidelines, and judicial actions affecting higher education.

Mautz sought to reduce the impact of "administrative absurdity" on the university system by locating responsibility at the scene of the action and setting up a conciliar process for planning and coordination with the state's executive and legislative agencies. A vice-chancellor worked with a council of university vice-presidents for each area of Administration, Academic, and Student Affairs, and the chancellor worked with the Council of Presidents. Committees with representative membership had functional assignments such as articulation with public schools and community colleges and development of management information, personnel, and budget systems.

To the dismay of some people, the chancellor's staff multiplied almost overnight. In 1969 its size approached that of the charter faculty of USF (about 100), prompting a disgruntled professor to suggest that removing the Chancellor's Office en bloc to set up a new university would be a great improvement in economy and efficiency. (Ironically, some of the more experienced staff did go to Miami to set up the new Florida International University that very year.) This staff, in fact, was none too large for the actual burden entailed in the manifold linkages among universities, communities, and government agencies.

Sometimes people tend to forget that administrators and trustees have a teaching job, too. Their work load cannot often be managed according to formula, either; the need to know and the volume of transactions involving external agencies are unpredictable. In Florida, state officials and university administrators confronted political power struggles inimical to the public interest and episodic decisions from the Cabinet and legislature that were generally dissonant with effective operations of the universities. They shared responsibility for developing more orderly, constructive ways of work. Together, they had to do a considerable amount of teaching and learning. In order to support this effort more effectively, both the University of South

Florida and the Chancellor's Office now had to catch up with the development of administrative resources that had been given low priority during the first decade of expansion.

Some analysts have predicted a more rapid increase in administrative positions than in other categories of university employment, well into the 1980s. As more extensive, effective linkages with all sorts of public and private undertakings consolidate, many universities and state systems will probably have to augment administrative staff and diversify their roles and functions. The responsibilities traditionally assigned to university administrators and trustees include this important function of collaborative study and action among many institutions serving the public interest. Strengthening resources for this important *institutional* dimension of "continuing education" may also involve new roles for faculty and students, along with a greater number and variety of administrative positions.

Productivity

When Dr. Mautz took office, there was a decided shift in state government from episodic, problem-solving actions toward a more orderly, constructive planning process. Governor Kirk was generating a flurry of legislative activity concerning principles of planning and accountability. He also appointed a blue-ribbon committee of executives from business and industry to study the educational system, charging them to improve its management efficiency and productivity.

One outcome of the committee's study was the "Twelve-Hour Teaching Law," F.S. 71.365, enacted in 1968. It was hailed as a means of "putting faculty back into the classroom" and improving the quality of higher education by introducing the sound management principle of productivity. The productivity formula for faculty assignment developed under this act was almost identical with the standard contract established by the Board of Control in 1963 and in effect translated its standard assignment of 12 credit hours of teaching into 12 "contact hours" per week in the classroom.

The productivity formulae are based on FTE enrollment, produced by dividing aggregate credit hours by 15 for undergraduate, 12 for graduate courses. The FTE enrollment figures are then divided by a *productivity factor*. It is the productivity *factor* that actually generates instructional time in FTE faculty lines to match enrollment, and dollars to match salary scales. This is not a standard formula but has to be a negotiated figure that takes salary into account. Set in 1968 at 395 for undergraduate and 290 for graduate FTE enrollment, its size has varied, mostly upward. The productivity factor loads undergraduate more heavily than graduate instructional lines, fixes each line at the undergraduate or graduate level, and influences the range in section size for each category of courses.

Similar formulae had been used by the Board of Control and were in general use in higher education. But many institutions were beginning to discover that these traditional formulae tended to impair the effectiveness of planning and program development, especially in urban universities. All across the country, administrators and faculties were trying to work out other approaches, more consistent with actual experience. The Florida universities suggested several alternatives to the regents, blue-ribbon committee, and legislature. In general, these proposals addressed shortcomings that might be corrected by examining the underlying assumptions.

First, the assumption that learning takes place in a classroom is consistent with the fact that students learn by taking courses. But course work involves learning that is also the result of advising, counseling, private study, studio and field work, and other activities that may or may not relate to "contact hours." Any adequate planning formulae should therefore take into account the broader scope and variety of learning inside and outside the classroom. Educational planning also confronts the fact that each course is unique and involves "piece work" that simply has to be done regardless of the differing amounts of real time that teachers and students may invest. The analogy to "hourly work" in an office or assembly line does not fit academic work; and classroom time alone will not measure adequately the resources and effort required.

Second, scalar models applied to level of instruction appear to have little rationale other than habit. In actual experience, the principal factors affecting the quality of teaching and learning appear to be developmental and relate more to teaching methods than to levels of courses. An inclination to reserve certain methods for a specific level of instruction goes along with habit but may be counterproductive.

For instance, students often carry into graduate school some imbalances in capabilities that entail an added burden for teachers who have to deal with them—traditionally in "hand-tooled," personalized ways. It is conceivable that some imbalances could be reduced by more effective, personalized ways of undergraduate instruction. To the extent that section size may affect the flexibility necessary for personalized instruction, the practice of loading undergraduate more heavily than graduate teaching assignments may work to the disadvantage of graduate education. Some gains at both levels might come from loading assignments equally or distributing load according to method instead of level.

Universities have developed a diversified repertory of instructional methods, including some that are traditional to graduate study and others drawn from early childhood education. Out of this repertory, teachers can fit ways of learning fairly compatibly to individual students' experience and expectations. This personalized approach seems effective in facilitating mature development of capabilities at any stage of progress toward a degree. The productivity principle emphasizes quality of education; the suggestion of developing planning formulae based on effective instructional methods appears consistent with this emphasis.

Third, the traditional pattern of continuous, full-time enrollment does not fit typical patterns in urban institutions—a significant proportion of part-time students, "swinging-door" enrollment at irregular intervals, and episodic participation in continuing education. In a residential setting, the difference between FTE and "head-count" enrollment has minimal effect on budget projections and teaching assignments. In urban institutions, with a large proportion of part-time students, slippage of FTE figures below whole-student figures tends to produce errors and discrepancies between actual needs and the distribution of resources, wherever student participation rather than enrollment status determines the functions and time required. Refinements in productivity models might profitably move toward sets of formulae, including some designed to capture effects of whole-student participation that escape formulae based on credit hours and FTE enrollment.

Part of the difficulty with the productivity principle appeared to come from the effort to simplify the planning process by adopting a single set of formulae. In practice, such an approach often tends to complicate rather than simplify matters. Complex processes often have been simplified more effectively by developing diversified techniques and formulae, each specific to a different set of conditions (or data base) while producing results related to some measurable commonality. For instance, time in clock hours can be produced out of real-time records, whole students, FTE enrollment, or contact hours in the classroom; the results should be reasonably commensurable and free from random error, if the relation of time to each variable is validated in experience.

Along this line, faculty and staff in each administrative area at USF were working on refinements that might both strengthen and simplify the planning process by applying more diversified sets of productivity formulae, capturing the effects of different functions, teaching repertory, and conditions of work.

Some groups canvassed refinements taking into account both whole-student and FTE enrollment and assessing the interactive effects of section size and instructional methods and settings. Some looked for sets of formulae that would combine teaching, research, advising, and community service as integrative functions rather than treat them as independent areas of faculty effort; such formulae might indicate ways to provide a better balance between resources and commitments in all areas. Others worked on diversified sets of formulae related to administrative functions, some affected by student participation, others directly related to timetables (e.g., accounting, construction, maintenance, and procurement schedules). These approaches generally centered on commensurable commonalities in process, such as time in clock hours, on which diversified formulae could converge in developing reasonable cost estimates.

This was not altogether an exercise in futility. Recommendations seemed to have little influence on the productivity principles eventually adopted under the "Twelve-Hour Act." But some did contribute to refinements in the systemwide process for defining commensurable factors, establishing a common data base, cumulating evidence, and generating budget estimates. Some techniques had internal uses in program planning at the departmental level, where the distribution of resources commensurate with effort has the most significant effect and can balance oversights and errors that will be produced by any generalized planning formulae. Pertinent questions for institutional research and planning surfaced, including the patent need for studies of faculty load and distribution of effort in real time, and the creation of methods dealing with factors related to "piece work" as the predominant pattern in teaching and learning.

In the general system of higher education, questions were surfacing about the compatibility of the educational process with some planning models that were coming into vogue during the 1950s and 1960s. For instance, the Department of Health, Education, and Welfare inclined toward a "delivery of service" model, which influenced the design of such programs as Student Financial Aid and Special Services for Disadvantaged Students. Taking students as clients or consumers, in keeping with this model, discounts their contributions to academic work on which universities necessarily rely in carrying out the responsibility at the heart of their mission, the advancement and sharing of knowledge.[6] The role of student as contributor or investor also escapes productivity models that do not correct the traditional concept of students as raw material, graduates as finished product. This "assembly-line" assumption inclines toward the fallacy of reification—treating people as things—which may be downright sinful.

Unless contributive roles are well-defined for both students and faculty, a productivity model may also mislead those interpreting results, by neglecting the actual products—goods, services, works of art, publications, and other benefits that colleges and universities pour out every day into the mainstream of community life. These returns exceed the investment almost beyond belief, and the costly effort to define real products and trace their diffusion may not be worthwhile. Even an informal study on a very small scale—for a department or program—will clearly indicate how any investigation of broader scope is likely to do little more than to confirm the common persuasion that education has incalculable value for communities and societies as well as individuals.

Even without such costly calculations, the fact that universities produce real valuables can be established in the assumptions undergirding planning models. This assumption confirms the role of faculty and students as producers, investors, or contributors, in keeping with experience. From this perspective, it may be possible to refine and simplify the overall planning process in several ways. For instance, the productivity formula for faculty load matches students' time with faculty time in the classroom. This necessary calculation can be done directly, without the two additional steps involved in calculating full-time equivalency and level of instruction, when questionable distinctions in enrollment status and value of performance in different types of academic work are disregarded.

Planning models tend to perpetuate such administrative artifacts and anachronisms, which can become redundant, inefficient, and misleading. A well-designed planning system will include adequate feedback from experience into a process for updating and refining the model itself and its underlying assumptions. In Florida's productivity model, feedback for cost control operates through budget and personnel audits. A process yielding evaluative information requisite to quality control in teaching and learning does not seem to be adequately developed. Neither does the model appear to provide useful indicators such as the goodness of fit between instructional methods and distribution of effort and resources, relating to design factors other than time.

Considering shortcomings in design, many people feared that the effects of the productivity model would fall short of expectations for developing academic work of high quality. Like the Merit System proposal, it seemed to supplant planning systems and neglect essential tests against experience that were more consistent with principles of cost and quality control and more effective in maintaining equilibrium in the process of program development.

Evaluation

The Twelve-Hour Act required the universities to establish a procedure for evaluation of instruction with student participation, and left the substantive design of criteria, evidence, and instruments to their staff and faculties. Systemwide procedure for faculty evaluation for promotion and tenure followed the steps outlined in the University's temporary organization and the Board of Control policy of 1963: peer review in the department proceeds to the dean, vice-president, and president, with recommendations for tenure and promotion going to the Board of Regents. Due process guarantees provide for appeal from evaluative decisions, or petition on any other complaint or grievance, to the chairman and dean, then to the Academic Relations Committee, with final action by the president.

USF continued to use much the same evaluative instruments and information adopted in 1960, including an annually updated curriculum vitae and an optional self-evaluation. Procedures for peer review vary among departments and colleges. In a fairly typical example, an elected committee rates each member of the department and prepares an Annual Faculty Evaluation Summary. Each instructor reviews the summary with the chairman, who adds his rating and forwards the documents for the remaining steps in the process.

Items on the summary call for ratings and percent of effort in each level of teaching, in research and creative activity, in advising and service to the University, profession, and public, and in administrative assignments and professional development in service or on leave of absence. Overall gains in productivity, effectiveness, and professional development are rated for the year. Small, average, and large salary increments, or none at all, may be recommended.

Instructions to raters call for "comparison with others in a similar position with similar assignments"—although similarity may be hard to find where almost every assignment involves a unique configuration of responsibilities. Faculty members and staff in Academic Affairs report that several departments solve this problem by sorting their members' documents according to rough assessments of quantity and quality of effort. Then they turn to the summary and assign ratings on each item within high, middle, and low groupings. Thus, they avoid to some degree the fallacious rank-order comparison of "apples with oranges" that Russell Cooper so earnestly wished to escape.

Faculty members generally agree that the evaluation system needs more thorough testing and refinement in design. Major points of dissatisfaction relate to the need for some weighting of each type of evidence in relation to program priorities; others relate to principles that have still not been settled for including, excluding, or weighting results from the students' Course and Instructor Evaluation, and to the need for criteria and measures for assessing progress in research, activity in the performing arts, and professional and community service. "Publish or perish" appears to operate in some fashion, but many people desire more clearly defined criteria, both quantitatitive and qualitative.

In general, a concern for procedures strengthening fairness and consistency in rating and interpretation predominates. Two refinements in design could provide some appropriate safeguards and capture more of the unique experience of each faculty member. Performance objectives could be established at the beginning of each year, and pertinent criteria and evidence could be specified for each task in the unique assignment, as a basis for comparison with actual performance at year's end. Principles of performance evaluation typically call for such a baseline, tested against the actual tasks assigned to each member, overall coverage of the department's responsibilities, and interaction with others in shared responsibilities.

Nothing appears to prevent any faculty, department, or college from developing such an approach to supplement or supplant an existing design. Few if any seem to have done so.

In general, the temporary evaluation system of 1960 still does duty and seems to have been refined minimally, although many of the faculty have extensive experience in evaluative design and research. The situation in 1975 resembled the case of the shoemaker's children: the University's own evaluation system was still going bootless in makeshift sandals with laces and straps dangling at loose ends.

One loose end appears in the gap between the evaluation process and the planning process out of which time and money for academic work are generated. Faculty evaluation primarily serves the internal rank-salary-tenure system. External connections to the process of general budget development and the appropriations process do not appear equally serviceable. These components of planning seem to need procedural safeguards for fair, adequate distribution of resources commensurate with the required effort.

This gap in the planning system tends to strengthen faculty perceptions that political finesse rather than educational effectiveness is the factor actually in operation in the evaluation system. By separating teaching from other activities, the productivity formula for faculty assignment has also aroused anxiety over a tendency for preoccupation with the classroom to attenuate resources for research, governance, and community service that must sustain the educational experience in equally important qualitative ways.

Experience with the productivity model tends to confirm anxieties over potentially regressive effects. In 1970, at the end of the first biennium under the new state planning system, a USF study of faculty effort indicated a shift toward teaching and away from research and community service.[7] Over the first five or six years, distribution of effort held fairly close to the 1959 model: approximately 70 percent in instruction, 10 percent each in research and publication, professional and community service, and advising and university service. In 1970, classroom instruction represented approximately 78 percent of faculty effort; research and publication, advising, and other university service took 6 percent each, and community service 4 percent. Apart from consultation and activity in professional associations, however, community service represented less than one-half of one percent of faculty effort—including adult and continuing education.

The marked shift toward the classroom is consistent with the intent of the Twelve-Hour Act; but it is out of line with equally important commitments to strengthen teaching and learning through research and community service. Faculty estimates of the *direction* of change proved correct, and raised many of the same questions that the Southern Association raised in 1973 about general evidence of a significant departure from commitments in the historic mission of universities.

Two direction indicators for refinement in the system stand out. First, the productivity model must be tested against the entire mission of the universities. Its emphasis on teaching requires particular attention to the generative processes in research and community service that actually sustain high quality in teaching and learning. Second, evaluative design should strengthen the criteria and evidence related to performance in teaching and should add measures of effectiveness in university and community service, in order to provide adequate coverage of the actual responsibilities of the faculty.

A Steady State

Another significant development during Governor Kirk's administration was the adoption of a new Florida Constitution in 1968. The new document provided a firm base for consolidating the state's organs and systems for planning and coordination. By 1970, the general planning system had settled on a zero-based budget framework with steady-state assumptions.

This planning model can operate on a number of different principles and assumptions about goals and processes. These elements of design, however, did not seem clearly defined and understood when the new budgeting procedure was first introduced, beyond the simple necessity for a balanced budget on the time-honored "pay-as-you-go" principle.

The universities, sus councils, and Board of Regents worked out the best assumptions they could draw from experience. In general they took "steady state" to mean zero-basing annual budgets and matching mid-range plans to inflation rate. Long-range plans, looking ahead for a decade or more, would have to be roughly outlined and held in abeyance. New departures in any range would have to be funded out of program cutbacks, cost-saving, resource-sharing, or new revenue.

Along these lines, each university developed an approach to program planning and budgeting consistent with its role and philosophy. As a general rule, each aimed to keep new, developing, and modified programs within a reasonable range around midpoint, when ranked in order of their productivity ratio (aggregate credit hours/faculty lines). None should have too heavy a burden (high productivity ratio) to be educationally effective, none too low a productivity ratio to be economically feasible. The upper and lower limits were checked against pertinent experience with design factors such as instructional methods.

The faculty of each program and college created several alternatives for each component of the University's general plan. These went forward through University and sus councils to closure on a systemwide plan that capitalized as fully as possible on resource-sharing within and between universities. Both internal and inter-university alternatives proved useful. For example, Classics and Ancient Studies found a home with Religious Studies at usf; and the regents approved a proposal from fsu to transfer its Ph.D. candidates in Engineering to the University of South Florida.

In allocating educational and general appropriations, the usf plans continued to set first priority on academic program. With the advent of the productivity formulae, Activities and Service fees (a surcharge on tuition for full-time students) came under increasing pressure. These funds were available for some discretionary outlay; they had been used to strengthen student services and student-initiated activities and also to supplement Educational and General (E.&G.) funds for some first-priority, academically related activities and events. Accordingly, Joe Howell, the new vice-president, mounted a study of Student Affairs programs, asking a task force to develop plans for each unit that would maintain high-quality programs and rely more heavily on A.&S. funding in order to relieve some pressure on E.&G. funds.

Reading the revenue estimates and planning documents was not exactly conducive to high morale. Members of task forces were also apprehensive about the possibility of cutbacks for administrative convenience, rather than as a consequence of financial pressures. Pressures toward conformity with uniform program-budget models as well as inflationary pressures occasioned considerable anxiety. Two examples may suggest the extent of these complex problems.

RESOURCE-SHARING

The task force for the Health Service recognized the urgent need for improving treatment facilities but confronted the skyrocketing cost of medical-nursing services in general. Howell suggested that the Ambulatory Care Center of the Colleges of Medicine and Nursing or the Outpatient Clinic of the University Community Hospital might share some resources. Neither option was likely to be practicable because of the exorbitant cost of change orders in facilities under construction; and in fact neither arrangement proved feasible.

Consequently, the University physician, Robert Egolf, sought some clarification of administrative intent. If the president and vice-president did not intend to consider more promising approaches, he was "not willing to preside over the elimination of my program and my job." No clarification was forthcoming, and Egolf resigned to resume private practice.

Then Dr. Howell informally worked out a three-part plan. In annual planning, first priority went to maintaining the present high quality in health education, preventive and consulting services for admissions-advising-orientation, residence halls, the Personal Resource Center, and recreation-athletics. Environmental health and safety services were transferred to facilities management. Second priority went to upgrading medical-nursing services (diagnosis, short-term treatment modalities, and referral to community inpatient and outpatient centers for long-term or intensive care). In mid-range planning, high priority in the general Student Affairs area went to relocation of the Health Center in improved facilities. Long-range alternatives could be explored for new approaches such as a Health Maintenance Organization for the USF membership or the whole neighborhood. The emphasis on educational and preventive programs was consistent with the principle of early intervention, well-tested as an effective way of capitalizing on shared resources and responsibilities.

FRONTIER SPIRIT

In Student Publications, Howell established a standing advisory board rather than a task force. The advisor, Leo Stalnaker, an experienced journalist, had strongly supported student editors and staff in developing a first-rate newspaper and yearbook and producing occasional publications on special topics. The *Oracle* had regularly won national awards for excellence, and circulation had increased over the University neighborhood with consequent increase in advertising revenues.

Within the year, the Publications Board had formally documented program planning, evaluative procedures, and professional standards of quality and ethical practice in reporting, editorials, and advertising. It had redesigned the program, replacing the costly yearbook with quarterly reviews published by a special staff as *Oracle* supplements. Adding a professional advisor for advertising gave reasonable expectation for revenues to approach full self-support in the near future.

Suddenly, in December 1973, President Mackey instructed the Publications Board to move the program off campus to function as a private enterprise. A number of universities had divested themselves of student publications, among them the University of Florida and Florida State University. Mackey forwarded a letter from Chancellor Mautz indicating that this action was an acceptable alternative.

The Publications Board was not disposed to dismantle an effective operation with a strong performance record. The members sympathized with the president in his dilemma: as publisher of record, a university president confronts a role conflict, wherein any prior censorship effecting his responsibility as publisher will compromise his commitment to academic freedom, in appearance if not in reality. But the board also had a dilemma: it could find no policy authorizing any executive action on its part, but it had to take some action on the president's directive. After prolonged deliberations, the members agreed that the board must respectfully decline to do anything at all about the directive. A faculty representative explained, "We can only delegate the responsibility back to the president."

After informal consideration of the problem, Dr. Howell proposed to continue the student publications program under year-to-year authorization. President Mackey agreed in June 1974 to authorize operation for the next fiscal year.

Centers of Responsibility

Some problems of locating responsibility seem to arise out of the scalar principle of organization—although people tend to look for their source in conditions of academic work. The assumption that an effective organization must have a single center of control seems to generate problems in organizations with diversified programs, especially on matters of prior approval from the center of authority. A corollary assumption, that degrees of authority and responsibility must necessarily diminish as the distance from the center increases, compounds these problems. Anxiety over weakening the center by taking away authority arouses counteractive apprehension over weakening capacities for responsible action on the periphery.

Consequently, organizations may develop a tendency to oscillate between overloading and frustrating first the peripheral agencies and then the administrative center. In the experience of the Florida universities, this tendency appeared from time to time, especially in their relations to state government. Decisions by the cabinet and legislature tended to swing back and forth between principles of centralizing and diffusing responsibility, between pyramid and network models for organization and planning. The universities held a fairly steady course, in keeping with standards and practices well-tested in the general system of higher education. But they had to cope with recurrent swings and episodic actions that often threatened to disrupt linkages with government and community agencies. To realize in practice the steady state assumed in the state's planning model of 1970 was a consummation devoutly to be wished, especially in terms of settling on consistent principles of locating responsibility and control.

USF resolved some problems and avoided others both internal and external by locating responsibility as close as possible to the scene of the action. As new universities came into being and the Board of Regents assumed greater responsibility in such matters as the administration of a general personnel system, the State University System followed the same principle to good effect.

Some advantages of locating responsibility according to function seem particularly clear in the case of the student publications program at USF. No single agency can even begin to carry the burden of prior approval for the enormous volume of published and broadcast material pouring out of a university every day. In actual practice, the president is the last person in a university who ever wants to do anything about its published material, except his own. On this reliable assumption, the editors and advisers had to act as if they also had the publisher's responsibility; and the backup system for planning, advice, counsel, and support by the Publications Board and vice-president left an appeal to the president as a last resort—should all systems fail by some extraordinary concatenation of circumstances.

There must be a last resort in any effective system—unless organizations are to continue oscillating, periodically overloading and frustrating some of their members. At some point, matters have to be brought to some sort of closure; and in the Florida universities, that point is located in the president's office. University presidents are fairly well accustomed to act on the extraordinary. It is the ordinary, everyday matters that can overwhelm a central administration, increasing costs and inefficiency in its work that tend to spread through the whole organization. Effective organizations provide the capability to bring everyday matters to closure as soon as possible, by diffusing responsibility and authority along with the work to be done. They usually save the resources of the central administration to cope with the extraordinary and the inevitable workings of Murphy's Law ("If anything can go wrong, it will").

Accreditation standards consequently emphasize the shared responsibility of students, faculties, administrators, and trustees for developing strong networks for teaching and research. These standards have stood up under recurrent pressure, and have steadily been refined over decades of experience. In making the transition from the Board of Control to the Board of Regents, the principle of shared responsibility embodied in educational standards helped to carry Florida's government and universities through a time of change and adaptation, in the midst of rapid growth and development.

Yet it often seems hard for people to understand the generative center for teaching and learning, on which universities also capitalize for planning and control—perhaps because it has multiple locations and can grow into many different forms. Learning involves a triadic configuration of people, process, and resources, which can be set up wherever shared responsibility for study and action may be required—at the top, bottom, or center of an organization, or out in the field. Such triadic configurations can vary quantitatively in any dimension and develop linkages with other configurations in any direction, without losing integrity and cohesiveness.

Almost as a matter of habit, universities generate multiple sets of triadic configurations (classes, committees, councils) and tie them together for a term, a year, or decades of collaborative work. Multiple linkages sustain cohesive networks both internal and external—for programs and disciplines within colleges within universities, across the general system of higher education and into other social systems of state, national, and international scope.

An ancient tradition of the community of scholars has carried down through the centuries the understanding of these generative centers and coherent networks that hold people together in shared responsibility. And the teaching repertory of universities is a veritable storehouse of techniques for planning and organizing all sorts of institutions and social systems.

During the period of expansion in higher education, the planning repertory was enriched, as governments, universities, and corporate enterprises shared their experience and expertise and drew on resources in the instructional repertory. Quantitative-statistical methods were being refined, diversified, and augmented by nonquantitative methods to improve "the art of navigation." Interdisciplinary approaches to planning proved especially useful in prefiguring new forms of organization, processes, and resources that would meet rising expectations and emerging problems and opportunities in the community and in higher education.

As the Florida universities, Cabinet, and legislature made the transition from centralized control under uniform regulations toward multiple centers following a common process, the test against experience proved to be as useful a guide in political decisions as in scholarly work. The design for planning, with its underlying assumptions, goals, and criteria, met the requirements for effective decision-making when it fit the conditions on the scene of the action. Multiple centers, diversifying the participants, process, and resources to fit the concerns of people for effective action, proved to embody "the spirit of things that *work*."

13
The University Repertory

Scenarios

Planning involves much more than facts and figures, resources and products. A plan tells a story of a future course of development, as an organization approaches new problems and opportunities. Affective, aesthetic tests apply in conjunction with quantitative assessment for an effective plan; it should ring true to "the spirit of things that *work*" to give the organization its identity. Each scenario—the new story for the next year or for a longer future—should continue its life history and ring true to known conditions of experience as well as future expectations for change, growth, and development. The roles of participants must ring true to each other, to their conditions of life and work, and to the mission of the organization. Their actions in shared responsibility should realize shared values for participants in each role and scene and for the organization as a whole.

Many people have suggested that aesthetic analogies represent significant commonalities in the whole history of human experience, on which all sorts of organizations may draw plans that stand the test of experience much better than the customary scalar analogies are likely to do. Along these lines, Erik H. Erikson has elaborated a general theory of organizational development around generative processes in three dimensions of shared experience:[1]

> • Shared values and shared visions by which people recognize an institution or organization and come together as members in a common mission.
> • Practical judgments, roles, and rules by which participants keep their action in line with the mission.

• Dramatic elaboration of shared visions, themes for performance in roles, and whole scenarios that promote solidarity of conviction and generative action to keep the institution alive and growing.

Universities will typically elaborate several different scenarios in their programs, and comparison to a repertory theatre seemed to fit the University of South Florida very well. Its "permanent company" produced both innovative and traditional works, on and off campus, and worked with students who were learning roles and themes for their future careers. Members worked in concert, exchanging roles and sharing responsibility according to capability and availability on the scene of the action, "on stage, backstage, or in the front of the house." For each production in the repertory, the accent on learning and the all-University approach set clear themes for the scenario and criteria of adequacy for performance in any role. People knew very well when they were learning and when they were just putting in classroom time, when their action was in tune or dissonant with the University's responsibilities and mission.

Higher education probably calls for at least two scenarios, on educational and enterprise themes. An enterprise scenario has to develop, for higher education is part of the world of work, and universities employ people who do educational work. They will have multiple roles; some may be enrolled as students and have university jobs at the same time, and teachers can never stop acting as students, never stop learning.

Consequently, the program plans for universities have to differentiate themes and roles very clearly in each of the scenarios in their repertory, in order to reduce the confusion and conflict entailed in multiple roles and role shifts. An educational scenario sets a unique, personalized role for each participant. Major themes will vary with the scholarly discipline, and participants will often improvise roles and themes to fit a particular setting or to link experience and expectations in a new way. An enterprise scenario draws themes and roles primarily from the world of commerce and industry, typically conforming to more stylized actions and transactions between customers and vendors, employers and employees, facilitators of processes and investors or contributors of resources.

Some roles will be fairly compatible with each scenario; for example, facilitator-contributor roles will often fit both the generative process of learning and the productive process of industry. This particular commonality made it possible for the University of South Florida to follow for several years a single, integrated, all-University scenario combining themes of learning, governance, and productive enterprise, for faculty, students, and staff in contributive roles.

ADMINISTRATIVE CHANGES

From 1960 to 1970, usf worked under its temporary plan of governance, capitalizing on the all-University scenario. Modifications usually involved fuller documentation of plans, policies, and actions, and the introduction of new roles for planning bodies, departments, and new colleges.

The Board of Regents continued to base systemwide policy on commonality in process, leaving substantive guidelines and decisions to the presidents and members of the universities. One change in this direction came in January 1965, shortly after the first regents took office, when some usf students appealed their suspension for violation of standards of conduct. The regents upheld President Allen's decision to let the suspension stand. Shortly thereafter, they amended current policy, eliminating any appeal to the Board of Regents.

Next, the regents reviewed and updated the entire policy on standards and discipline, due process guarantees, and rights of appeal, for all members of the universities. Shortcomings had surfaced when the usf administration came under censure by aaup, and changes were anticipated when colleges and universities came under the wage and hour acts. A revised policy established consistent procedures for academic, student, and administrative affairs and at last set the keystone for academic freedom and responsibility that was so sorely needed in the support system. The principal change at usf came in Academic Affairs, where the Committee on Educational Problems and Academic Relations replaced the ad hoc hearing panels that had been used under the temporary organization.

During the flurry of activity in Governor Kirk's administration in 1967, usf added two deliberative bodies to facilitate feedback on external matters requiring internal study and action. The Administrative Council functioned as an augmented Executive Committee, bringing together division and department heads from colleges and administrative areas to meet with the president, deans, and vice-presidents. It provided a time-saving "loop"; assembling on short notice, its members could bring a matter to closure for the president's action in a single session that combined the two to four steps otherwise required in the planning process. The elective Senate Council served as an interim body for the University Senate and filled a gap between the Executive Committee and the senate's Planning and Policies Committee by monitoring the timetable for planning and providing fast turnaround on urgent universitywide decisions. It met regularly with the president to plan the senate's agenda and take interim action subject to senate confirmation.

The University Senate modified the committee structure as new tasks emerged. For instance, the Council of the Computer Research Center was created to develop new data-processing configurations in keeping with local needs and the state's comprehensive plan. A separate Committee on Athletics was created to develop the third-priority program of intercollegiate competition under General Policy No. 48, preparing for USF's entry into NCAA in 1965. A Traffic Committee was separated from the Committee on Physical Plant to hear appeals from on-campus citations; it terminated in 1970 after a court ruling that appeals should go to a circuit judge in the first instance.

Changes fitted fairly comfortably into the all-University scenario. But there were grumblings with political undertones from the day the University opened. From year to year, governmental actions seemed to create "administrative absurdity" that sometimes appeared to increase by something more than the square of the distance between Tampa and Tallahassee. The pride of its members in the University's accomplishments reinforced their desire to counteract absurdities and irrationals and to win from state government and politics the recognition and support merited by their effective work.

But Florida had a "little Hatch Act" that barred faculty and staff from much of the action in the political arena. The concept of internal organization on a governmental model, matching the state apparatus power-for-power, began to gain wider appeal as an alternative way to generate political strength equal to the task of securing strong support and preventing arbitrary interference. Just how replicating political organization, roles, themes, and scenarios in the University would make state executive and legislative action more supportive of higher education was not clear; but many people seemed to be persuaded that such a reorganization would have this effect.

THE ENTERPRISE SCENARIO

Compliance with the wage and hour acts in 1967 introduced a more distinct enterprise scenario with themes from the production line, career ladder, and bureaucratic roles in management. Like many other teachers and administrators, Russell Cooper remarked regretfully on the consequent shift of themes from teaching and learning to job security, competition, and finesse in dealing with colleagues. He considered that these technocratic themes spoiled the enjoyment of learning for students and faculty.

At all events, employer–employee roles were brought into line with major themes in the enterprise scenario: productivity, equality of opportunity, fair practices, job security against arbitrary changes, and due process guarantees for rights and responsibilities. Employee roles were supposed to follow serial ranks within job classifications, so that enterprise themes combined with bureaucratic roles in the call for a new design of governance. Replacing the University Senate with a separate legislative body for each employment category, the new organization was complete by 1973, and the educational and enterprise scenarios were becoming fairly well differentiated.

FACULTY ORGANIZATION

The general faculty chose to follow almost precisely those concepts in the Working Paper of February 26, 1959, that President Allen and the planning staff discarded. Its constitution and bylaws established a Faculty Senate of 100 members apportioned according to the number of tenure-earning positions in each college. Eligibility to vote in elections and serve in the senate was reserved for the ranks of assistant professor and above. The senators elected Committees on Elections, Agenda, and Bylaws, and a Committee on Committees which makes up the list of nominees to be approved by the senate and presented to the president for appointments to all-University committees.

The right to vote for senators, and especially the right for the senate to vote on policy, program, and committee membership, seemed to satisfy most of the concerns about faculty participation in governance. Otherwise the systems for planning and administration continued with little modification.

ADMINISTRATIVE AND PROFESSIONAL ORGANIZATION

Administrative personnel felt themselves to be in a rather anomalous position. They coordinated major segments of the academic and administrative organization and often supervised teaching, research, and other professional positions. Their ranks represented almost every profession and field of study; many people had dual appointments in teaching and research. All were strongly committed to the educational component of educational administration. But they often felt that they were positioned in the academic pecking order as second-class administrators and second-rate educators.

The Administrative and Professional (A.&P.) staff decided to adopt a simple plan of work rather than a constitution and senate. Accenting their important educational role, they developed an agenda on such matters as parity with faculty in rank and salary and clarification of administrative procedures and responsibilities in USF and the state system. In 1976 the A.&P. staff went into the same collective bargaining unit as the Teaching and Research staff.

CAREER SERVICE ORGANIZATION

The Career Service adopted a constitution and bylaws and organized a senate paralleling the faculty organization; 50 senators were apportioned among academic, administrative, and regional centers. The principal agenda related to conditions of work, and the senate adopted an extensive set of work rules with a long list of specific offenses and fixed penalties.

The general staff had earned the prominence that came with reorganization. Their ingenuity and proficiency in the art of making brick without straw had carried the University through many a manpower and budget shortage. The Career Service included many professional positions, some having dual teaching or research assignments, many having responsibility for planning and training. Staff were generally knowledgeable about the whole University and often participated in many of its activities outside of their jobs.

Reorganization seemed neither to impair nor to enhance these assets very much. Some people felt that interaction with faculty and administrators became more difficult; others were disappointed that a bicameral system had not been set up so that Faculty and Career Service Senates must concur in proposals. But organization of the separate senate seemed to satisfy most of the staff's concerns for participation in governance.

STUDENT GOVERNMENT

One version of an enterprise scenario follows a rather simplistic "production-line" analogy: faculty and staff have to be working on something; their work centers on the classroom; students go into classrooms and come out with a degree; obviously, faculty and staff must be working on students to produce graduates. This commonplace fallacy of reification gave a distinct countervision to the educational scenario with the accent on learning and to any enterprise scenario emphasizing the students' generative roles as contributors or investors in academic work.

Activists of the 1960s vigorously protested against this fallacy. ("Do not bend, fold, staple, or mutilate this student," said one slogan.) As an alternative, some elaborated political themes of student power under the jurisdiction of an autonomous student government, immune to faculty and administrative intervention. Adoption of the Twenty-sixth Amendment to the U.S. Constitution in 1971 and concurrent Florida statutes making 18 both the voting age and the age of majority reinforced the appeal of political themes and scenarios for student government.

During the reorganization of 1971–72, the Student Association prepared a new constitution to organize the student body under a Student Government. With some misgivings, Joe Howell, the new Vice-President for Student Affairs, agreed to accept that title and approved the new Student Government constitution. The document established an executive branch under an elected Student Government President; an elected Student Government Senate apportioned according to enrollment in each college; and an appointed Student Government Court of Review to hear questions involving constitutional interpretation and cases involving charges of misconduct of the organization's affairs by its officers and other functionaries.

At last, USF students had come into the tradition handed down from the older universities, regarding Student Government as a training ground for political careers. The stage was set for a political scenario to be added to the enterprise and educational scenarios in the University repertory.

Equalitarian Themes

Few changes proved to be as far-reaching as some advocates of reorganization expected them to be. Some people found that the new requirements for seeking an elective or appointive office and securing approval of a representative body cramped their style. They had become accustomed to regard USF as a voluntary association, where any individual could contribute or any two or three members could gather together to propose a new departure, without necessarily having to represent any particular group. The political themes bespoke time-honored democratic values, however, and grew out of equalitarian concerns for access to education and employment, consistent with the University's philosophy and the concerns of its membership. Changes in roles and themes thus appeared to be tolerable for most people, if not satisfactory in all instances.

Reconciling real and perceived roles and themes for students continued to present difficult tasks. Meritocratic and equalitarian themes intermingled in academic policy, practice, and folklore with considerable disharmony. In meritocratic tradition, students (especially the most talented) represent a precious national asset to be protected, nurtured, and brought into fully mature powers under the care of the university; national policy exempting students from the military draft was consistent with this approach. Such special privilege, however, was not consonant with equalitarian themes of shared responsibility for contributing to the life and work of the community; and on educational themes, students must share responsibility with faculty as peers among peers in the mission to advance and share knowledge.

In this mingling of themes, students were just as likely as faculty and administrators to try to take things both ways; to enjoy both dependent and independent roles; to benefit from special privileges and services in protected roles; and also to maintain in the postadolescent subculture the traditional posture of protest and resistance toward officialdom on campus and in the community. In this mingling of themes of protection and antagonism, student power and student responsibility, the period of the quiet campus came to an end. Political and equalitarian themes emerged in student protest; exemption from the draft did not exempt students from the voice of conscience, which led many to protest the involvement of the nation in the Vietnam War, the inequities in the draft, or the caste system with its abuses of civil rights in campus and community.

In clarifying students' roles and developing equalitarian themes, universities had some clear guidelines. The courts had made it quite clear that neither students nor universities could expect to take things both ways. Universities had to decide what they could provide in the way of academic programs, services, privileges, and care for the welfare, regulation, and conduct of their members. Students who chose to enroll could enjoy the programs and services offered, but the responsibilities for academic work under standards and regulations went along with the privileges of membership and the care for their welfare. Students could not claim care and protection that universities could not give; neither could universities impose regulations or offer privileges infringing upon the equality, rights, and responsibilities of students as citizens.

In any event, all members of universities had equal responsibility to respect each other's rights and support the exercise of these rights in the work of teaching and learning and in community life beyond the college walls. The courts emphasized the task of developing clearly defined roles and positive rules for mutual support of adult rights and responsibilities, which must accommodate individual differences in experience and conditions of work. Standards must include safeguards for due process in disciplinary action and positive ways to amend conduct and correct errors.[2]

During the 1960s, both the American Association of University Professors and a consortium of professional associations in administration produced declarations of student rights and responsibilities.[3] These documents took a developmental-counseling approach to shared responsibilities, based on contributive roles for students as adults, peers among peers in university membership. Collaborating with NSA, fraternity councils, and honor societies, the professional groups sought to bring student roles into line with standards of academic freedom, responsibility, performance, and integrity, common to all members of universities.

In some areas, the Student Affairs staff at USF had comparatively little difficulty in developing policy and practice consonant with equalitarian themes. Much of the original planning stood up firmly in the test of experience with demonstrations and confrontations in the student protest movement and with judicial proceedings. Guidelines facilitating the exercise of free speech and assembly stood with little modification; little change was necessary in standards and regulations for voluntary associations and campus activities, where, from the outset, self-direction and collaborative roles had been established. Special services and regulations for fraternities and special controls over fund-raising by recognized groups on campus were revised or eliminated with little objection. Safeguards for due process in disciplinary action required little modification, aside from continuing refinement of procedures and documentation. Little difficulty was encountered in eliminating the procedure for approval of off-campus housing.

In other areas, however, the development of equalitarian themes of shared responsibility in collaborative roles made headway with difficulty against dissonant themes of political power and centralized control. In the process of eliminating the curfew and sign-out system in women's residence halls and developing a more extensive visitation program, the Student Association claimed the prerogative to administer the entire system of residence hall standards and discipline. Vice-President Wunderlich firmly withstood this pressure. He and President Allen kept the decision-making process within the original framework of self-governance for each living unit, and kept the residence halls within the general University system of standards and discipline. It seemed difficult, however, for the principle of diffusing responsibility to the scene of the action to penetrate the deliberations of the Student Association, against the persuasion that some central agency must take control in order for the system to work at all.

A similar paradox seemed to escape recognition by the Student Association during its deliberations in 1969 concerning the increasingly frequent involvement of students in the courts and the safeguards for due process in disciplinary action. At one point, the student legislature adopted a resolution declaring the right of students to have legal counsel take part in disciplinary hearings, and another calling upon Student Affairs to provide legal advice and counsel to students free of charge. Wunderlich rejected both proposals on legal and financial grounds. But the Student Association was trying to respond to real needs for which students turned to the University for special service. The problem was to find some way to meet needs without some central power and control inimical to students' rights as citizens and without imposing costs that neither the students nor the University could afford.

One outcome was an initiative by the Student Association to develop a commuter affairs service and publish a handbook for off-campus living. These actions responded to appeals for assistance with landlord-tenant problems and other matters of personal and property rights. The commuter service also facilitated study and action on other matters such as the construction of bicycle paths, provision of public transportation in the university neighborhood, organization of car pools and child care services, and development of special events and activities for commuter students and their families.

HELPING SERVICES

There was good reason for turning to Alma Mater for help in coping with conditions of personal life and work that affected academic performance. Faculty and staff had the necessary professional expertise and provided a major resource for the community in developing similar services for the general welfare. There was no reason to prevent these skilled people from helping their students, in whose personal and professional development they had particular interest. The partnership of student volunteers and paraprofessionals with faculty and staff in helping services and other activities provided a major resource for teaching and learning on which USF capitalized heavily. These collaborative roles not only realized educational values but also provided a way of resource-sharing and cost-saving that made many campus and community services possible in the first place.

Claims for power, autonomy, and centralized control by a student government ran counter to this course of action in some respects, reinforced by two rather simplistic approaches sometimes advanced in the community and the faculty. Some people proposed that the University divest itself altogether of helping services; they often pointed to a European tradition of purely intellectual encounter of students and professors, unsullied by mundane considerations of personal health and welfare. This tradition was honored more in folklore than in practice; during the 1950s and 1960s, leaders of European universities often conferred with student personnel workers in the U.S. on plans to develop similar advising, counseling, and health services for their own students.

Others proposed that the University simply transfer responsibility to students for any helping services they might desire, withdrawing professional support by faculty and staff. This approach would be tantamount to shifting the whole responsibility to the community, contrary to the University's responsibility for community service inherent in its mission. Some rather dubious assumptions underlay this approach. For instance, some people assumed that students created the problems and should simply muddle through as best they could. Substance abuse, in particular, was sometimes considered to be just another fad of the youth subculture, on a par with rock concerts and more traditional fads and rituals such as football bonfires and fraternity "beer busts." The assumption that students alone were involved in problems of anxiety and alienation, substance abuse, suicide, and other crises was false on its face. Simplistic solutions, such as expelling those involved in these situations, in disruptive demonstrations, or in violations of laws and regulations, did not touch the underlying problems throughout society.

Shared problems involved shared responsibilities for students and universities, communities and governments. Prefigurative approaches were clearly necessary in dealing with conditions new to experience. Universities could draw on ample experience with prefigurative ways of work; at USF the "Accent on Lagniappe" and personalized ways of work provided for unique, unpredictable factors in fairly orderly procedures for planning and risk-taking.

The Dean of Men and Dean of Women carried particular responsibility for dealing with the extraordinary in prefigurative ways. They administered the system of standards and discipline, which necessarily provided personalized approaches to errors, misadventures, and violations. They gave advice and assistance to students making special arrangements to continue study if possible despite illness, financial difficulty, and other unexpected changes in conditions of life and work. The central office of Student Affairs gave information, advice, and referral to campus and community services, in person or by telephone. Around the clock the operators on the main University switchboard gave invaluable support, helping to relay messages, secure assistance from police and other emergency services, or locate one of the deans for special assistance.

In helping students under arrest, the deans had fairly clear roles and rules to follow, as well as considerable discretionary judgment. Under constitutional and statutory guidelines, any person could call for help and any citizen could help a friend, colleague, or relative to exercise the right to equal protection of laws and due process in hearing complaints and charges against them. In any event, assistance was primarily a matter of grace and favor; no person had any particular obligation to accept any cost or risk at all in answering a call for help.

The decision to build residence halls meant that USF should offer some help to students involved in an arrest or other crisis or emergency. The deans agreed that they should at least receive any call for help and then try to locate some relative or close friend who would come to the student's aid. If they provided help for residents, they should also assist commuters who were not able to reach their families or friends for some reason. They agreed that any further help should be given on the basis of a plan worked out with the student, and of course they would give advice on appropriate procedure to any student on request at any time.

Before USF opened, the deans worked out these procedures with local law enforcement officers, and they also considered procedures involving investigations on campus requiring information from official records and interviews, where both ethical and legal protections of privacy and confidentiality must be observed. Student Affairs and campus security staff also worked with community agencies and law enforcement officers on such matters as crowd control, emergency procedures, fire drill, hurricane drill, civil defense, protection against assault, theft, vandalism, and problems related to substance abuse.

These arrangements naturally involved rather intricate problems, but the deans found no particular lack of clarity in their role and responsibility. They had to give students information and orientation to their roles, rights, and responsibilities in the USF system of standards and discipline, in state and federal systems of civil and criminal justice, and in emergency procedures. They offered information, advice, and referral such as any citizen might give to those under arrest or in other emergency situations, upon request. And they had to exercise discretionary judgment on the student's readiness to cope, access to necessary assistance, and past conduct and academic performance—and their own willingness to accept a degree of cost and risk for themselves and the University.

From other perspectives, however, the deans were cast in quite different roles. Some people perceived their action as capricious and inequitable on at least two counts: residents needed and got more help than commuters; and assistance in any case was largely a matter of grace and favor. Two common persuasions were equally fallacious: one depicted the deans as conniving with students to cover up violations and protect offenders from the full authority of the law; the other held that they were secretly in league with undercover agents to entrap and apprehend students, interfering with their rights under the law. As the student protest movement spread, some of its themes of oppressive authority, police brutality, and interference with civil rights reinforced a fallacious persuasion that law enforcement was not a helping service at all—but an authoritarian instrumentality subversive of people's liberties.

Some role conflicts for the deans were involved in the combination of responsibility for disciplinary action and assistance to those under arrest. These were minimal and manageable without much difficulty from the administrative standpoint. From the standpoint of student protest and folklore, conflicts were built into the whole "establishment" and the deans, playing equivocal, capricious roles, merely appeared to be on the side of students while actually acting as their adversaries, putting them twice in jeopardy from campus and community authority. There was just enough political and social fact in evidence on the American scene to make such themes of mistrust and resistance appear plausible.

In the face of common fallacies, dissonant themes, and mistrustful resistance, the helping services of universities and communities had to continue in their shared responsibilities and address many problems and issues new to their experience. Perhaps none taxed their commitments and their ingenuity more than did the problem of substance abuse.

DRUG AND CRISIS INTERVENTION

To the extent that the state of the art and the resources available made any action possible, the health and counseling services at USF had coped with problems of substance abuse involving alcohol, marijuana, drugs, and other hazardous substances. Such problems often surfaced as one of many factors involved in medical treatment, counseling referrals on disciplinary matters, cases of arrest, and other crises of personal and academic life. But no services in the University or the community had resources sufficient to the need presented in the extensive problems of substance abuse in the late 1960s.

In dealing with substance abuse, people in all the helping services, from law enforcement on down, needed considerable clarification of their roles and responsibilities and considerable improvement in the state of the art, as well as additional resources. Legal obstacles to the possession of proscribed substances stood in the way of research needed to advance the state of the art. Legal remedies were also needed to open the way to referral for health and counseling services in cases where possession of prohibited substances was involved.

Following the lead of the Congress, the Florida legislature took action on some of these needs. First, it amended the statutes to prohibit the possession and provision of marijuana, an additional list of drugs and chemicals such as LSD, and other substances frequently abused or hazardous when misused. Three sections of the act were particularly intended to clarify the relation of university systems of standards and discipline to law enforcement and the system of criminal justice.

One section required the president (or an officer acting under his authorization) summarily to suspend any student arrested for violation of drug laws. On its face, this section was inconsistent with statutes and judicial principles safeguarding due process. In 1970 Vice-President Wunderlich perforce suspended a USF student immediately upon his arrest on drug charges. The student brought suit, and the court found F.S. 293.582 defective with respect to due process guarantees. The legislature quickly amended the statute to specify hearing prior to disciplinary action and to authorize rather than require suspension or dismissal as a penalty.

A second section authorized waiver of disciplinary penalty when a student gave information to law enforcement agencies concerning providers of drugs and other proscribed substances. Many students, faculty, and staff found this section offensive because it seemed to co-opt the university system of standards and discipline into the criminal justice system with its ways of plea bargaining for information on matters under investigation. To be sure, disclosure would concern the student, legal counsel, police, courts, and public prosecutors. University officers would have no part in the matter until they received information from some officer of the law or the court. Any consideration of waiver would be at the discretion of hearing panels, deans, and presidents, in keeping with their responsibility under university regulations. Nevertheless, this section of the act tended to strengthen the false persuasion that university officers were participating in plea bargaining and welcoming if not actually recruiting informers and undercover agents.

On the other hand, the statute also authorized waiver of penalty when a student voluntarily disclosed personal problems of substance abuse. This cleared up many vexing questions of referral to health and counseling agencies for people in law enforcement and other helping services on campus and in the community.

The waiver of penalty facilitated development of drug intervention programs, which the legislature now required universities to provide. One of the most useful contributions of the Student Association to USF came through its initiative in developing a comprehensive program of drug and crisis intervention. In 1968–69, the association organized a task force in cooperation with the Student Affairs staff, to prepare plans that President Mackey eventually authorized in 1971. Since no funds came with the mandate from the legislature, the University once again had to fall back on its prime resources: the ingenuity of its members and their voluntary contributions in developing special programs and services. The expanded program capitalized on existing resources in a tripartite effort of information and referral, early intervention and peer support of special services, and outreach and cultivation of participation in shared responsibilities.

With the advent of new technology for direct dialing, the special support provided by the resourceful operators on the main University switchboard was lost. Now HELPline came into service as a dusk-to-dawn and weekend source of information and referral on any sort of need to know; backing up the Deans of Men and Women, HELP covered a wider spectrum than the typical specialized "hot line." Volunteer operators cross-trained with the staff in all areas, who shared their knowledge and experience concerning information and referral. Of some 500 calls during the first term, more than 100 involved suicide, drug, and crisis intervention. But the very first caller, on September 6, 1971, needed to know how to operate the new type of washing machines in the residence hall laundries.

The Counseling Center for Human Development organized Rap Cadre, whose paraprofessionally trained volunteers and student assistants conducted formal and informal discussions in residence halls, off-campus housing centers, classes, organizations, and other gatherings. They dealt with matters concerning substance abuse, suicide, and underlying problems of anxiety, alienation, and mistrust. They gave advice and information on ways of helping friends to cope with crises and facilitated referral to helping services in the University and the community.

Rap Cadre, HELPline, and the residence hall councils collaborated in opening the Night Owl coffee shop in Andros as an alternative gathering place for people who abhorred the drug scene but were attracted to the music, camaraderie, and life style of the subculture. As an *Oracle* supplement, Rap Cadre published the "Free Nickel

Bag" of information on substance abuse and the special services available on campus and in the community.

The task force also developed a drug information service. Rap Cadre received samples submitted anonymously and reported results of laboratory analysis, indicating any hazards to users through the *Oracle* and special bulletins. The local State's Attorney helped to arrange a lawful procedure for receiving and forwarding substances with protection for confidentiality. He gave other helpful advice on general problems of referral to helping services in ways that were consistent with the statutes and the role of the police and the courts.

All of these drug and crisis intervention services were extensively used. They capitalized on the experience developed by professional staff and students in information, training, and services of intervention and referral, from the time the University opened. With no considerable addition to funds and other resources, the services in drug and crisis intervention expanded substantially in variety and scope. The best available quantitative indicator of their effectiveness came from HELPline, where the number of calls mounted by substantial increments from term to term beyond the 500 or more registered during the first 10 weeks of operation.

Assessing overall effects, however, was very difficult, partly because of student resistance and mistrust, partly because of shortcomings in the state of the art. During the late 1960s, students tended to rise up in indignation over any evaluative survey, seeing it as a device to trick them into self-incrimination. And experienced counselors and student personnel administrators considered typical statistical indicators likely to show little more than "the tip of the iceberg" in view of the anxiety and alienation underlying the problem.

In developing the drug and crisis intervention programs, the task force in Student Affairs took a prefigurative approach to a whole set of problems that had defied other remedies for generations, perhaps for centuries. With very few clear patterns to follow, students, staff, faculty, and professional people in the community had to develop a new scenario with new roles and themes.

Dealing with deep-seated problems of anxiety, alienation, mistrust, and hostility, the prefigurative course of action was hard to maintain. Deans and counselors, faculty and students, officers of the law and the courts, and legislators and other public officials were all in the same bind. They could cope with shared responsibilities in their various roles; they could do very little about the widespread

misunderstanding and misperception of their actions. Students sharing responsibilities with staff were inevitably going to be perceived
in some circles as autocrats, junior grade—as puppets of administrative authority, betraying their whole generation to the oppressive
"establishment." Confusion, anxiety, and mistrust aggravated tragic
problems needing no further complication.

Going by the Book

With many new programs and many changes in University policy,
statutes, and judicial action beginning to crystallize into new themes
and scenarios, Vice-President Howell decided in the summer of 1971
to get a comprehensive review and update of documents for the
whole system of standards and discipline. President Mackey agreed
to appoint a Task Force on Student Rights and Responsibilities and
charged its members to "compile all statements concerning offenses,
policies, and procedures."

This Task Force published *The Book,* whose four parts covered
offenses and penalties, policies and procedures, rights and responsibilities, and complaints and grievances—with appendices citing
selected portions of the U.S. and Florida Statutes and the Board of
Regents Operating Manual. In preparing the material, the committee followed the developmental-counseling approach commended
by judicial and professional analysts and adopted for USF in 1960—
except on one matter that it considered trivial. It transposed positive
statements of standards into a list of offenses with fixed penalties,
reverting to a practice obsolete before USF was ever conceived.

For more than two decades, the best available legal and educational
advice had underlined the advantages of positive statements (some of
these being known at least from the time of Aristotle) in giving more
information about a matter than negative or prohibitive standards
can provide and indicating ways to correct errors on the spot or to
reduce the probability of error and misconduct. Judicial and professional deliberations had repeatedly emphasized the importance of
"enabling rather than merely restricting action" and facilitating the
positive exercise of rights and freedoms in producing useful academic work. Experience had confirmed the effectiveness of ways of
teaching and learning, in which universities excel, for correcting
errors on the spot and avoiding recourse to adversary proceedings.[4]

Nevertheless, the Task Force rewrote the documents on standards and procedures, producing a negatively stated list of offenses and penalties. This "trivial" modification yielded results consistent with several centuries of human experience: "Going by the Book" produced more confusion, errors, protests, and grievances than it settled—including a good many questions that had never been raised about the positive standards and procedures that it replaced.

Accordingly, a Student Government officer, Paul Bradley, undertook an independent study project, in which he revised *The Book,* deleted obsolete and redundant items, and restored positive statements on standards, policy, and procedure. His manuscript was published in the 1972–73 Student Handbook.

Political Themes

In the American experience, self-governance by voluntary associations has almost been a necessity, especially in frontier communities remote from established centers of power and authority. Meriam's dictum, "Any institution which makes rules to govern the conduct of individuals is in itself a government,"[5] sums up this general experience and the democratic persuasion that people sharing responsibility for self-governance can cope effectively with all sorts of crises and opportunities.

During the time of the quiet campus before World War II, many universities had sought a stronger foundation in democratic values for their ways of governance and instruction. The era of unchallenged supremacy of presidents and trustees was passing. Students and faculty were moving into shared responsibility for determining standards of conduct on campus as well as maintaining high standards of academic work.

In 1947 the President's Commission on Higher Education called for the nation's colleges and universities to strengthen the democratic experience on campus and to share its spirit with each student generation, taking up the challenges emerging out of World War II and its horrors of tyranny, terrorism, and holocaust. The report urged colleges and universities to study both the accomplishments and the shortcomings of democracy, to cultivate democratic values through self-governance in academic life and work, and to examine and revise academic programs, policies, and practices in order to "give students every possible experience in democratic processes within the college community."

In this call for developing democratic themes, roles, and values, the commission recommended a developmental approach, embodying the concept of shared responsibility expressed in the tradition of the community of scholars. It envisioned a worldwide network of public and private organizations, in which colleges and universities, state educational systems, the federal Office of Education, and other agencies both public and private would represent multiple centers of shared responsibility—just as self-governing departments, colleges, and student activities would hold institutions together in a network of shared responsibility. The recommendations centered on commonalities in the self-governing process as the essential element of the democratic experience that the commission wished to cultivate.[6]

During the 1950s, studies such as Corson's and Dennison's reported how institutions tended to take this challenge simplistically by adopting governmental models and political scenarios for the academic organization. In 1970, W. Max Wise conducted a similar study of governance in colleges and universities.[7] He found a similar trend toward the adoption of governmental-political themes and roles, with special emphasis on documentation of institutional policy, rules, and regulations consistent with the actual distribution of power and authority and on equal representation in decision-making bodies with the right to vote on policies and programs.

Wise was particularly apprehensive about fragmenting the organization of colleges and universities beyond any legitimate power of presidents and trustees to hold them together. The tendency to involve faculty and students in more and more administrative functions seemed to present at least two hazards: attenuating the integrative capabilities of central administrations and multiplying rival centers of power and control in parallel structures representing occupational classifications, scholarly disciplines, or membership categories.

The effects could go beyond any conceivable capability for integration by any internal or external agency. Wise observed that this trend "carries syndicalism on the campus several steps beyond what we have known, and raises serious questions especially in light of the performance of other representations of syndicalism, which have consistently ignored the public trust and have been insensitive to questions of justice and equity."

Syndicalist theories of organization, social stratification, and social change have elaborated themes of politics as a power struggle within and between parallel hierarchies in feudal systems or parallel bureaucracies in modern urban-industrial societies and their institutions. Max Wise found many distressing signs of a political scenario for higher education that inclined toward syndicalist rather than democratic principles, roles, and themes.

USF had avoided syndicalist proclivities, primarily by developing generative, self-directing centers for concerted study and action wherever teaching and learning, planning and administration were conducted. As a more explicit political scenario developed, the elaboration of democratic themes had centered on equalitarian principles such as the positive exercise of rights and freedoms and shared responsibility for academic work. From 1970 forward, a political scenario was more fully elaborated at USF, and syndicalist themes of power struggle within and between parallel "power structures" began to clash with democratic themes of voluntary initiative and self-reliance in sharing responsibilities on the scene of the action.

14
Politics in Education

Student Rights and Responsibilities

Especially in the aftermath of war, developments in American higher education have generally tended toward diversifying the roles and themes for academic life and work. Veterans returning to study and teaching have strongly influenced this trend. For example, they formed voluntary associations to study American history and literature after the Civil War and developed resources and programs that universities eventually brought into the curriculum. Returning veterans of World War II similarly raised questions about the values and issues underlying Western civilization, modern science, and technology, questions that influenced the development of general education thereafter.

After World War II, the recommendations of the President's Commission of 1947 were very much in keeping with the concerns of many veterans on many campuses, emphasizing the shared values of democracy in the whole experience of academic life and work. A stronger emphasis on student participation in all aspects of academic work and governance emerged. In many universities, veterans in the student body and faculty emphasized political roles and themes in the democratic experience and developed political scenarios for student government.

At the University of Florida and Florida State University, student governments had replicated the political apparatus of the state in their constitutions, election campaigns, and party organizations. The only missing element was the power of the purse. After World War II, student-body leaders capitalized on a wealth of experience in developing a campaign to secure this power. Beginning in 1947, each successive generation of officers arranged to have a bill introduced at each legislative session, authorizing student government to administer allocations from the Activities and Service (A.&S.) fee, a tuition surcharge casually referred to as "the students' own money."

Only once did such a bill pass, and the governor promptly vetoed it. In 1967 the Board of Regents assumed discretionary authority over the allocation and transfer of funds in the SUS budget. Accordingly, student-body officers turned from the legislature to the Board of Regents in their campaign for control over A.&S. fees.

Neither the Board of Control nor the Board of Regents had developed a general policy on student rights, responsibilities, and participation in academic and administrative affairs. They had simply delegated responsibility to each president for organizing the membership of the university. In keeping with this principle of diffusing responsibility to the scene of the action, the Council of Vice-Presidents for Student Affairs recommended that the chancellor and Board of Regents deal with the student governments' proposal on A.&S. fees in a broader context. General policies, guidelines, and procedures were needed in the SUS to document roles, rights, and responsibilities for all students as members of the universities and participants in their governance.

The vice-presidents considered a student government to provide only one of many centers required for participation in university affairs. Some of the new universities, including USF, had no student government; they had organized a network of multiple self-governing councils representing student interests in all areas of their operations. The two venerable universities had also developed such networks with multiple centers of participation and coordination—in addition to their student governments, which were minimally oriented toward academic life and work.

The regents took up the proposal from student-body presidents on the A.&S. fees in this broad context, and on October 3, 1969, adopted a comprehensive policy, including the following sections of the Operating Manual referring to student government and its role.

7.3 Institutional Responsibility for Student Life
    A. Each institution shall develop, publish, and enforce appropriate rules and regulations governing student life. The Student Government should have clear and defined means to participate in the formulation of institutional policy affecting academic and student affairs.

B. The Board requires that the penalty for serious violations
of university regulations shall be recorded in the record of
the individual concerned. The administration of discipline
should provide, whenever possible, for the correction and
positive guidance of students who have violated such standards.

7.4 Student Freedom and Responsibility
Student Government shall be the representative of all students
and is encouraged to function on campus, with the recognition
that ultimate authority for university affairs rests with the
administration of each university.

Student Government may propose to the president written
recommendations covering the allocation of that portion of the
university fees fixed by law or designated by the Board of
Regents for student activities.

Student Government is authorized to propose student social
regulations.

Specific mention of student government answered three specific
questions from the student-body presidents about participation in
policy, regulation of conduct, and program planning. It also encouraged them to interpret the policy as a mandate to create an autonomous Student Government in each university, controlling student
affairs programs and the allocation of Activities and Service fees.

The most judicious, realistic interpretation considered the policy
to authorize organization of the student body, delegation of responsibility and authority to students in particular roles, and general
participation by students in program planning and governance. In
this context, "student government" had to be understood as a traditional term convenient for referring to a number of different ways in
which the student body could organize. In designating student government as a representative agency, the regents had no apparent
intention to dismantle other agencies in operation or to keep students
from representing their interests and sharing responsibility in other
centers for planning and coordination. Apparently, the regents had
followed a tradition strong in their own experience and understood
the present situation much as the student-body presidents saw it.
Any student-body organization would just naturally adopt a constitution and make rules to govern the conduct of members. In effect, it
would be a student government and might as well be called by that
name and have a specific area of jurisdiction—especially since no

general title for other configurations, based on function rather than "territory," had come into customary use.

Herbert Wunderlich had worked especially hard to develop a general policy consistent with state and federal statutes and regulations. He particularly desired a policy documenting the principle of self-governance in voluntary associations and in such areas as residence halls. He considered the developmental approach of "correction and positive guidance" to need a stronger foundation in the policy on standards and discipline. The Council of Vice-Presidents shared these concerns and particularly made sure that the policy would include safeguards for administrative accountability for action in the public interest, especially the clause in Article 7.4.

These efforts were decisive in preventing the perpetration of an administrative absurdity by creating a student government free from accountability to the university administration, the Board of Regents, the state and federal statutes—and the educational absurdity of separating students from the rest of the academic enterprise and encapsulating them in a subculture having only a single channel for participation in the university's life and work.

With the adoption of this policy, the campaign for student government control over Activities and Service fees returned to the legislative arena.

Financial Resources

Regarding Activities and Service fees as "the students' own money" was a considerable error. All fees were levied and all funds expended under legislative or constitutional authority exercised through the Board of Regents. Once students paid tuition, the money belonged to them just about as much as did the money they spent in the cafeteria or bookstore—or in their neighborhood supermarket.

In recommending a more comprehensive policy, the Student Affairs administrators responded to genuine concerns going beyond the Student Government campaign. They found a general need for students to play more active, self-directing roles in shared responsibility for academic life and work. Designating funds for Student Government control appeared very likely to counteract efforts to open more ways for student participation. By putting additional burdens and restrictions on financial resources and budget planning systems that were already under severe constraints and pressures, the flexibility and degrees of freedom for change and growth into new ways of work would be reduced.

In 1967 tuition included the matriculation fee, a "block tuition" charge for full-time enrollment in 9 or more credit hours per term (part-time students paid a proportionate fee per credit hour), plus surcharges designated for capital improvements and financial aid, with an undesignated "Activities and Service" portion. Undesignated funds could be allocated among prepaid services, admission to cultural and athletic events, and other activities, according to the program plans for each university.

In urban universities, the substantial number and percentage of part-time students produced disparities between actual burden and income from both the Activities and Service fees and the Educational and General appropriations under FTE formulae. On the theory that part-time students would use community services and take part in community rather than campus activities, they did not pay the A.&S. fee and supposedly would not participate in funded services and activities—even though these often included publications, orientation, recreation, student unions, and other programs open to one and all. Some USF services such as health and counseling could and did exclude part-time students. There was no "blanket tax," but admission charges for some cultural and athletic events helped to offset some of their cost and applied to all comers. In other events and activities, aside from requirements for elective office or other special responsibilities, there was usually no practicable way to exclude part-time students even if anyone wished to do so.

USF had to use A.&S. funds for some programs that older universities supported out of E.&G. appropriations. This move partly compensated for slippage in converting whole-student enrollment to full-time equivalents for the purpose of budget projections. For example, in 1960 E.&G. funds based on estimates of 1,200 FTE enrollment were about 16 percent short of actual burden, with 1,997 individuals enrolled and producing 1,400.4 FTE. Some burden could be shifted to A.&S. funds for some program categories in the areas of Academic and Student Affairs. But the enrollment mix also produced a slippage of some 35 percent below estimates for these discretionary funds.

The Board of Control and the Cabinet made some allowances for this situation, peculiar to USF as the first urban university in the system. After 1967, the Board of Regents had greater discretionary authority for planning and revising allocations for expenditure from all income sources in all the universities. At USF, the Vice-President and Business Manager in Administrative Affairs ingeniously managed to provide funds reasonably commensurate with program plans, by varying the pattern of discretionary allocations as much as possible under the guidelines as well as by cheerful cheese-paring and resource-sharing. The whole membership helped to take up some of the slack, through volunteer service where employed staff could not be provided and by special charges or contributions to particular activities and special events.

The general trend in the state toward uniform planning formulae and strict budget controls steadily reduced the degrees of freedom allowed for discretionary outlay. The universities also moved toward more consistent designation of the funding source for each portion of the academic and administrative program. The advent of productivity formulae for Educational and General funding shifted more resources toward classroom teaching and reduced the flexibility in allocating this portion of the budget. These effects increased pressures on A.&S. funds, even as the undesignated sum diminished under the formal and informal "earmarking" of allocations.

In order to reduce some of these pressures and constraints, in 1971 the Board of Regents undertook to redesign the whole fee structure. First, it authorized each president to levy a special fee for health services, not to exceed $10.00 per term. The income could be used to supplement or supplant allocations from A.&S. fees. Part-time students could be given the option to pay the fee and use the service, at the president's discretion. But they still paid no activity fee, and the board considered overall revision of the fee structure to be necessary in order for all students to share more equitably in both costs and benefits of activities and services.

The fee-per-credit-hour proposed in 1972 followed this principle. The plan was worked over by university and SUS councils very carefully because of the values at stake: fitting the plan to the actual enrollment mix; differentiating the charges for undergraduate and graduate tuition; and stabilizing the system for program and budget planning. They also wished to save for students some of the flexibility in program planning under block tuition payment, through choices of extra courses beyond the degree requirements without extra cost for such enrichment of their studies.

These values were not mutually exclusive, and alternatives combining block tuition and fee-per-credit were considered. The USF Vice-President for Academic Affairs, Carl Riggs, suggested a general allowance of one course per term at no extra charge, or a "freebie" for each A or each term with a high GPR, up to a limit of five or six courses beyond the 180 required credits.

The legislature ultimately adopted a straight fee-per-credit-hour, including a proportionate share of the Activities and Service fee and other surcharges, and charging more for graduate than for undergraduate courses. The change gave budget planners a somewhat more reliable base for projections. It deprived students of the opportunity for enlarging and enriching their programs without extra cost; and many faculty and students considered this change counterproductive in relation to concerns for quality education.

One root of the problem seemed to lie in the traditional scenario for the passage to a degree by continuous, full-time study, on which the concepts of full- and part-time enrollment and different levels of instruction were based. Few alternatives suggested any inclination to examine the assumptions underlying this scenario, with a view to developing another approach more consistent with actual enrollment mix and the variable timetable for completing a degree.

STUDENT PARTICIPATION IN PLANNING

Vice-President Howell, responding to concerns and themes underlying the concept of Student Government as the voice of the student body, wanted to enlarge the scope of student participation in planning Student Affairs programs. With the advent of the new fee structure, he established SAPBE, the Student Affairs Program-Budget-Evaluation System, whose design fitted the typical two-stage planning process at USF. The system required extensive student participation in the first, most decisive stage of designing program-budget proposals and organizing them into a coherent plan.

Charles Hewitt, Assistant to the Vice-President, administered the system and worked out the general design with the Finance Committee of Student Government and the staff of the University's Administrative Planning Division. The process started with formative evaluation, linked to the performance evaluation of Student Affairs staff and program units, as a basis for program and budget projections.[1] Each program unit and funded activity developed a yearly plan based on its annual evaluative report, and documented budget projections according to program objectives, schedule of activity, participant capacity, and resource requirements, with performance criteria established for the next round of evaluation and planning.

The committees directing voluntary activities eligible for funding from Activities and Service fees reviewed their program-budget plans with the Council on Student Activities, which presented a composite plan. Its own Finance Committee reviewed plans for Student Government operations and the special events and activities under its auspices and prepared a program-budget plan for the S.G. president, who presented this "appropriations bill" to the S.G. Senate for study, amendment, and adoption. The S.G. president had veto power over senate action, with provision for override by the senate, under the constitution. Administrative units under Student Affairs staff sent their plans to Dr. Hewitt for compilation and review, and Academic Affairs sent the section of the budget using A.&S. funds to his office for inclusion in the general budget for the Student Affairs area. Composite proposals from all four sources were compiled by Dr. Hewitt for hearings and recommendations by a Student Affairs Committee on Program-Budget-Evaluation (SACPBE). This planning body had predominantly student membership, nominated by the Student Government president with senate concurrence and representing each college and major activity area, to be officially appointed by President Mackey in the customary way. When SACPBE completed hearings and adopted recommendations, the plan went to the vice-president for review, refinement, and approval, then to Administrative Planning for incorporation into the general University budget for presidential action.

The Student Association's Finance Committee had previously given informal advice on general program and budget planning to the Business Manager and Student Affairs staff. Now that committee became a formal planning agency in Student Government; through cross-representation on SACPBE, it shared formal responsibility for comprehensive review of the whole Student Affairs program and budget.

Through two planning cycles, the SAPBE system developed into a fairly smooth operation. However, it had to be modified in 1974, as a consequence of action in the Florida legislature.

A GRAND STRATEGY

In 1970 the Student Government's campaign for the power of the purse returned to the legislature, and in the 1974 session the customary bill was filed as S.B. 1004. It proposed to authorize each Student

Government to allocate those portions of the A.&S. fees (represented in the tuition payment per credit hour) that were not otherwise dedicated by the legislature or regents. A university president might veto any allocation but could reassign funds only to intercollegiate athletics or health services; otherwise, deleted funds should go into reserve.

Vice-President Howell immediately conferred with the chancellor, vice-chancellor, and Council for Student Affairs. He urged action to block the passage of the bill at the earliest possible stage. Few people in Tallahassee took very much notice of Howell's concerns; they had become accustomed to such a bill as a standard political exercise for student body presidents. To judge from past experience, studied neglect should lead to the demise of S.B. 1004.

Howell and the USF staff in Student Affairs thought otherwise. Political conditions had changed; voters aged 18 to 21 had now come into the picture, and legislators were likely to be especially attentive to interests of any new voters in an election year. Moreover, there was rumor on campus and among legislative aides of some grand strategy to secure passage of S.B. 1004. The strategy was not hard to predict, and the bill passed as anticipated.

At the end of the session both houses, as usual, were taking bills en bloc with limited debate. In committee hearings, Senator Robert Graham moved to amend H.B. 2892 (a main motion passed by the house that authorized payment by credit card) by attaching S.B. 1004, the activity-fee bill. The committee approved and on the last day of the session, the senate passed H.B. 2892 back to the house with the activity-fee amendment. The bill was adopted and sent to Governor Reubin Askew, almost before anyone except the authors of the strategy noticed what was going on.

A former Student Government president at FSU, serving as a legislative aide in 1974, participated in the action and discussed it with the 1976 conference of the National Association of Student Personnel Administrators. He related how "Senator Graham pulled a very swift parliamentary move with the support of the Senate President. . . . it was definitely a parliamentary maneuver. . . . I don't know that any of the politicians were all that worried because I had insisted from the very start that the president have veto power over allocation and expenditure." He considered the veto to provide all the necessary safeguards against irresponsible action. "I am glad it was there then, I'm glad it's there now, it needs to be."

At least seven of the regents and all of the nine presidents urged Governor Askew to veto H.B. 2892. The matter of fairness to administrators also had to be considered. A president could correct unreasonable or inequitable allocations only in two programs, health services and athletics, leaving other activities without the same protections; a president could reduce their allocation, but could not transfer funds to them in correcting errors and inequities. This limitation seemed to put the presidents in a position where they could not act with fairness and equity. President Mackey pointed out that it also reduced their capability to comply with statutes and policies in other areas for which they were accountable, especially fair employment practices.

Attorney-General Robert Shevin gave an advisory opinion that the act delegated legitimate authority to Student Government as a recognized agency under the Board of Regents' policy. But the university presidents, the Speaker of the House, and some other legislators did not see how any presidential veto could cut through the legal, administrative, and financial tangles that could develop, even with the most responsible actions under provisions of the bill. The president of Florida Atlantic University considered H.B. 2892 also to create "an undesirable adversary relationship between the president and the Student Government Association," where cooperation was preferred, not confrontation.

Governor Askew had been president of the student body at Florida State University, had encouraged participation of the student-body presidents in SUS councils and legislative hearings, and had supported the extension of the vote to age 18 and also the act making 18 the age of majority. He considered the matter very carefully and wrote both a veto message and a rationale for approval. On balance, he decided to sign the bill, and it became effective as of July 1, 1974, as F.S. 290.0951—effective, that is, except for the fact that credit card corporations will not accept tuition charges on their accounts, and the main article cannot be implemented.

Now the Student Affairs planning system had to be revised. The functions of SACPBE in recommending allocations of A.&S. funds passed to ASFAC, the Activities and Service Fee Allocation Committee of Student Government. Academic and Student Affairs programs with multiple funding sources filed plans with Dr. Hewitt. He reviewed and polished the overall program and budget plans, then separated those portions under A.&S. funding which were sent to

ASFAC. All other proposals for A.&S. monies went to ASFAC in the first instance. Otherwise the action steps and timetable remained the same, and President Mackey's directive on the new procedure stated that he would continue to consider allocations as part of the general University budget. Whatever the president might do with a veto, he had to determine the best course of action in the context of the University's whole program and budget, for which he was accountable in every respect.

DISSONANCE AND DYSFUNCTION

Planning for fiscal 1975 went smoothly through the first round under F.S. 290.0951. Planning for fiscal 1976 came almost to a standstill—or standoff.

The sequence of events, beginning at the first of February 1976, covers 85 or more action steps documented in the log for the Student Affairs planning system. Complications came precisely where legislators, regents, and presidents had advised the governor they were most likely to develop—over conflicting roles and power plays in attempts to control the planning system, and over interference with the funds necessary for compliance with Budget Commission and Merit System guidelines, SUS personnel and financial policy, and state and federal regulations on fiscal and employment practices.

When the planning cycle started in February, the chairman of ASFAC sent a letter instructing heads of all units eligible for A.&S. funds to send their full program-budget projections to that office, regardless of funding source. This procedure would, in effect, extend oversight by Student Government to almost the entire program and budget in Academic and Student Affairs. This costly, meaningless duplication of functions was neither contemplated nor required under F.S. 290.0951. Charles Hewitt promptly sent a letter of correction, reiterating the established procedure.

By the April 1 deadline, Dr. Hewitt had compiled and refined requests for A.&S. funds to be submitted to ASFAC; and almost all eligible organizations and activities had filed requests with that committee. But the ASFAC chairman now circulated another letter, objecting to the filing procedure and calling once more for all proposals to go first to ASFAC, regardless of type of unit or activity, or type and source of funding. This time Vice-President Howell responded, reiterating the procedure and underlining his responsibility for recommending the overall Student Affairs budget.

Besides challenging the procedure, ASFAC was also running behind schedule. Hearings on proposals had not been conducted during March or scheduled for April, but all remaining steps had to be completed by June 25, the last day for expenditures on accounts for fiscal 1975. The S.G. president and senate could compensate for slippage in the timetable through a resolution requesting President Mackey to authorize expenditures on a contingency plan based on the 1975 budget. Hewitt and Howell worked with ASFAC and S.G. officers on this procedure; but the resolution was not forthcoming, and Howell froze all A.&S. expenditure accounts on June 25.

On June 29, the S.G. Senate took up an ASFAC appropriations bill in a prolonged, tumultuous session. Amendments deleted several programs and staff positions and applied a 13 percent cut across the board. The S.G. President vetoed the bill on the spot because "some figures needed revision," but the senate overrode the veto.

Vice-President Howell returned the proposed allocations to the S.G. president and published an open letter to the whole University community, written in "sincere anger." The S.G. Senate had struck off 35 permanent Career Service positions, zero-funded student publications, the drug and crisis intervention program, CAUSE, the Child Care Center, the Tape Bank for visually handicapped, all the college councils, and some other well-established organizations and services; many had been initiated by the Student Association or by Student Government itself. It had allocated some $300,000 to a "Common Learning Network" (for student-directed "alternative instruction") and other activities neither registered nor recognized under University policy.

Howell described the action as suggesting "insensitivity unparalleled by any action I have observed in over twenty years of work in higher education. . . . motivations of squelching and mugging of the freedom of the press and free speech. . . . irresponsibility at a level which cannot be tolerated." He returned the entire list of allocations and asked Student Government again to consider a resolution to release contingency funds. On July 12, the S.G. president delivered a senate resolution observing that students "dependent on income from A.&S. funds are being evicted from their dwellings or are starving," and requesting release of contingency funds up to 20 percent of the 1975 budget. Howell then released up to 15 percent of 1975 funds and required his signature or that of Dan Walbolt, Assistant Vice-President, on all purchase orders against A.&S. accounts.

The S.G. president now sent a message to the senate, objecting to the elimination of Career Service positions and the allocations to organizations that "have not met their stated objectives of serving the Student Body." On July 20, the senate adopted a revised appropriations bill, modified only by a schedule that would eliminate the positions after six months. On July 30, Dr. Howell announced that essential activities and services would continue on the 1975 plan and budget; action on all other accounts would be frozen. He added, "The spirit of the law surely did not support the stripping of accountability from the University and/or the firing of state employees over some whim or shortlived preferences by a small group of students."

On August 5 he sent a recommendation that President Mackey accepted, cutting through some of the absurdities. A set of recommendations acceptable to both Student Government and Howell were approved. A second set funded all Career Service positions on Howell's recommendation alone. A third set of accounts for health services and athletics included funds reallocated in keeping with the statute. A set of accounts that did not meet University or sus policy and standards was vetoed, and another set was returned to Student Government for adequate documentation and reconsideration.

On August 31 the final listings came back from the S.G. president. Howell recommended and President Mackey confirmed the formal allocation of some $2 million in A.&S. funds for fiscal 1976.

Politics in the University Repertory

Generally speaking, people who were not particularly involved in this imbroglio tended to shrug it off as "one of those crazy things that are always going on out there at usf." In this instance, as on many other occasions, the action at usf did not follow traditional assumptions, roles, and themes. Often the University's plans would not work out according to scenarios traditionally drawn from politics and government, business and industrial enterprise, or theories in the academic disciplines.

Universities often tolerate inequities, equivocal policies, adversary roles, and dissonant themes, unfavorable to effective teaching and learning, by informal, temporizing arrangements. At usf these appeared right on the surface, and its members had to cope with them directly in order to sustain its identity, growth, and development. Created out of a shared vision in the Florida Plan for a system of higher education accessible to all adults, the University's very existence depended on the experience, resources, and responsibilities to be shared in a support network involving the community, the government, and the general system of higher education. It had to keep both its internal and external ways of work consonant with values, themes, and scenarios embodied in that vision.

A common persuasion that politics and education do not mix has deep roots in American higher education. Yet universities, both public and private, have connections with government, and they share concerns of all citizens for political dealings that will be consistent with principles of fairness, openness, and effectiveness in serving the general welfare. Accordingly, a political scenario centered on shared values of freedom, equality, and responsibility for the public interest should fit comfortably into a university's repertory and facilitate its linkages to government.

Indeed, traditional ways of work in both higher education and parliamentary government share themes and values that have grown out of long experience in synagogue, church, and intentional communities both worldly and enclosed. Universities and parliamentary bodies share commonalities in congregational methods of study and action, to which members contribute out of differing but equally important roles, talents, and resources. The organization of USF paralleled in many respects the organization of parliamentary bodies, with standing and ad hoc committees and councils that move the process of study and action along to closure in "the committee of the whole." Formal parliamentary organization and procedure will not always fit conditions of work in universities; but they share with parliamentary bodies many themes and values in the process of concerted study and action.

Shortcomings of the scalar principle of organization have often surfaced in both higher education and government. For example, some shortcomings surfaced in the expansion of the state's Merit System, and the incompatibility of scalar analogies with academic responsibilities was decidedly involved in the problems with A.&S. allocations. The Student Affairs planning system depended heavily on student participation in the first and most decisive stage, where Student Government had major responsibility to facilitate the process and produce a composite plan. Looking at the planning process as a bureaucratic ladder, however, Student Government seemed to be on the lowest rung, subordinate to presidential authority and power of the veto and having little power in its own right. The log of the 1976 planning process suggests that ASFAC and Student Senate leaders were reacting to this misperception of the planning process and were simply trying to take the upper hand in a bureaucratic power play.

In actual operation, the roles of students, faculty, and staff in program-budget planning called for highly effective disciplines of study and action with high quality of performance. In the end these disciplines prevailed against a political scenario with themes of power struggle, inimical to academic and democratic values.

As Corson observed, "administrative absurdity" tends to go along with the scalar principle of organization. "The theatre of the absurd" has often enacted themes of helplessness against absurdities perpetrated in depersonalized power structures,[3] and the "revolutionary theatre wing" of the protest movement often improvised on such themes at USF. The 1976 log suggests a scenario for the theatre of the absurd, and a theatrical convention it sometimes employs—in which the players fade away one by one, leaving one poor soul to struggle for some meaningful conclusion in a situation utterly indifferent to the human condition.[4] In much the same fashion, the Student Government actors seemed to fade into the audience and watch the vice-president's struggle to cut through the absurdities of the A.&S. allocations.

According to this scenario he would inevitably take dictatorial action, pointing the moral of the absolute indifference of universities to students, with the autocratic administrators behind the equalitarian facade, playing false to democratic themes and values. But somehow, the administrative absurdity seemed to be going on primarily in Student Government. Enacting themes of power struggle tended to dishonor and disrupt both the educational and enterprise scenarios in the University repertory. The act did not do well at the box office; like the actors, the audience seemed to fade away, and the *Oracle* editors and other critics panned the whole production.

Syndicalist scenarios, elaborated in student protest movements around the world during the twentieth century, often included themes of power struggle, depersonalized bureaucracy, and administrative absurdity. In theories of social change, syndicalist philosophies[5] often deal with a hypothesis that obsolete, irrational habits, myths, and folklore tend to erupt out of deeply rooted patterns of culture, and charismatic leaders can capitalize on this upheaval to mobilize revolutionary action around a more or less spontaneous "deed of the moment." This upsurge of irrational energy can immobilize established institutions, disrupt patterns of culture, dissipate energies for constructive work, and may prevail over rational and historical forces in society.

In the United States, syndicalist themes appeared in strategies of Students for a Democratic Society.[6] S.D.S. considered student government weak, uncertain of its role, and vulnerable to capture by a small, well-knit cadre of activists appealing to the student body as a reform movement. Strategies could capitalize on a claim for student power over campus activities and control of activity fees as an issue for "consciousness-raising" in the student body. Activists could capitalize on interaction of student government with university administration to disrupt and immobilize the academic organization. Then the leadership could use the power base in student government to seize control of universities, which would in turn serve as a power base in a similar strategy for immobilizing other institutions that would be captured, reordered, and controlled from a strong center by a well-disciplined intellectual elite.

This syndicalist scenario appeared similar in some respects to some of the experience at USF; at least, a small group of activitists, some active in Student Government, were skilled in confrontation and in perpetrating absurdity with a straight face, and the ructions in the Student Senate very nearly immobilized the budget process for the entire University. Any syndicalist scenario, however, seems absurd on its face in proposing rational ways to mobilize irrational urges; and at USF syndicalist themes did not prevail and did not seem to fit the actual situation at all. The contretemps over A.&S. fees at USF stood well within the American tradition of struggle for equality and freedom against power blocs and arbitrary, insensitive authority. The democratic theme of contending against irrational power structures was elaborated in Student Government and the Student Affairs staff as well as in protest demonstrations. The majority of students and other members who took any part in the matter followed the traditional themes of equality and responsibility for contending against power politics—as they were responsible to do under law, SUS policy, University governance, and long-established principles of academic freedom.

In the social sciences, syndicalist theory has been useful in explaining some effects of social stratification and social change, such as alienation, administrative absurdities, and political power struggles. Max Wise was concerned for syndicalist proclivities in higher education, partly because of their tendency to increase role conflicts and power struggles that increase the burden of responsibility for extraordinary matters, even as they reduce the capability of presidents and trustees to cope with such conflicts and dysfunctions.

Action on the extraordinary, when all systems fail, cannot easily employ some of the usual checks against experience and the balancing of the special interests of different parties involved. Providing the typical model for organizing anything, American government also provides a typical model for exercising the power to cut through checks and balances in order to deal with the extraordinary—a power located primarily in the presidency.

Over the entire period 1950–75, and especially during the course of the Vietnam War, concerns over this center of power and the potentials for its abuse were very much in the forefront of American government and politics. Analogies between developments in government and in the University in many respects rang true to a common experience with the adverse effects of power politics.

From April 1 to July 31, 1974, the activity-fee bill proceeded to enactment and promulgation. Through these months people everywhere were preoccupied with the unique drama of Watergate unfolding in Washington and on TV. On August 8, 1974, this political scenario worked its way to closure, and the *Oracle* published its first "extra" covering the resignation of the President of the United States, Richard M. Nixon. The Board of Student Publications decided to present a plaque to honor the *Oracle* staff for this unique edition with its grave and scholarly coverage of extraordinary news; the board members may also have been moved partly by euphoria, having recently learned that the program would continue under University auspices.

At its August 14 meeting, a representative of Student Government reviewed concerns among its leaders over the conduct of the *Oracle,* especially its editorial criticism of senate and committee proceedings and its practice of endorsing candidates for office. He reminded the board that the governor had signed the activity-fee bill, and now the S.G. Senate had the power to "keep the *Oracle* in line or throw it off campus."

The board went on to clear the program and budget for fiscal 1975 to the vice-president and award the plaque to the *Oracle* editor. The entire board shared the concerns expressed about the new role of Student Government, and they were also sensitive to the denouement of Watergate—showing the extent to which the persuasion that all politics is power politics has pervaded the American experience, even as it had surfaced in the complaints against the *Oracle*. The issues raised in the Watergate affair, and the issues raised in this meeting of the board, strengthened the board members in their commitment to the freedoms, rights, and responsibilities, shared by the press and the people, that hold the United States and its institutions together.

In June 1976, the S.G. Senate in fact fulfilled the prediction that the publications program must "raise its consciousness" and "politicize" or else be zero-funded by the power brokers. The publications program operated on reduced funds for one quarter of 1976, but it did not get "kicked off campus." Similarly, the United States survived the crises of 1974–75 and preserved its democratic political institutions.

But the Watergate affair had an ironic twist, from an academic perspective. Some actions looked very much like the familiar antics in the student government of Old Siwash U., "where the boys will have their fun with their political games." Some of the principal actors had in fact worked in student government at the University of Southern California (Ziegler, Chapin, Porter, Strachan, Segretti, and others). Investigations traced this shared experience through a recurring pattern of dirty tricks and absurdities, an "enemies list," capricious action "just because the power was there," and some key words that were not so elegant as syndicalist terms for "consciousness-raising" and "politicizing."[7]

Like the experience with the activity-fee bill and the impasse in planning the 1976 budget at USF, part of the story of Watergate appeared to have the same roots in a tradition of student government as the first step in a political career that can go all the way to the top, even on the national scene. The scenario included themes of power struggle and political gamesmanship that confronted the nation and its universities with very grave questions about the compatibility of power politics with the public interest and the general welfare. There seemed to be little choice between democratic and syndicalist themes for power politics; the Watergate scenario simply turned syndicalist strategies of student protest upside down. Instead of the universities being "politicized," it suggested that American politics might be "universitized."

Politics and Power

The years of expansion in American higher education, 1950 to 1975, were also years of industrial development, social turmoil, and warfare around the world. Universities strove to keep pace with social change, economic development, and the knowledge explosion, even while some of them suffered violence and terrorism, oppression and disruption. Some universities became tragic symbols of a time of tribulation: venerable foundations such as Charles University of Prague, the French university system, the University of Mexico, and the University of California at Berkeley and Columbia University in the United States; and new and developing ones known beyond their constituency only in the moment of agony, such as the Free University at Stanleyville in the Congo (Zaire), and Jackson State University and Kent State University in the U.S.

There is no occasion for self-congratulation by the Florida universities or any others for passing through these years with minimal distress. The experience of universities throughout history clearly outlines the ever-present danger of irrational, mindless power struggles, disrupting their organization and destroying their capability to advance and share knowledge. The intervention of oppressive power, violence, and terrorism, whether the source be on the campus or in the community, presents a perennial hazard.

Many themes in higher education and politics concern the idea of power and its location, action, direction, and pressure, drawing analogies from the physical sciences. But in higher education, contributive roles in reconciling interests across diversified fields of study and generating multiple configurations for learning, planning, and governance are at a premium; they seem to follow themes and scenarios that are not consonant with traditional metaphors of power. The succession of twentieth-century wars, revolutions, and crises has suggested to many people that something may be wanting in metaphors of power when tested against experience in higher education and in politics alike.[8] Developing scenarios for a more civilized world, in which people can live and work constructively together with less recourse to power struggles, strikes many people as a necessity obvious to any reasonable person.

Out of the period of expansion and turmoil in higher education comes considerable evidence that more effective alternatives are needed. For example, Lewis Feuer studied the experience of student movements, worldwide, from the early nineteenth century forward. He found an apparent commonality in their ideologies and scenarios: a fixation on the dramatic theme that student power is foreordained to confront and disrupt oppressive power structures, generating political upheavals that will in the end liberate and reorder societies in equity and justice. As to the outcome of nearly two centuries of action on this conviction, he concluded that "wherever student movements have flourished academic freedom has consequently declined."[9]

Jacques Ellul, a noted French philosopher, analyzed some commonplace fallacies pervading French society after World War II, fallacies which surfaced in the protest movement of university students in the late 1960s.[10] He observed that the ancient Means-End fallacy becomes particularly obvious to people who have to put up with benefactors claiming to use power "for your own good"— especially the power of the sword. Nowadays, the fallacy of justifying means by the ends may have deadly effect on benefactor and beneficiary alike, especially when the means include contemporary weapons of mass destruction. Ellul concludes, "The use of violence leads inevitably to the establishment of a dictatorship and to the denial of freedom. *Means corrupt Ends*. This is the precise meaning of the slogan of those admirably lucid Polish socialists who announced in 1961: 'Yes, we are *for* socialism, but we are *against* all paths that lead to it.' This is the most profound wisdom and the most precise truth."

In politics, if they have any choice, Americans appear to have a distinct preference for the power of the purse over the power of the sword. In neither case, however, do they particularly favor arbitrary action cuting off participants or imposing obligations on them "for their own good." They prize the principle of equal representation in the process of political action. They value protections for the right of due process under law that facilitate use of the freedom to assemble for concerted study and action. These positive safeguards, capitalizing on academic freedom and responsibility and on concerted action by citizens for their own common good, cannot depend purely on the power of the sword and the purse. Conventional concepts of power in general have little pertinence to effective action in the community, in its politics and its other institutions.

Teaching and learning have other tests of effectiveness in producing good academic work, developing and implementing effective plans, recognizing and correcting errors and shortcomings, improving quality and sharpening skills for high performance. No sovereign power can enforce the responsibility to test, correct, and improve the quality of academic work. Tests for quality and integrity have to be made where the work is done and be built into the learning process at each step.

From the perspective of learning as a process that sustains life in individuals and societies, the experience of the past three decades may appear in a new light. As people turn from themes and scenarios of power, this shared experience in campus and community may provide a rich resource for a new political repertory, centered on the process of learning as a more peaceable way for concerted study and action to bring people together throughout society.

Shared Values and Shared Visions

Capitalizing on Experience

At the end of June 1961, a faculty member remarked that starting the University of South Florida had been a once-in-a-lifetime experience. Another replied, "Once is enough." Together they spoke a simple truth.

Like the people who create them, universities and other institutions have a life history that follows much the same stages of development from conception and gestation to birth and growth to full maturity. Each university is unique in its identity and life history, and the experience unique to each stage of its development could not be replicated—even if anyone *really* wanted to repeat it. In any event, people rarely expect to repeat exactly the same experience but desire to realize even more of the values that rewarded the first venture. Once is enough to open new dimensions of experience with prospects for enlarging and enriching its values. Shortcomings and errors also accompany even the most exciting and rewarding experience; and once in a lifetime gives people more than enough of these misadventures. The desire to do better next time strengthens the urge to do it all over again.

Some of the strongest habits of thought and action develop out of this desire to capitalize on the values of experience both old and new. In this process, errors, shortcomings, and null and negative results have at least as much value as rewards and satisfactions. Irving Lorge used to point to those things that "smart people do *once*" (if at all) as constituting perhaps the most important body of knowledge, having inestimable value in helping people to think *otherwise*—to look for other perspectives, assumptions, and techniques more consonant with values known to experience. Russell Cooper liked to remind people that no learning is ever useless; the knowledge of errors to be avoided may represent the larger, more valuable part of a university's contribution to a community.

Out of the values tested in shared experience grow shared visions that carry into the future the patterns of culture shaping the life history of individuals and institutions. Capitalizing on shared values enriched over generations of life and work, shared visions also prefigure the appearance of new experience in the next stage of life and learning and shape expectations of new opportunities and risks just beginning to come over the horizon. Just as people capitalize on experience to sustain life and learning, so they develop around shared visions those institutions and patterns of culture that will outlive them and sustain the generations to come.

The new University of South Florida grew out of this generative process. The 1956 Florida Plan for higher education, and the program embodied in the 1960 *Accent on Learning,* created a vision of a contemporary university capitalizing on values enriched out of millenia of learning about the learning process itself, centuries of universities, and at least a decade of concerted study and action by thousands of people in the community, across Florida, and throughout the United States. To be a contemporary university meant that its identity, role, and program would link this experience to new expectations for the advancement of knowledge, through each stage of its growth and development. This would be a university—and all of its members, together with the community, would almost literally have to *learn* it into life.

The Enjoyment of Learning

Creating and sharing visions may represent the essential work of higher education. In a university, if nowhere else, people work together to develop shared visions and values that sustain the vitality of the whole human experience and carry the culture of cities into the future.

The *Accent on Learning* emphasized particularly the shared values in academic work—and took particular pains to make clear that this work was the most important responsibility of adults. The University offered neither youthful "fun in the sun" nor an express trip to a prestigious professional position. Contrary to some prevailing folklore, at USF the enjoyment of learning itself made the work worthwhile and generated the values of lifelong learning and lifetime careers for students and faculty.

As far as anyone can tell, learning comes naturally and continues for a lifetime; to stop the process altogether seems almost impossible, though people may get stuck on a plateau at some point or avoid particular ways of learning more or less successfully. In any case, the University planners were determined to share the enjoyment of learning and to interfere as little as possible with other participants in the learning process.

Of all the shared values and visions sustaining USF in its growth and development, the founders and charter members may have capitalized most fully on the personal enjoyment of learning. New, small, untested, of unknown quality on any count, operating on slim resources, the University of South Florida had little more to offer than the spirit of sharing in a new opportunity to enjoy learning as the vocation and recreation of adults. And the enjoyment of learning may be all that anyone could ask of higher education.

Equality

Among the visions of equality shared in the American experience, the values of *a birthright in lifelong learning* join naturally with the values of life, liberty, and the pursuit of happiness. Assuming that learning is an essential part of the life process, this birthright has values that ring true to the whole human experience and a growing body of knowledge.

Lifelong learning is already a fact of life and a responsibility of American higher education. On the horizon the vision of a learning society is already appearing, with centers for teaching and learning dispersed into workplaces, homes, and community gathering places. Equal access, the principle particularly emphasized in plans for expansion in the 1950s, called for the general system of higher education to diversify as well as expand. Creating more types of institutions, programs, and places for learning offered more options, more pathways, and more access for people in all walks of life to participate in the system.

Developing more pathways for learning has required new models for the organization of educational institutions and systems, alternative to scalar, monolithic configurations of traditional form. Analogies to a network of organs and systems, to a road map with many connections between fields of study, to a fabric woven or knitted together, to an orchestra or repertory theatre, seem to describe more fully the shape and form of a university and the functions involved in its organization.

Many of the "process models" that are being developed for a variety of institutions and systems capitalize on such metaphors, tested against experience and consistent with expectations for future performance in shared responsibilities. The general understanding of the many ways to integrate different configurations of people, process, and resources into a coherent pattern of shared responsibility has steadily grown. The recognition that each unique configuration is equally important, that each unique person has equal responsibility to hold together the configuration for life and work, capitalizes on much of the experience of equality as an integrative factor in patterns of culture.

Americans generally incline toward a fair-minded persuasion that people have to be "equal to the tasks" they are asked to undertake and the risks they have to run. Along with this persuasion comes an expectation that learning can provide some way for people to develop capabilities equal to new tasks. People generally view education as a way to close the gap between experience and expectations in the next stage of personal, community, and national development— as far as the state of the art makes any closure possible.

In this context a general "merit principle" seems to have developed and to have been applied in several different ways in government, education, and the enterprise system. This principle is not an American invention, but in the American experience it seems to have had particular survival value. It may have been the only feasible approach for people organizing a new society remote from European centers of sovereign power and authority. In the frontier experience, rank and nobility, power and authority had very little pertinence to the actual responsibilities and risks with which people and communities had to cope. Coming together in voluntary association on the scene of the action, people were able to share resources and authorize responsibility specific to actual tasks. Voluntary association put a premium on learning and capitalized on diversified experience in order to meet the expectations of performance in many new tasks in a new way of life.

Sharing responsibility equal to "merit" involved much the same process as organizing for teaching and learning: developing threefold configurations in which the combination of people, process, and resources could be modified in various ways to fit differing conditions and requirements for effective performance of necessary roles and responsibilities. The equalitarian "merit principle" that people should be equal to their tasks had to be applied in all walks of life, not just at the apex of the social pyramid or the bureaucratic ladder embodied in *meritocratic* principles of social organization. Many of the network and process models for higher education and other social systems have applied the equalitarian principle of merit in a prefigurative approach that calls for people to share out of diversified talents and experience in developing effective ways to cope with opportunities and tasks both new and old.

These habits of thought and action give a fairly clear vision of equality, tested against more than two centuries of American experience. Some blurred edges appear, and some clouded visions that seem to pit an earned right against a birthright in opportunities for learning and career development. For instance, when the University of South Florida tested the quality of academic work by students and faculty, its approach appeared to equivocate on traditional meritocratic standards for student and faculty selection, to mix administrative and faculty roles and ranks, and to blur the lines between scholarly disciplines and levels of instruction. When USF tested its program and budget against the mission to advance and share knowledge throughout the community and society, its approach often appeared to diverge from the traditional academic lockstep, the professional career ladder, and the generally accepted principles of efficiency, equilibrium, and control in administrative operations. The University's personalized approach to participation in learning, planning, and organization often seemed to skirt equalitarian issues of racism and sexism, academic freedom and democratic governance. In these respects, the University was decidedly in the mainstream of higher education and national life.

The plans for expansion and development in higher education addressed many shortcomings and equivocal approaches. In general, the approach taken by national bodies and state authorities was farsighted and large-minded. But in many respects, the outcomes fell short of expectations. In conversation about the constraints on resources for education and some of the factors involved in the "generation gap," Margaret Mead made an offhand comment that young Americans have learned one thing for sure: grownups cannot count. . . . but they can usually be depended upon to come up short.

In keeping with this observation, experience suggests that growth and development in American education have been coming up short, but not for lack of commitment or for lack of inclination to share resources generously. Nor have shared values in the enjoyment of learning, principles of freedom and equality, and diversified responsibilities required in a culture of cities been disregarded or neglected. Shortcomings most frequently appear to arise from some ingrained meritocratic habits of planning: counting only the places at the top of occupational rankings, career ladders, and the social pyramid in planning for higher education; and counting only each cohort of new births, disregarding the adult population, in planning the entire system of education.

As one indicator of this tendency, a metaphor of "the talented tenth" recurs in higher education from Thomas Jefferson's notes on his proposed educational system for Virginia,[1] through the talent search of the 1950s, to the founders' approach in recruiting top-ranking students for USF. Even before World War II, this metaphor became incongruent with the growing needs for well-educated people in all walks of life. And long before World War II, the assumption that formal education ended with the beginning of adulthood became invalid in light of the growing need for access to lifelong learning by a populace challenged with change and opportunity in almost every aspect of personal and national life.

Despite shortcomings, the course of development in national life and in higher education has moved toward a shared vision of equality as "the spirit of things that *work.*" Embodied in this vision is the birthright of all Americans: the freedom and opportunity for learning equal to the tasks of life and work, in a nation equal to its growing and diversifying responsibilities in a changing, turbulent world.

Community Is a Verb

Planning for the University of South Florida capitalized on an ancient vision of the community of scholars. The insight that "community is a verb" centered planning on the process of bringing people together in shared responsibility. Themes developing out of modern experience—the sharing of resources and contributions to learning among members of a university, the cultivation of a network of scholars, voluntary associations in the learned professions, and universities around the world, sharing a common mission to advance knowledge—all were manifestations of visions deeply rooted in the Judaeo-Christian heritage.

The shared vision of a community at once distinctive in identity and integrated into a worldwide network, sharing responsibilities with other communities in a single mission, emerged from the experience of congregational life and intentional communities. Even a cursory review of the history of intentional communities gives an immediate impression of the extraordinary diversity in their forms, rules, themes, and ways of life and work. Those of enclosed or monastic form moved away from the cities during the great persecutions, seeking to distance and protect themselves somewhat from a hostile society. The American model for residential colleges capitalized on this experience, inherited from European institutions similarly self-contained and self-governing. The residential college followed in some ways the tradition of distancing the community of scholars, protecting them from the distractions of external affairs and guarding them against interference from disorder or oppressive powers in the body politic. In similar ways of nurturing members in a special environment and integrating life, learning, and work, the residential colleges and universities adopted strict parietal rules and disciplines ordering the life style of all students, faculty, and staff.

Centers that typically became known as universities, for their hospitality to scholars from all Christendom, frequently developed out of more worldly forms of intentional community, especially cathedral chapters and their schools in urban settings. Out of this heritage, both urban and residential colleges in the United States shared common concerns for developing their distinctive identity, role, and scope, their autonomy in self-governance, and the commitment to teaching and learning shared with the community of scholars throughout the world.

The Florida Plan for higher education capitalized on much of this tradition in establishing integrative principles guiding the development of new autonomous colleges and universities, diversified in role and in the scope of their commitments to serve urban constituencies. Traditional models could sometimes be replicated in a contemporary university, but frequently the underlying principles, themes, and values had to be transformed into new patterns and ways of work. It was the process of *doing* community that most often rang true to contemporary experience and expectations.

For instance, plans for USF could not replicate a cluster-college model with the smallness and close personal knowledge characteristic of enclosed communities and American residential colleges. Its design for academic organization did capitalize on the process of personalizing academic work and forming small disciplinary configurations in the faculty that gave mutual support to their members. The personalized approach and disciplinary configurations, with little modification, have come down through the centuries in the heritage from intentional communities, the oldest universities, and the American residential college; and they have served USF well.

The *Accent on Learning* emphasized personal commitment and planning for a course of study by each student, to be assessed for consistency with the University's mission and facilitated by an advisor. This approach saved the principle of shared responsibility and mutual support honored by generations of scholars and practiced by American universities in ways of work that are both rigid and prescriptive, flexible and self-directed. This process of choice, program design, and personal commitment must reconcile threefold expectations: of students for a career, of the university for its mission, and of the community for developing effective social systems.

Such shared responsibility for students and faculty requires a continuing process of performance evaluation for correcting errors and testing learning against experience and expectations, both personal and social. At the very heart of the shared vision of a community of scholars stands a shared value of integrity—realized in an integrative process generating trustworthy knowledge and reliable ways of work—that has sustained the commitment to learn and to share knowledge across the generations and through the centuries of human experience.

"Community is a verb" accents the primary commitment to the process of integrating life, learning, and work, which stands at the center of the American heritage of higher education. Manifold themes, models, and scenarios have grown out of long experience with this process of reconciling the diversified experience and expectations that must be integrated into effective ways of life and work. These values and visions have been shared with organizations and enterprises throughout society, strengthening universities and other institutions in formal and informal ways.

For example, some corporations have adopted performance contracting by teams of employees who share functions in a distinctive process. They capitalize on interaction in these small, mutually supportive configurations, by assigning individual responsibilities that will accomplish a general plan for the whole enterprise. From corporate experience, ways of performance contracting and evaluation have flowed back into universities, enriching both academic and administrative ways of planning and organization. And the conciliar process familiar to the academic community has facilitated countless tasks of planning and problem-solving by committees, commissions, and advisory bodies serving government, corporate enterprise, and other institutions in manifold ways.

Many community and national interests converge on such ways to bring people together in shared responsibility. The principle of "community is a verb" undergirds many effective ways of work and generates many shared visions of a more peaceable and civil way of civilization.

Epilogue

Studies of the half-century of comparatively peaceful American campuses sometimes suggested that an appalling countervision lay under the quiet surface. Signs of apathy and a pervasive sense of helplessness under insensitive authority concerned some observers of the "silent generation" of the 1950s. Disaffection and disillusion with the academic lockstep and occupational rat race distressed many teachers and students alike.

A postwar generation was growing up with the dispiriting knowledge that atomic and biochemical weapons systems had the same death-dealing effects on winners and losers alike in wars and power struggles. To some observers, the calm campus atmosphere sometimes seemed closer to the sorrowful hush of a funeral than to the quietness of living and growing things. Wylie Sypher summed up recurrent themes in the literature of the period that seemed to ring true to the mood of sorrow and apathy in society and on the quiet campus:

> To adapt the self to the new realities of power is to feel a new kind of dread, to sense a new kind of guilt, to be weighted by a new kind of helplessness quite different from our helplessness before either the gods or the natural order.[1]

In the universities and in society, however, shared visions of life provide more than optimistic alternatives to the awareness of death and despair. These visions grow out of long human experience with genuine, life-sustaining values shared in personal identity, productive work, and mature enjoyment of ways to learn and act in community.

In his developmental study of America at the time of the Bicentennial, Erik Erikson suggested that even now some new scenarios, elaborating upon shared visions of life, may prefigure "a century of the adult" coming over the horizon of the year 2000.[2] Just as the vision of childhood seemed to flower in the nineteenth century and the twentieth century gravitated towards visions of adolescence and youth, the new century may center in generative themes and mature, adult roles, in processes that sustain life in all forms and stages.

In small ways the experience of the University of South Florida may prefigure some dimensions of higher education in "a century of the adult." Lifelong learning became a reality. Some of the lines and scales dividing people of different rank, level of education, occupation, age, sex, and color began to blur and dissipate. Postfigurative ways of prescribing courses of study, roles and rules, and standards of conduct began to give way to prefigurative ways of planning and learning how to cope with conditions new to the experience of all concerned.

A new dimension of community service came into the mission of higher education, expanding beyond immediate concerns for educational and economic development into more extensive concerns for the environment, the quality of life, and the culture of cities. In the Tampa Bay area, these concerns took visible, palpable form in the campus environment and in the surrounding city, rural hinterland, and seashores. Ecological study of the fragile network of land, air, and water sustaining the life of the sea, the cities, and the countryside became more than mere abstract exercise of scientific expertise. People could see and feel changes, gains, and losses from day to day. This shared experience opened shared values that would clearly be saved and enriched, or lost and forgotten, according to the course of study and action chosen in the University and community.

Recalling those experiences that had the greatest impact on their learning at the University, members of the charter class often recount an especially sharp contrast in vision and countervision.

They were among the first human beings to see the whole Earth. NASA's photographs from space shared the vision of its whole life, bright against the black firmament, incredibly beautiful.

They read Rachel Carson's *Silent Spring*.[3] They considered some sobering implications of her quiet, scholarly analysis of a nightmare world, where no birds might be left to sing, no fish, no dolphins, perhaps no people to be sad that they were gone.

Against these images, some academic folklore, some commonplace issues and stresses of life and learning, seemed significant primarily as indicators for new directions, signals for an urgent effort to learn how to sustain all creatures in the unique environment of Earth. Now that they could see it whole, Earth appeared incredibly alive, very dear and worth caring for.

Beyond equality of rights there was a birthright of all life in this Earth, of incalculable value. Beyond freedom and responsibility, there was a commitment to learn how to care for life. Beyond rules and statutes stood the knowledge that no punishment for error, mischief, or insult to the environment will suffice to sustain a living world against irreparable loss.

Against all risks, against all hazards of ignorance, carelessness, and obsolescent folklore, there was also a kind of confidence in "the spirit of things that *work*" to sustain people in their life and learning. These charter members had the experience of learning how to create and develop a new university, in addition to planning for their own growth in knowledge and expertise. Their choices made a difference in their careers; their participation contributed to the life of the University. They enjoyed themselves as they learned how much people can accomplish when they join in concerted study and action. The pioneering spirit of adventure in opening up new worlds of experience imparted also the spirit of caring and sharing in the vital responsibility to sustain a new university, their community, and their world.

Their visions and values rang true to the expectations and experience they shared with one another as the University visibly grew around them, sustained by their own effort. The community, their families, and the state had cared enough to give them the opportunity to learn; they learned how to take full advantage of it and contribute in return. Taking care for learning opened the way to sustain, share, and enjoy the values given in their heritage of shared visions for a whole, living Earth.

Erik Erikson closed his Jefferson Lectures with a watchword for "a century of the adult," a commonplace phrase that students of these decades often used as they took leave of each other. For the next century in higher education, this watchword may well serve all who love learning and choose life.

Take care.

Notes

Chapter 1

1. *Report of the President's Commission on Higher Education*, vol. 1, *Establishing the Goals* (Washington: U.S. Government Printing Office, 1947), pp. 39–43, 101, and passim.
2. U.S. Department of Health, Education and Welfare, *Digest of Educational Statistics: 1968* (Washington: U.S. Government Printing Office, 1968), p. 63.
3. Clark Kerr, "The Frantic Race to Remain Contemporary," in *The Contemporary University, U.S.A.*, ed. by Robert S. Morison (Cambridge: Riverside Press, 1966), p. 24.
4. K. Patricia Cross, *Beyond the Open Door* (San Francisco: Jossey-Bass, 1971), pp. 1–11.
5. A.J. Brumbaugh and Myron Blee, *Higher Education and Florida's Future* (Gainesville: University of Florida Press, 1956), p. 4.
6. Ibid., pp. 73–74.
7. Lewis B. Mayhew, *Colleges Today and Tomorrow* (San Francisco: Jossey-Bass, 1969), p. 21.
8. Seymour Harris, *A Statistical Portrait of Higher Education* (New York: McGraw-Hill, 1972), p. 3.
9. Clark Kerr, *The Uses of the University* (Cambridge: Harvard University Press, 1963), p. 89.
Note: Gerald Grant and David Riesman, *The Perpetual Dream: Reform and Experiment in the American College* (Chicago: The University of Chicago Press, 1978), includes an assessment of the development of the cluster colleges in the University of California at Santa Cruz, and also of New College, now incorporated in the University of South Florida.

Chapter 2

1. Speech by President John S. Allen, inserted by the Honorable Charles E. Bennett in the *Congressional Record*, 9 February 1959.
2. President's Commission on Education beyond the High School, *Summary Report* (Washington: U.S. Government Printing Office, 1957), pp. 5ff.
3. Gerard Piel, *The Acceleration of History* (New York: Alfred A. Knopf, 1972), pp. 21–31, is an exceptionally graphic account of this developmental process in distinctive scholarly and practical realms and in overall knowledge.
4. Floyd W. Reeves, "Comments on Faculty Matters," attachment to "Working Paper on Staffing Problems," typescript (February 1959), University of South Florida Archives, Florida Collection.

5. *St. Petersburg Times,* October 17, 1957.

6. "Working Paper on Staffing Problems," typescript (February 1959), University of South Florida Archives, Florida Collection.

7. Reeves, "Comments on Faculty Matters."

Chapter 3

1. Cross, pp.163–65, suggests alternative approaches to certification, departing from this meritocratic assumption.

2. James D. Mooney, *The Principles of Organization* (New York: Harper, 1947), p. 14.

3. John J. Corson, *Governance of Colleges and Universities,* Carnegie Series in American Education (New York: McGraw-Hill, 1960).

4. Ibid., p. 18.

5. Ibid., pp. 9–11.

6. "Working Paper on Staffing Problems," with attachment, "A Suggested Plan" (for faculty organization), typescript (February 1959), University of South Florida Archives. (Marginal notes identified as Elliot Hardaway's handwriting by Jay Dobkin, librarian of the Florida Collection, University of South Florida Archives.)

7. Esther Lloyd-Jones and Margaret Ruth Smith, *Student Personnel Work as Deeper Teaching* (New York: Harper and Row, 1954).

8. Kate Hevner Mueller, *Student Personnel Work in Higher Education* (Boston: Houghton Mifflin, 1961), pp. 386–94, gives a detailed outline of a complex report prepared by a joint committee for the American College Personnel Association, the National Association of Women Deans and Counselors, and the National Association of Student Personnel Administrators.

9. Lewis B. Mayhew, ed., "Intellectual Tone for a State University," *University of South Florida Bulletin,* vol. 3, no. 4 (February 1960), University of South Florida Archives.

10. Philip E. Jacob, *Changing Values in College* (New York: Harper, 1957)

11. Eliot Friedson, ed., *Student Government, Student Leaders and the American College* (Philadelphia: United States National Student Association, 1955).

12. Margaret B. Fisher and Jeanne L. Noble, *College Education as Personal Development* (Englewood Cliffs, N.J.: Prentice-Hall, 1960). This orientation textbook, published about six months before Dr. Fisher came to USF, had been adopted for scores of such courses by September 1960.

Chapter 4

1. Lyn. H. Lofland, *A World of Strangers* (New York: Basic Books, 1973), p. 82.

2. Jacques Barzun, *The American University* (New York: Harper and Row, 1968).

3. W. Storrs Lee, *God Bless Our Queer Old Dean* (New York: G. P. Putnam's Sons, 1959).

4. *Pseudepigraphica Academica* cannot be located in any catalog, reference, or index; the late Howard Johnshoy had the only copy I ever saw of this wonderful, scurrilous work on the Greek revival in America, which I believe to have been published by Williams and Wilkins of Baltimore.

5. Censure was published in the *American Association of University Professors Bulletin* (March 1964), pp. 40–57; hereafter cited as AAUP *Bulletin.* Removal of censure was reported in the AAUP *Bulletin* (Summer 1968), p. 178.

6. Charles E. Dennison, *Faculty Rights and Responsibilities in Eight Independent Colleges* (New York: Bureau of Publications, Teachers College, Columbia University, 1955).

7. Earl S. McGrath, *The Graduate School and the Decline of Liberal Education* (New York: Bureau of Publications, Teachers College, Columbia University, 1959).

8. Kerr, *The Uses of the University.*

9. Alain Touraine, *The Academic System in American Society* (New York: McGraw-Hill, 1974); see especially the chapter "Protest," describing the U.S. movement in the context of worldwide student protest and intervention in politics; Lewis S. Feuer, *The Conflict of Generations* (New York: Basic Books, 1969); a cross-cultural analysis from psychosocial perspectives of student protest since the nineteenth century.

10. Correspondence, August 1973.

Chapter 5

1. Harvard Committee, *General Education in a Free Society* (Cambridge: Harvard University Press, 1945), pp. xiv–xv.

2. Report of the President's Commission on Higher Education, *Higher Education for American Democracy,* vol. 1, *Establishing the Goals* (Washington: U.S. Government Printing Office, 1947), pp. 49–50 passim.

3. J. B. Lon Hefferlin, *Dynamics of Academic Reform* (San Francisco: Jossey-Bass, 1969), p. 71.

4. Southern Association of Colleges and Schools, *Report on the University of South Florida,* mimeographed (October 1963), p. 6, University of South Florida Archives.

5. University of South Florida Committee on University Organization, Minutes (December 1970), University of South Florida Archives.

6. Hefferlin, pp. 67–68.

7. University College, *General Education and Integrative Studies, 1973–74* (East Lansing: Michigan State University, 1973); Daniel Bell, *The Reforming of General Education* (New York: Columbia University Press, 1966); "DeBary Proposes Major Academic Reorganization," *Columbia Reports* (April 1973), p. 1.

8. Margaret Mead, *Culture and Commitment: The New Relationships between the Generations in the 1970s* (New York: Doubleday and Co., 1970); rev. and updated ed. (New York: Columbia University Press, 1978), pp. 65–94, 147–58.

Chapter 6

1. Jacques Barzun, "College to University—and After," *The American Scholar* (Spring 1964), p. 215.

2. Earl McGrath, *The Graduate School and the Decline of Liberal Education* (New York: Teachers College, 1959). Also pertinent and useful are Daniel Bell, *The Reforming of General Education* (New York: Columbia University Press, 1966), and Nevitt Sanford, *Where Colleges Fail* (San Francisco: Jossey-Bass, 1967).

3. University of South Florida Bulletin, *Accent on Learning* (1961–63), vol. 3, no. 2.

4. Cecil Mackey, "Memorandum on Academic Reorganization," (June 1971), University of South Florida Archives.

Chapter 7

1. Mead, pp. 65–94, 147–58.
2. Lloyd E. Blauch, ed., *Education for the Professions* (Washington: U.S. Government Printing Office, 1955), p. 5.
3. Paul L. Dressel, "Developments of Professional Education," in *College and University Curriculum* (Berkeley: McCutchan Publishing Corporation, 1971), p. 153.
4. Edgar H. Schein, *Professional Education* (New York: McGraw-Hill, 1972), pp. 59–70.
5. Carnegie Commission on Higher Education, *Less Time, More Options* (New York: McGraw-Hill, 1971), p. 1.
6. Frank C. Pierson, *The Education of American Businessmen* (New York: McGraw-Hill, 1959); Robert A. Gordon and James E. Howell, *Higher Education for Business* (New York: Columbia University Press, 1959).
7. L. E. Grinter, "Report of the Committee on Evaluation of Engineering Education," *Journal of Engineering Education* (1974).
8. Newman A. Hall, ed., *The Britannica Review of Developments in Engineering Education* (Chicago: Encyclopedia Britannica, Inc., 1970).
9. B. A. Walker, "Goals of Engineering Education," *Journal of Engineering Education* (1974), p. 34.
10. Oliver Cope and Jerrold Zacharias, *Medical Education Reconsidered* (Philadelphia: J. P. Lipponcott and Co., 1966); Hans Popper, ed., *Trends in New Medical Schools*, A Mount Sinai Hospital Monograph (New York: Grune and Stratton, 1967); Barrie Thorne, "Professional Education in Medicine," in *Education for the Professions of Medicine, Law, Theology, and Social Welfare*, ed. Everett C. Hughes (New York: McGraw-Hill, 1973).

Chapter 8

1. Florida Board of Regents, "Comprehensive Development Plan of the State University System of Florida, 1969–1980," University of South Florida Archives.
2. Lewis B. Mayhew, *Graduate and Professional Education, 1980: A Survey of Institutional Plans* (New York: McGraw-Hill, 1970), p. 5.
3. National Board on Graduate Education, "Federal Policy Alternatives toward Graduate Education," *Chronicle of Higher Education,* (February 11, 1974).
4. Ann M. Heiss, *Challenges to Graduate Schools* (San Francisco: Jossey-Bass, 1970), pp. 73, 76ff.; a report of trends in the organization for graduate education and interdisciplinary program design. Several alternative approaches to planning and administration are consistent with the usf plan, or follow similar trends toward resource-sharing and diffusion of responsibilities.

Chapter 9

1. Lewis B. Mayhew to John S. Allen, memorandum, Office of Institutional Research and Evaluation Services, (August 11, 1961), University of South Florida Archives.
2. University of South Florida, Self-Study, 1965: A Report to the Southern Association of Colleges and Schools, mimeographed, p. 87, University of South Florida Archives.

3. The analysis of the University's relationship to the black community and its approach to racial integration has been greatly facilitated by interviews granted by John S. Allen, Grace Allen, Jean Battle, Ed Kopp, Donn Smith, Frank Spain, Henry Robertson, William H. Taft, and Richard Pride, of the University of South Florida; by Augusta Thomas, Claudia Silas, and Jesse Artest, of the Tampa Urban League board and staff, who in 1960 were working in the Hillsborough County Public Schools to recruit black students; and by the late Johnnie Ruth Clark, dean, St. Petersburg Junior College; Sondra Wilson, Altamease Hamilton, and Eva Pride of Hillsborough Community College, among many other students and educators.

4. Cross, pp. 157, 171. Her study includes extensive data from the talent search and other nationwide inventories of academic achievement. The human rights strategy for "pathfinders" to test the segregation laws and pave the way for black students in schools and colleges, and the difficulties of coping with their stressful experience, have been analyzed in depth by Robert Coles, *Children of Crisis* (Boston: Little, Brown and Co., 1964).

5. Committee on Institutional Research, "Analysis of Marginal Student Program, USF, Trimester IIIB, 1964," Institutional Research Report No. 6, prepared by Edmund E. Allen, mimeographed (University of South Florida, November 1964), University of South Florida Archives.

6. Robert M. Roth and H. Arnold Meyersburg, "The Non-Achievement Syndrome," *Personnel and Guidance Journal* (1963), pp. 535–40. This study, one of the first such investigations at the college level, aimed to develop some counseling techniques to help non-achieving students (those who make high test scores and low grades, and improve in basic skills without showing corresponding improvement in academic work). The technique of developing sliding scales combining grades and test scores, employed by the Committee on Academic Standards, was brought to USF by Margaret Fisher, who assisted in the research project by Roth and Meyersburg at Hampton Institute.

7. The figures and reports cited in these sections come from annual reports, memoranda, and minutes of the Committee on Academic Standards, 1960–72, and the Committee on Academic Regulations, 1972–75, in the USF Office of the Registrar.

Chapter 10

1. Cross, pp. 18–31.

2. Christopher Jencks, *Inequality: A Reassessment of the Effects of Family and Schooling in America* (New York: Basic Books, 1972), pp. 3–41.

3. Cf. B. F. Skinner, *Science and Human Behavior* (New York: Macmillan, 1953).

4. L. F. Malpass et al., *Human Behavior*, vols. 1 and 2 (Dubuque, Iowa: William C. Brown Co., 1962; rev. ed., New York: McGraw-Hill, 1963).

5. L. F. Malpass, A. Gilmore, M. Hardy, and C. Williams, *Comparisons of Two Automated Teaching Procedures for Retarded Children*, CRP #1267 (Washington: U.S. Office of Education, 1963).

6. M. B. Fisher and L. F. Malpass, *A Comparison of Programed and Standard Textbooks in College Instruction*, CRP #1921, U.S. Office of Education (Tampa: University of South Florida, 1963).

7. Morton Deutsch, "Education and Distributive Justice: Some Reflections on Grading Systems," *The American Psychologist*, vol. 34, no. 5 (May 1979), pp. 391–401. The author analyzes an "artificially created shortage of symbols of merit" and suggests alternatives applicable to honors programs and other special awards and opportunities.

8. C. M. Warnath, *New Myths and Old Realities* (San Francisco: Jossey-Bass, 1971).

Chapter 11

1. "Working Paper on Staffing Problems"; attachment: Floyd Reeves, "Comments."

2. A. E. Bayer, *Teaching Faculty in Academe,* 1972–73, ACE Research Report No. 8 (Washington: American Council on Education, 1973); A. E. Bayer and Helen S. Astin, "Sex Differentials in the Academic Reward System," *Science* (May 23, 1975), pp. 796–802.

3. "Working Paper" and attachment: Floyd Reeves, "Comments."

4. Dana L. Farnsworth, *Mental Health in College and University* (Cambridge: Harvard University Press, 1957), p. 79.

5. Office of Institutional Research and Evaluation Services, "Correlation Coefficients, Instructor and Examination Grades," mimeographed (University of South Florida, February 1961), University of South Florida Archives.

6. Office of Institutional Research and Evaluation Services, "Student Evaluation of Courses and Faculty," mimeographed (University of South Florida, July 1961), University of South Florida Archives.

7. Office of Institutional Research and Evaluation Services, "Students' Perceptions of the University of South Florida Environment: A Preliminary Report," Institutional Research Report No. 1, mimeographed (University of South Florida, September 1964), University of South Florida Archives.

8. Office of Institutional Research and Evaluation Services, "Quality of Students and Grading Practices at the University of South Florida," Institutional Research Report No. 23, mimeographed (University of South Florida, 1965), University of South Florida Archives.

9. Office of Evaluation Services, "Grade Distributions by College," mimeographed (University of South Florida, March 1962), University of South Florida Archives.

10. Office of Evaluation Services, "Grades of Junior and Senior Students, 'Native' to the University of South Florida, by Major," mimeographed (University of South Florida, April 1963), University of South Florida Archives.

Chapter 12

1. *Report of the Visiting Committee of the Southern Association of Colleges and Schools for Accreditation of the University of South Florida, February 28–March 2, 1965.* University of South Florida Archives. This report includes an attachment, "Political Interference and Red Tape" (pp. 52–66), giving particulars and including a series of articles by Sam Mase for the *St. Petersburg Times,* an accurate, comprehensive account of the issues and conditions involved in the transition from the Board of Control to the Board of Regents.

2. Correspondence, John S. Allen to T. B. Castiglia, April 11, May 20, 1966, Personnel Services files, University of South Florida.

3. Correspondence and memoranda from various universities in the State University System to T. B. Castiglia, April–May 1966, Personnel Services files, University of South Florida.

4. Corson, p. 15.

5. Laurence J. Peter and Raymond Hull, *The Peter Principle* (New York: William Morrow & Co., 1969).

6. Willard F. Enteman, "The Integrity of the Student," in Clarence C. Walton and Frederick de W. Bolman, *Disorders in Higher Education* (Englewood Cliffs: Prentice-Hall, 1979), pp. 151–52.

7. Office of Academic Services, "Selected Statistics on Faculty Effort, Productivity and Teaching Load at the University of South Florida, Fall Quarter 1970," Office of Academic Services (University of South Florida, 1971).

Chapter 13

1. Erik H. Erikson, *Toys and Reasons,* the Godkin Lectures of 1972 (New York: William Morrow & Co., 1977); Erikson, *Dimensions of a New Identity,* The Jefferson Lectures of 1973 (New York: William Morrow & Co., 1974). On the testing of analogy against experience, see also J. Bronowski, *Science and Human Values* (New York: Harper and Row, 1956).

2. Terrence N. Tice, *Student Rights, Decisionmaking and the Law,* ERIC/Higher Education Research Report No. 10 (Washington: The American Association of Higher Education, 1975).

3. The American Association of University Professors developed a "Statement on Faculty Responsibility for the Academic Freedom of Students," published in its *Bulletin* (Summer 1964), pp. 254–57. With a consortium of ten professional associations in higher education, the AAUP participated in developing another model for students' roles and responsibilities, "The Joint Statement of Rights and Freedoms of Students," published in its *Bulletin* (Winter 1967), pp. 365–68.

4. Cf. Tice.

5. Charles Meriam, *Public and Private Government* (New Haven: Yale University Press, 1944).

6. *Report of the President's Commission on Higher Education* (1947), vol. 1, pp. 12–14, and vol. 3, passim.

7. W. Max Wise, "New Configurations in Governance," in *The Troubled Campus,* ed. G. Kerry Smith (San Francisco: Jossey-Bass, 1970), pp. 131–36. A more detailed account appears in W. Max Wise's *The Politics of the Private College* (New Haven: Hazen Foundation, 1968).

Chapter 14

1. Margaret B. Fisher and Joe A. Howell, "Evaluation and Accountability," *National Association of Student Personnel Administrators Journal,* vol. 10 (October 1972), pp. 118–23.

2. Walton and Bolman, eds., *Disorders in Higher Education.* 1979) A recent symposium examined several models for organizing higher education, outlining role conflicts, dissonant themes and scenarios affecting students, faculty and administration. An exceptionally useful analysis of student roles is included in Enteman's "The Integrity of the Student."

3. Kafka's works are well-known examples; "beat" literature of the 1950s elaborated similar themes. Examples of existentialist themes of alienation are surveyed in an excellent study by Martin Esslin, *Theatre of the Absurd* (New York: Viking Press, 1973).

4. Among several plays capitalizing on the device of disappearing actors to accentuate the effect of loneliness, alienation, and helplessness, one of the earliest examples comes from Pirandello, *Six Characters in Search of an Author,* where only the stage manager remains to cope with the historic sense that things somehow have to come to meaningful closure. Eugene Ionesco gives this device a comic or tragicomic turn in such plays as *Exit the King.* In *The Chairs,* he creates a special effect by inverting the device; the chairs people the stage with all sorts of actors, audible but invisible, waiting for the one player to apppear. . .

5. Georges Sorel, *The Illusions of Progress* (Berkeley: The University of California Press, 1959); Sorel, *Reflections on Violence* (New York: Peter Smith, 1941); Vilfredo Pareto, *The Mind and Society* (New York: Harcourt Brace, 1935).

6. Touraine, *The Academic System in American Society,* pp. 222, 230–35.

7. Carl Bernstein and Bob Woodward, *All the President's Men* (New York: Warner Books, 1974), pp. 132–38.

8. Gregory Bateson has recently published his letter to fellow regents of the University of California, analyzing analogies to power and suggesting that the myth of power is obsolete.

Gregory Bateson, *Mind and Nature* (New York: E. P. Dutton, 1979), pp. 217ff.

9. Lewis S. Feuer, *The Conflict of Generations* (New York: Basic Books, 1969), p. 44.

10. Jacques Ellul, *Critique of the New Commonplaces* (New York: Alfred A. Knopf, 1968), pp. 300, 302.

Chapter 15

1. Thomas Jefferson, *Notes on the State of Virginia,* ed. William Peden (Chapel Hill: University of North Carolina Press, 1955), pp. 146–151, 289.

Epilogue

1. Wylie Sypher, *Loss of Self in Modern Literature and Art* (New York: Random House, 1962), p. 14.

2. Erikson, passim.

3. Rachel Carson, *Silent Spring* (New York: Houghton Mifflin, 1962).

Index